TWENTIETH-CENTURY JOURNALISTS

TWENTIETH-CENTURY JOURNALISTS

America's Opinionmakers

S. L. Harrison

University Press of America,® Inc.
Lanham · New York · Oxford

Copyright © 2002 by
University Press of America,® Inc.
4720 Boston Way
Lanham, Maryland 20706
UPA Acquisitions Department (301) 459-3366

12 Hid's Copse Rd.
Cumnor Hill, Oxford OX2 9JJ

ISBN 0-7618-2193-7 (cloth : alk. paper)

Dedicated to

Harold A. Williams

*a twentieth-century journalist–reporter, correspondent, editor,
historian and author–and a thorough professional who
exemplifies all the best qualities of newspaper talent,
with warm friendship.*

Contents

Acknowledgments

A lifetime of reading–a silent, solitary activity with dubious reward–resulted in the selection of the several people who are discussed in the pages following, All individuals here are included because of the author's sole decision; no opinion polls, focus groups. or mass surveys should be blamed for the inclusion–or omission–of persons deemed worthy. If discerning readers object to the admittedly idiosyncratic method of selections, they are free to write their own book. Without question, however, each of the extraordinary individuals examined here made a significant journalistic contribution–for good or ill–to twentieth-century American thought and opinion.

The author explored some of these figures in earlier articles and is grateful to indulgent editors of journals hospitable to those comments: *American Journalism* for Eugene Field, Franklin P. Adams, Ring Lardner, Ernest Hemingway, and H.L. Mencken; *Journalism History* for Robert Benchley; *Menckeniana* for Edmund Duffy and Mencken. Selected material was drawn from: *H.L. Mencken Revisited: Author, Editor & Newspaperman* (University Press of America) and *The Editorial Art of Edmund Duffy* (Fairleigh Dickinson University Press). Further research and biographical material was drawn from the extensive bibliography cited that crowds my bookshelves to overflowing. Additional material was drawn from obituaries, especially from the *New York Times.* Since the author began his newspaper apprenticeship in this final summation of lives, it is appropriate to note that this is a department lamentably deficient in many of today's newspapers.

The author is grateful to Gail Shivel for her many suggestions, editorial assistance and guidance through the Quark's quagmire and to Frances June for coping with someone lost in the past, often an elusive territory.

All interpretations and opinions rest with the author and any errors of fact are his alone.

S.L. Harrison

Introduction: An Overview

Disturbing the Dust of History

Each century produces three generations—perhaps four—and inevitably many events and participants in that passing parade are forgotten. Memory is brief. Neither fame nor performance assure enduring remembrance. The distant past dims and memories grow hazy, recall falters, events fade, people die; current happenings fill the consciousness and crowd the past aside. This brief exploration of some significant figures of twentieth-century journalism may prove interesting, especially as an introduction to some men and women who recorded the past when it was new. Each of these individuals influenced several generations of Americans of the last century, one that may be remembered for being, among other things, the last, most prolific era of the printed word.

Forgetfulness is not a recent phenomenon. Arthur Krock, once a respected political columnist for the *New York Times,* admonished "the American people—and especially newspaper workers—to not allow the dust of forgetfulness to gather." Implicit in his advice is a charge to the news media to exercise stewardship of the past. "Memory and intelligence are closely connected," E.M. Forster observed, "for unless we remember we cannot understand."

Newspapers early on contained more than news. Newspapers play a pivotal role in chronicling our national events, ideas and information beyond mere happenings. The *Federalist Papers,* explaining the proposed Constitution, appeared in the New York newspapers. The columnist existed in the nineteenth century. By the time of the Civil War two were well-known: Charles Farrar Browne, of the Cleveland *Plain Dealer,* who wrote a series of comic sketches as Artemus Ward; and D. R. Locke, of the Toledo *Blade,* created Petroleum V. Nasby. Both columnists were favorites of President Abraham Lincoln. By the 1880s syndicated columns featured writers such as the poet James Whitcomb Riley, novelist Booth Tarkington and humorist Bill Nye, a Chicago columnist. In that era Eugene Field began his career. Field's column "Sharps and Flats," with comment on politics and baseball but also featuring poetry, set a standard that influenced the content of newspapers for the next fifty years. Field's poetry–sentimental and poignant–established a standard rarely met by others; poetry columns became a staple of America's newspapers. For example, the Baltimore *Sun* featured Folger McKinsey–the "Bentztown Bard"–and William Randolph Hearst syndicated poets Edgar A. Guest and Nick Kenny to all of his newspapers.

Those early years of the twentieth century, between America's coming of age and its entry into the international sphere of the 1914-1918 war, are often recalled as a halcyon interlude for the United States. In reality, the times were turbulent: mass immigration brought new people and new ideas to America; the Progressive movement in the West provoked opportunity to comment on the changing economic and social forces; the myth of the idyllic garden gave way to the wasteland described by newsman E.W. Howe in *The Story of a Country Town.* Populism and change produced books that described the harsh inequities: Frank Norris' *The Octopus;* Upton Sinclair's *The Jungle;* and Marie van Vorst's *The World's Work* documented the exploitation of farmers, manual workers, and women, respectively.

Newspaperman L. Frank Baum, witnessing the contending movements that pitted labor and management, agrarian and city-dweller into conflict, wrote *The Wonderful Wizard of Oz,* an allegory of contemporary issues. It became a best-seller, but only as a children's book—rather like Lewis Carroll's *Alice in Wonderland.*

Reality prevailed for a brief decade when the muckrakers took center stage. The issues that prompted the rise of the journalists who chronicled the ills of society are worth recall. Muckrakers—the epithet was applied by President Theodore Roosevelt—sought to inform and arouse the public, of the way things really were.

Muckraking was a moral, radical movement that exposed graft, corruption, and other harmful business practices. Newspapers were not silent: E. W. Scripps, founder of United Press, supported labor reform; Joseph Pulitzer's newspapers declared war on "government of the trusts"; and even Hearst's newspapers supported reform selectively. But magazines led the way: *McClure's Magazine, Everybody's, Munsey's Magazine,* and *Cosmopolitan* were a few. Lincoln Steffens began his series that became *The Shame of the Cities* in *McClure's.* Ray Stannard Baker exposed the railroad trusts in *Collier's Weekly;* David Graham Phillips' *The Treason of the Senate* had its beginnings in *Cosmopolitan.* Ida Tarbell, the greatest of the muckrakers, wrote the *History of the Standard Oil Company* for *McClure's,* and was instrumental in the breakup of the

oil trust created by John D. Rockefeller. But the muckrakers' time was brief. That interlude of reform ended
with the outbreak of the World War, aided by the concentrated efforts of business to control the magazines,
the rise of mass advertising, and the desire to please a
diverse audience.

Before the First World War, Howard Garis a Newark
newspaperman who free-lanced children's adventure
books, created an animal character who was destined to
become a staple of newspapers nationwide. Uncle
Wiggily began in 1910 and remained a favorite of readers for more than a half century. The old gentleman rabbit became known through games, toys, and books.
Garis also won fame as the creator of Tom Swift and a
host of other adventure books. Newspaper readers,
young and old, found escape in these columns. America's
middle class majority was growing larger and more literate, with time to read. Early motion pictures were in
their infancy, radio was yet to be heard, and the major
source of communication was the printed word.

Increasingly, women of the growing middle class
became a group recognized with specific interests and
needs; in modern terms, they became a market. A number of womens' publications flourished, but under the
editorship of Edward Bok, the *Ladies' Home Journal*
captured the largest-circulation and became the most-
influential women's magazine in America. After an early
enterprise into muckraking–Bok initially engaged Mark
Sullivan to investigate patent medicine frauds–the
Journal settled into safe writing about well-known
celebrities by recognized, first-rank writers–Rudyard
Kipling and William Dean Howells, for example.
Through advertising and subscription prizes, Bok built
the *Journal's* circulation to more than a million– one in
fifteen Americans read the *Journal*–and made it a vehicle to improve taste and middle-class culture. During

the first World War, editor Bok was proud to declare that the *Journal* was the "unofficial" voice of government policy– i.e., a propaganda instrument, for which he won the gratitude of President Woodrow Wilson.

For editors who questioned America's participation in the European war of 1914, however, the First Amendment guarantee of free speech and free press brought little protection. For some, including H.L. Mencken at the Baltimore *Evening Sun,* publishers refused to print their anti-war commentary; for others, like the Socialist *Masses,* the federal government simply put the magazine out of business and prosecuted the staff under the Espionage and Sedition Acts. In all forty-four newspapers and magazines were put out of business (sixty-odd were allowed to continue, provided the war not be mentioned) and the First Amendment slumbered during the war years. George Creel, once a reputable newsman, was charged with the government's propaganda apparatus; the Creel Commission thoughtfully suggested topics for editorial writers and subjects for newspaper cartoonists. World War I was an unhappy interlude for freedom of the press in America.

After the war years, a number of distinguished newspaper columnists provided readers fare for America in the Twenties. Franklin P. Adams conducted "The Conning Tower" in the New York *World,* with verve and wit that made FPA a household word in literary circles. Don Marquis' "Sun Dial" column in the New York *Sun* featured poetry and prose heavy with theological overtones, yet light enough to delight average readers, especially with the commentary of Archy, a cockroach with claims to Shakespearean lineage. Ring Lardner emerged after his Chicago apprenticeship, as a sportswriter who captured the nation's attention with his comic tales of baseball. The 1919 Chicago Black Sox World Series scandal embittered Lardner, however, who went on to become a writer with outstanding literary contributions that looked with acerbic perspective on American personality and behavior. The 1920s were a golden age for a number of newspaper columnists centered in New York and Chicago.

The black press, which began to emerge in significant numbers in the early 1900s, had its share of outstanding contributors–Robert S. Abbott, of the Chicago *Defender* and W.E.B. DuBois of the *Crisis,* for example–but none had the fervor of George S. Schuyler, of the Pittsburgh *Courier.* An iconoclast without apology, Schuyler derided the tactics of most black movements that sought social and economic equality: he exposed the modern African slave trade as an enterprise controlled by blacks that exploited blacks, for example. He deplored the demonstrations of black protest and attacked the tactics of Dr. Martin Luther King Jr. George Schuyler was a newspaperman of courage and conviction who wrote the truths that people did not wish to hear.

Myth is often preferred. Ernest Hemingway's reputation as a great reporter was a myth largely of his own making, and the myth endures. Like many myths, however, the legendary newsman Hemingway contributed to America's belief in the journalist as expert in war and peace. Hemingway, a novelist of unquestioned merit, ironically helped create the image of the journalist as an adventurer–perhaps more so than genuine reporters who often lacked the dash and self-promotion abilities of Hemingway. This extraordinary story-teller did not hesitate to allow fact to impede any tale he told.

Journalism as art was exemplified by the editorial cartoons of Edmund Duffy, a three-time Pulitzer Prize-winner. Duffy worked for the Baltimore *Sun,* the *Saturday Evening Post, Newsday,* and in his last years, for the *Washington Post.* Editorial cartoonists, since the early newspapers of the Republic, played a significant role in shaping and influencing–or reflecting–opinion: readers need only look to understand a powerful editorial message. A number of excellent cartoonists made an impact on millions of readers: "Ding" Darling, Cliff Berryman, Art Young, Daniel Fitzpatrick, Bill Mauldin, Herb Block, to mention a few of the best. Duffy, with his audience of millions (and not through syndication), held a steady courageous course, with integrity and independence that established a standard of uncommon excellence for editorial artists.

In the later part of the past century, the number of editorial artists were reduced to little more than a hundred–rising costs, fewer newspapers, increased syndication are some of the culprits cited–and many of those remaining are content with gag humor and mildly comic commentary, calculated to reduce confrontation. Humor is welcome, but more properly belongs on the comic pages; strong feeling and a passionate stance often stirs controversy, an unwanted element avoided by most modern newspapers fearful of offending readers.

Editorials in pictures became a provenance of the photojournalists when the picture magazines emerged– *Look,* the *National Geographic,* and most especially, Henry Luce's *Life* and *Fortune.* Luce began with the newsweekly *Time* that became after a short time a widely popular publication that people believed printed factual news. *Time* was fact as Luce defined truth as it should be. Luce was an editor who read copy carefully and did not for a moment hesitate to alter to his personal interpretation of what should be printed. He created a print journalism empire with *Fortune,* a magazine that became a leader in photojournalism: stories were written only after the photographs were produced. His picture magazine, *Life* showed Americans how they looked at work and at play, in good times and bad.

The photographs that enabled Americans to see

themselves–and the world–were the product of a number of creative artists with a camera, but one of the best
was Margaret Bourke-White, a staff member for
Fortune and *Life*. She was an autodidact with a talent
for capturing unique images of machines and humans in
dramatic and poignant fashion. Bourke-White portrayed people and the events of the Great Depression, a
world at war, and its aftermath with accurate authen-
ticity and a conscience.

Passion was once an integral part of newspaper commentary. Heywood Broun held outspoken liberal
views–it was said that Broun set the Hudson afire every
morning. Broun had a cause and a point of view that
irritated some readers; his crusade for a fair trial for
accused murderers Sacco and Vanzetti caused his column to be suspended by the New York *World* when publisher Ralph Pulitzer disagreed with Broun's views.
Broun was an outspoken disciple of President Franklin
Roosevelt's New Deal policies. Broun did not hesitate to
confront the strong Roman Catholic bloc in New York
City over the sensitive issue of birth control. That stand
finally cost him his job with the *World*. Other columnists
have sustained censure from their publisher, but no one
exceeded Broun in his dedication to battle for the
courage of his convictions. Broun's lasting legacy for
journalists, however, remains the Newspaper Guild, an
organization he helped organize and nurture into a
union that protected jobs and enabled newspaper people
to earn a decent salary and regulated hours. Broun was
a crusader whose impressive contribution has never
been fully recognized.

Dorothy Thompson, another columnist with extreme
views, was one of the most influential women in
America, second only to Eleanor Roosevelt, according to
opinion polls of the time. Thompson was an avid and
active critic of the growing fascist threat to United

States security in the 1930s, an early supporter of a
Jewish state, and a vigorous voice for women's independence. An extremist, a self-promoter, and a domineering
person, Thompson was less than lovable, and she sometimes erred. She dismissed Hitler as ineffectual,
described Jewish patriots as terrorists, promoted
woman's role in the kitchen and garden, and dismissed
ardent feminists as zealots. Thompson paid a price for
her style, personally and professionally (she freely used
exclamation marks and italics), critics mocked her, but
readers loved her and listened to her. Thompson was a
positive journalistic force through newspapers, magazines, books–and radio. Radio became another form of
journalism.

Radio provided an outlet for another kind of newspaperman. Walter Winchell produced a personal interpretation of journalism through rumor, gossip, and celebrity chit-chat that appealed to many Americans. His
columns, initially show business and Broadway talk,
grew increasingly popular and began to include more
personal and intimate elements concerning people–
items of salacious interest heretofore ignored by family
newspapers. His popularity increased circulation in an
era when newspapers were losing financial solvency.
Winchell added radio as an outlet and increased his
audience by millions. Winchell set into motion a trend
employed increasingly by television. Gossip, rumor, and
speculation concerning the rich and famous provides
standard fare today for many television shows, and the
formula is similarly beneficial to significant areas of
print media. Winchell, no adornment to journalism,
undeniably made his influence felt in twentieth-century
America. Winchell's brand of journalism crossed the line
of bad taste and added to the faults of journalism.

Honest, intelligent criticism of the press, especially
by the press, is rare. Harold Ross' *New Yorker,* a saucy

and impertinent venture when it began in 1925, nevertheless undertook this kind of examination from its earliest days. Robert Benchley, writing under the pseudonym "Guy Fawkes," began "The Wayward Press" in 1927. Benchley, a former newspaperman and magazine editor for *Vanity Fair,* became drama critic for the *New Yorker* and went on to motion picture success in Hollywood. Nevertheless, he continued his newspaper criticism for the next dozen years. Benchley's examinations, witty and whimsical, were on target and perceptive. A.J. Liebling resumed the column with another perspective after World War II. Occasionally, H.L. Mencken or Walter Lippmann would task the press for error and bias, but the *New Yorker* provided the only continuous forum for press criticism.

The press's main job is reporting the news. During the pre-war years and for two decades thereafter the journalist who made the greatest impact on readers was Chicago *Daily News* newspaperman and author John Gunther, who presented the complex issues of the day in an accesible format. Gunther's *Inside Europe* launched a series that examined continents and he became one of the most prolific and well-paid authors in twentieth-century America.

Day-to-day reporting was not H.L. Mencken's stock in trade, but for more than a half-century HLM was a potent force on American thought. Journalism, when he turned his attention to it, came under heavy fire, from its inept schools and faculty to the toadyism of editors, publishers, and journalists themselves. But all of America offered an inviting target for Mencken's baleful examination. Mencken led the attack on literary Puritanism. His influence, Walter Lippmann observed, embraced an entire generation of educated Americans. Newspaperman, author, and editor, Mencken was a one-man gang who assessed American Democracy itself, its system, its people and politics, and its literary tastes–all were found wanting. Mencken was the best newspaperman of twentieth century America.

Ranking with Mencken, however, was Walter Lippmann, a first-rate thinker and philosopher; a journalist (Mencken would have scoffed at the term) of merit. Lippmann's intellect and perceptive analyses dominated American journalism, for more than fifty years. Lippmann's columns for the *New Republic,* the *Herald Tribune* and later the *Washington Post* and *Newsweek* were read by the nation's leaders and millions of readers for their even-handed presentation of world and national happenings. His books continue to be read today and provide fresh tools for thinking.

The legacy of the twentieth century, however, is television. Philo T. Farnsworth invented electronic television in 1921; World War II impeded its development, underway in the late 1930s, but television finally emerged as a journalism tool by 1948. One of the best practitioners, however, began in radio. Edward R. Murrow made his early claim on fame with wartime broadcasts for CBS covering the London blitz. Murrow, a master of delivery himself, recruited a group of talented people. His criteria for broadcast was an ability to write and capability to get news. Consequently, CBS earned a reputation for quality broadcast reporting. Television held slight attraction for Murrow, but television provided the promise of a network future for audiences and revenue. Consequently, Murrow moved to television and became a master of programming substantial issues. His record is unmatched for excellence; Murrow was a broadcast journalist without peer.

Murrow presciently warned of what television could become: wires and lights in a box, devoid of much substance or meaning. Television holds the capacity to illuminate, educate, and entertain but the operative word today is entertain. Much news reporting today, especially at the local level, has become little more than rumor and idle chit-chat similar to a Winchell-like gossip column with pictures. National network news is similarly deficient. Walter Cronkite, Murrow's successor at CBS who served nineteen years as anchorman, complained after his retirement in 1981 that news reporting had become "trivialized." The networks largely abandoned reportage for easier and cheaper "infotainment" features. Consequenty, much broadcast news reporting is little more than tabloid journalism.

Perhaps an examination of the past and the people who made news events and ideas come alive–and how information was reported–may enable future media people to become better journalists if they look into the recesses of history and "not allow the dust of forgetfulness to gather."

The individuals discussed in these pages in some detail–some who provide excellent examples of outstanding journalistic achievement, others perhaps less so–made significant contributions to American thought and opinion; their stories provide a useful introduction to the legacy of American journalism in the past century.

1

Eugene Field

Bridge to the Twentieth Century

Journalism is endowed with a rich legacy, but people who once dominated the profession are now often forgotten. Eugene Field, once known to every school child when grammar schools across the nation celebrated "Eugene Field" days each Spring, influenced the content of newspapers for a half century. Columns that contained poetry–for which he is best known–were a staple of newspapers for the first half of the twentieth century, primarily because of Field's popularity. As renowned as some contemporary journalism luminaries are, none hold the universal affection once enjoyed by Field. One of his best-remembered poems is the chronicle of the bedtime adventures of "Wynken, Blynken, and Nod" [the *Dutch Lullaby*], who–

> *Sailed off in a wooden shoe–*
> *Sailed off in a river of crystal light,*
> *Into a sea of dew.*

Eugene Field: Chronology

1850   born, St. Louis, Mo.

1870   Attends Williams College, Knox College, University of
        Missouri; did not graduate

1873   Joins St. Louis *Evening Journal* as reporter, city editor

1875   Joins St. Joseph (Missouri) *Gazette,* city editor

1877   St. Louis *Journal* and *Times-Journal,* paragrapher
        and editorial writer

1879   "Christmas Treasures,"first verse published;
        "Little Peach" gains national attention

1880   Kansas City (Missouri) *Times,* managing editor

1881   Denver *Tribune,* managing editor; *Tribune Printer*
        published

1881   Chicago *Daily News,* begins column "Sharps and Flats"

1889   Cambridge University Press publishes *A Little Book of
        Western Verse* and *A Little Book of Profitable Talks*

1895   dies, Chicago, Illinois

Eugene Field (1850-1895), an American author and poet, was a newsaperman and most of his career was devoted to journalism. Only a few of his books and collected poems remain in print, however. Once Field was America's dominant popular poet—exceeding even the fame of James Whitcomb Riley—who celebrated children and childhood.

Field was born in St. Louis, Missouri, in a financially secure family. His father defended Dred Scott before the Supreme Court. Field pursued his higher education at a number of institutions: Williams College, Amherst, Mass.; Knox College, Galesville, Illinois; and finally at the University of Missouri, Columbia. He finished his junior year and then abandoned formal education.

During his college years, however, Field gave promise of his calling with frequent contributions to the Galesville *Register,* on college life and personalities. He was gregarious and well-liked and comparatively well off. In 1873, he joined the staff of the St. Louis *Evening Journal* as a reporter and rose to city editor within two years. His first assignment was drama critic and, with little training, his early tendency toward humor manifested itself. Field could be acerbic as well. It was Field, and not one of the Algonquin Circle (as is often said), who wrote of an inept actor's dramatic effort that he "played the king as if he was afraid somebody would play the ace."

Field's beat was politics and he covered the campaign of Carl Schurz, the legendary newspaper editor (with the New York *Tribune* and the Detroit *Post*), who was then serving as United States senator from Missouri. In 1875, Field joined the St. Joseph *Gazette* as city editor, holding that post for eighteen months and conducted a lively column, "The St. Jo Gazette." In 1876, Field won national recognition as a reporter. Field broke the story of General George Armstrong Custer and his troops' anniliation at the Little Big Horn; his habit of hanging about the telegraphers' office at the rail depot paid off. By 1877, Field was back in St. Louis as an editorial writer (called paragrapher in that era) for the *Journal* and *Times-Journal*. His first verse, "Christmas Treasures," was published in the *Journal* in 1879, and Field began to acquire a reputation beyond St. Louis as a good newspaper poet. His "Little Peach" was widely reprinted and Field's verse began to attract notice.

In 1880, he moved to the Kansas City *Times* as managing editor, then, in 1881, to the Denver *Tribune,* where he also served as managing editor. A collection of his writings from his column, "Odds and Ends," was published as *The Tribune Primer*. Many of Field's verses ridiculed the state governor, who sued the newspaper, unsuccessfully, for libel.

Field continued his drama reviews–all his life Field was attracted to the stage and performers. He became friends with many theater personalities who toured extensively: Oscar Wilde, Sarah Bernhardt, Henry Irving, Ellen Terry, and Lillian Russell, a special favorite. An inveterate theatergoer, Field continued his drama reviews in his Denver column along with verse. His "Nonpareil Column" later became "Odd Gossip." The items were increasingly reprinted in Eastern newspapers, particularly by Charles A. Dana's New York *Sun.* One of Field's prize possessions was Dana's editorial scissors. (Before syndicates, a primary editorial tool was a good pair of shears to clip items from rival newspapers.) Dana admired Field and sought in vain to hire him for the New York *Sun*. Field declined; he believed that New York might not offer the scope and latitude for expression that he enjoyed in the West.

Melville E. Stone, of the Chicago *Daily News*, lured Field away from Denver with a ten-dollar-a-week raise (to a princely $50) and the promise of a special column of whatever topics he chose. Field was remembered in Denver, however. After his death, the city erected a monument in his honor.

In August 1881, Field joined the Chicago *Daily News* and began a column, "Current Gossip," but within a month his column appeared under the title he made famous, "Sharps and Flats." He continued to write of theatrical people and drama, music, and politics and to perpetrate hoaxes and practical jokes (a popular art form of newspaper and theatrical people in those innocent times). Increasingly, Field's verse drew attention. In those early years Field wrote a good deal about baseball, America's passion. Politics was another consistent ingredient of Field's columns and his comment, whether prose or poetry, was pointed and partisan, without apology. He also wrote verse like "Jest 'Fore Christmas," with its child-like and winning words. Many people remember the opening lines

> *Father calls me William, Sister calls me Will,*
> *Mother calls me Willie,*
> *but the fellers call me Bill!*

without knowing who wrote them. Field loved Christmas as a theme; in those sentimental and Victorian times Christmas was formed into the holiday season we know. "Christmas Treasures," written in

1879, his first published poem, deals with Christmas and a child's early death, both typical Victorian themes:

> *I count my treasures o'er with care,–*
> *The little toy my darling knew,*
> *A little sock of faded hue,*
> *A little lock of golden hair.*
>
> ....

Field was a writer who evoked emotions. The love for animals, especially dogs, another Victorian sentiment, was a favorite Field theme. His elegy for Snip, a co-worker's dog, affected readers everywhere. Ironically, the remembrance of "Old Snip," placed the only dog that Field ever thoroughly detested among the pantheon of dogs remembered in song and story. The "real" Field is unknown; he could parody and stir sentiment. He wrote poems extolling childhood and children, but was not particularly fond of children. He once admitted that he "did not like all children." He wrote in the *Tribune Primer*–

> *Why is this little girl crying? Because her*
> *Mamma will not let her put Molasses and*
> *Feathers on the Baby's face. What a bad*
> *Mamma!....Never mind. When Mamma goes*
> *out of the room, Slap the horrid Baby and if*
> *it Cries, you can tell your Mamma it has the*
> *Colic.*

–an acerbic parody of the *McGuffey Eclectic Reader's* saccharine prose. Field could, of course, love children, but he could also dislike a child, and say so.

Emotions did not control his writing; Field admired

the classics and was inspired by Malory and the Roman poet Horace, and kept their works by his desk to study and emulate. He spent little time at his desk writing. As managing editor, office work was taken up with proofs and checking out-of-town papers. He did most of his writing at home, alone and mostly late at night in bed. He was a meticulous worker and would revise and rework a piece for months. His immortal "Little Boy Blue" was well-worked before it was published. It begins

> *The little toy dog is covered with dust,*
>   *But sturdy and staunch he stands;*
> *And the little toy soldier is red with rust,*
>   *And his musket moulds in his hand.*
> ....
> *What has become of our Little Boy Blue,*
>   *Since he kissed them and put them there.*

and concludes with melancholy sadness. The poem was not written upon the death of his son, as one of his colleagues remembers (leading to a myth still believed). Field's son died a year later. Field wrote the poem, as an assignment for the first issue of the magazine *America*. He knew the verse was good. James Russell Lowell also wrote a poem for that issue, and Field kept careful accounting of his poem's popularity by checking reprints. "Little Boy Blue" was everyone's favorite over his pretentious rival's "St. Michael the Weighter."

Field did not pursue publishers. He never solicited a manuscript or book for publication. In 1889, University Press of Cambridge approached him for two volumes, *A Little Book of Western Verse* and *A Little Book of Profitable Tales,* as subscription books. Subscription publishing was a popular means of marketing at that time, used by well-known writers like Mark Twain and William Dean Howells. Both books were subsequently published in popular editions by Scribner's Sons. Field was a bibliophile who loved and collected books, and took great care that all of his books were well produced typographically with quality illustrations. A dozen of his works were published.

Field died in November 1895, of a heart attack in his sleep. His obituary in the Chicago *Record* (the *Daily News* had changed names for its morning edition) was written by Ray Stannard Baker, a colleague who admired Field, and described him as "the poet laureate of the children of the land."

In Chicago, a monument stands today in Lincoln Park. A bronze statue of Field, with the magic boat of Wynken, Blynken, and Nod and the Sugar Plum Tree, stands on a massive granite base. His home in St. Louis, where he wrote for the *Evening Journal* and the *Times-Journal,* was restored as the Eugene Field House and Toy Museum. Field was unpretentious, a sentimental but hard working journalist, whose last column appeared the day before he died, and a man who brought joy and inspiration to millions. Field was the leader in a journalistic tradition–the columnist-as-poet–that endured for nearly fifty years in American newspapers.

Eugene Field was a prominent newspaper columnist who played a major role in American journalism. He helped shape this nation's perception of itself, and was an integral part of that process. He was a major influence in newspaper columns through the twentieth century; he bridged that era to our own. He raised journalism to a higher level in America.

Newspapers have changed, interests have changed, readers have changed, the times have changed. Poetry is anathema to readers, most of whom have little time to devote to light verse, or indeed lack the fundamental reading skills to appreciate it. Modern newspapers, indeed, few magazines, find space for poetry or verse. Newspapers have a different agenda or so their reader surveys reveal.

Eugene Field set a standard that a great number of newspapers attempted to emulate and his work influenced an army of imitators. The standard established by Field endured for more than half a century and influenced modern American journalism.

SOURCES:

Geoge Ade, *The America of George Ade: 1866-1944* Jean Shepherd, ed. (New York: G. B. Putnam, 1960).

James DeMuth, *Small Town Chicago* (Port Washington: Kennikat Press, 1980).

Charles H. Dennis, *Eugene Field's Creative Years* (Garden City, N.Y.: Doubleday, Page and Co., 1924).

Melville E. Stone, *Fifty Years a Journalist* (Garden City: Doubleday, Page and Co., 1921).

Slason Thompson, *The Life of Eugene Field* (New York: D. Appleton and Co., 1927).

SELECTED BOOKS BY FIELD:

Poems of Childhood (New York: Scribner and Sons, 1904
    and/Atheneum/Simon and Schuster, 1996). A replica of
    the 1904 edition with illustrations by Maxfield Parrish.
The Tribune Primer (Boston: H. A. Dickerman & Son,
    1900/Reprint Services, 1992).

The Eugene Field Book (New York: Charles Scribner's Sons,
    1900).

2

L. Frank Baum

Creator of an American Metaphor

At the outset of the twentieth century, a struggling newspaperman, L. Frank Baum, wrote a book that made his name immortal. *The Wonderful Wizard of Oz,* a uniquely American fairy tale, contains a deeper meaning beyond the story of a little girl's adventure from drab Kansas to the magic land of Oz.

A hundred years ago America was confronting the vexing problems of economics and finance and an elusive goal of prosperity, the subtle themes in *Oz.* Baum, wrote his book he said, "solely to please children." But *Oz,* published in 1900, and immediately widely popular, encompassed more than the modest goal of pleasing youngsters. Baum's appealing story communicated a deeper message beyond the whimsy of a childhood tale.

The Populist platform of "cheap" money and "free silver" became a rallying cry for millions who saw relief in abundant money. America was a divided nation of debtor farmers at one end and lavish-living millionaires on the other. William Jennings Bryan electrified the Democratic convention and the nation with his "Cross of

L. Frank Baum: Chronology

1856   Born, May 15, Chittenango, New York

1873   joins New York *World,* general assignment reporter

1875   joins Bradford, Pa. *New Era,* reporter

1878   tours as actor, writing and producing plays

1882   tours with his play "The Maid of Arran"

1886   publishes first book, *The Book of the Hamburgs*

1888   opens "Baum's Bazaar," retail store, Aberdeen, S.D.

1889   editor of Aberdeen (S.D.) *Saturday Pioneer*

1891   joins Chicago *Post;* Chicago *Evening News*

1897   *Mother Goose in Prose, By the Candelabra's Glare*

1898   founds National Association of Window Trimmers;
       publishes *Father Goose: His Book*

1900   *The Wonderful Wizard of Oz*

1901   *Dot and Tot of Merryland; American Fairy Tales; The
       Master Key*

1902   *The Life and Adventures of Santa Claus*

1903   *The Enchanted Island of Yew*

1904   *The Marvelous Land of Oz*

Gold" speech, calling for the coinage of silver at a 16-1 ratio. Bryan was defeated and the winner, President William McKinley, put the nation on the gold standard in 1900 to stabilize currency.

Influences other than economic also shaped Baum's outlook. America, in the wake of the Spanish-American War, emerged as a world power and industrialization was underway. Literature in 1900 reflected pessimism: Mark Twain exposed venality in *The Man That Corrupted Hadleyburg* and flummery in *A Connecticut Yankee in King Arthur's Court;* Theodore Dreiser's *Sister Carrie* and Frank Norris' *McTeague* both explored life's gritty realism.

Lyman Frank Baum (1856-1919) was born in New York state of prosperous parents, privileged enough to indulge in travels with a Shakespearean acting troupe (his father owned a string of theaters and oil well interests). Young Baum toured with his own play, from Kansas to Canada. Baum was not a playwright, but he displayed a decided ability for writing.

Baum gained an early introduction to newspaper work with a monthly chronicle, the Rose Lawn *Home Journal,* that he and his brother printed and produced. Baum gained admission to the professional world at the age of seventeen, when he managed to get a job with the New York *World.* Two years later, Baum founded *The New Era,* a newspaper that is still thriving in Bradford, Pennsylvania. Advertising and selling provided Baum with additional areas of opportunity as he sought to establish himself. This was the era of Phineas T. Barnum, the showman and promoter, and advertising in its infancy was gaudy and spectacular.

Later, Baum worked for two years as a salesman for his father's oil business, which eventually failed. Afterward, young Baum set out for the Dakota Territory, running a variety store. Financial setbacks ended that

1905　*Queen Zixi of Ix; The Woggle-Bug Book*

1906　*John Dough and the Cherub*

1907　*Ozma of Oz; Father Goose's Year Book: Quaint Quacks and Feathered Shafts for Mature Children*

1908　*Dorothy and the Wizard of Oz; Baum's American Fairy Tales*

1909　*The Road to Oz*

1910　*The Emerald City of Oz; L. Frank Baum's Juvenile Speaker*

1911　*The Sea Fairies; The Daring Twins*

1912　*Sky Island; Phoebe Daring*

1913　*The Patchwork Girl of Oz*

1914　*Tik-Tok of Oz; Little Wizard Stories of Oz*

1915　*The Scarecrow of Oz*

1916　*Rinkitink in Oz; The Snuggle Tales*

1917　*The Lost Princess of Oz*

1918　*The Tin Woodman of Oz*

1919　*The Magic of Oz;* dies, Los Angeles, Calif., May 19

1920　*Glinda of Oz*

brief enterprise. By 1890, Baum landed a job as editor of the Aberdeen *Saturday Pioneer,* and like most editors of that era, he wrote a great deal, of the copy. Early in his bleak prairie existence, Baum experienced a devastating cyclone. Eventually, the newspaper failed and in 1891 Baum returned East to continue his newspaper career with the Chicago *Post.*

After business hours Baum pursued his writing. He published his first book in 1886, a book about chickens, *The Book of the Hamburgs.* It was a commercial enterprise that appealed to the "chicken farmer," as Baum described himself. His second book, in 1897, *Mother Goose in Prose,* contained twenty-two stories based on Mother Goose verses. Graced with illustrations by Maxfield Parrish, the last story featured a little farm girl named Dorothy. The book was a commercial success and sold well enough to finance Baum's next venture, a self-published book of verse, *By The Candelabra's Glare.* Two more books of verse were followed by another commercial effort, *The Art of Decorating Dry Goods Windows and Interiors,* drawn from his commercial selling and advertising experience.

Baum wrote books to make money. He had a talent for writing and had tried many venues. No real financial benefits accrued. Often the profits went into financing other, hopefully more promising ventures. His earlier newspaper writing commented on topical issues, but with little passion or political ideology. These efforts helped him launch another personally financed book, *The Wonderful Wizard of Oz.* Illustrated by Baum's colleague, newspaper cartoonist William Wallace Denslow (the two owned joint copyright of the enterprise). The illustrations helped identify Dorothy and her friends.

Baum used his sense of advertising and promotion in conjunction with the improved printing presses that allowed frequent use of color through the pages with

Denslow's quaint line illustrations. Baum used the new technology that produced yellow journalism. The cover was a bright, attractive green, an important motif; Baum had originally titled his book *The Emerald City*. Color was an important element throughout the book. The opening pages set in bleak Kansas were a dull, dun-colored gray. Later chapters featured bright splashes of color to heighten the adventures of Dorothy and her companions, Toto, the Scarecrow, the Tin Woodman and the Cowardly Lion.

The book was an outstanding success; before the year was out it sold over 90,000 copies. Within two years, a musical-comedy version appeared on the Chicago stage. Comedian Fred Stone mounted a successful Broadway production that ran for a year and a half in New York, then toured the nation until 1911. Oz became a classic, and remains part of the American psyche. Several movie adaptations were made and Baum took a hand in several stage and movie productions. The classic (and only successful) version, Metro-Goldwyn-Mayer's motion picture released in 1939, perpetuated Oz and its characters for millions who have never read any of the dozens of Oz adventures. This screen treatment more or less follows the story. The title, in fact, follows Baum, who eliminated "wonderful" from the book in every edition after the first. This deletion eliminates some irony, because the Wizard was not at all wonderful. He was a humbug, a con-man, a bluster, a fraud. In the movie, Dorothy meets the traveling medicine man, a type known to every American of that era, when she runs away from home to protect Toto. Neither event occurs in the book. (During Baum's lifetime, Toto became a pig in stage productions.)

The M-G-M motion picture depicts the events during and after the cyclone as a dream. Dorothy does sleep while the house is borne away, but her adventure depicted by Baum, is no dream. Moreover, Oz does not lie "somewhere over the rainbow," but is surrounded by a desert many miles from home, and as Dorothy observes, Oz is certainly not Kansas.

The motion picture retains a sense of the book in that early events in bleak Kansas, with its hard-scrabble farm, are filmed in black-and-white. When Dorothy opens the door, a marvelous and colorful world awaits. The moviemakers made one significant change. The magic slippers are ruby red, not silver, as in the book. Silver slippers are important because they relate to the Populist symbolism in Baum's story. The silver motif relates to the Yellow (gold) Brick Road. Baum was following themes, but his goal was simple: to make money, to write a popular book appealing to children. Baum carefully studied the traditional children's classics and sought a new formula. But he was aware of the ideological forces in America.

Baum was a man of his time influenced by the events and people around him. Inevitably, and perhaps unconsciously, some of these influences emerged in his story, that was written, he explained in his introduction, "solely to pleasure children of today." But readers see more in Oz and its characters than Baum's simply stated purpose. Baum was a writer of prose, sometimes poorly written prose lacking polish, that told a story and kept action going with text that children appreciated. He often included gentle jokes and puns that children understood; his word-play was uncomplicated and his puns and jokes one-dimensional. But Oz contained a deeper theme.

Baum's story is more than the "modernized fairy tale" he ingeniously described. It is that, and more. Oz imparts a subtle message to the discerning reader. Interpretations differ. One may detect a Communist manifesto in Oz, which would have astonished Baum, a solid upper-class citizen who never ceased to seek to acquire as much capitalistic reward for himself as he could amass in his lifetime. Baum was no socialist; his estate collected royalties on his Oz enterprises until these expired in 1956.

Some observers with less of a sense of humor and more of a sense of mission see a significant feminist theme through the Oz sagas. Baum's story line, with its heroine, Dorothy and the powerful figures of the several witches influence much of the action and events. But Baum was no feminist. Some of his columns and newspaper commentary expressed sympathy for female suffrage, but in other writings Baum makes clear his opposition to possible threat of female domination, with mocking allusions to requirements for men to cook and sew and perform housework. Baum's sequel to the Wizard, *The Marvelous Land of Oz,* is a clear satire and an unkind parody of the suffrage movement.

In another reading a religious theme of Puritanism and high idealism, with a universal element of related symbols, renders Baum's magic land into an Eden. Virtue and goodness are present in Baum's moralistic tale—he proposes that a heart is needed for love—but religion was not Baum's theme. Baum had dabbled in Theosophy, but Oz is no morality tale. He originally called his Wizard "wonderful," a character who was a very bad Wizard. The Wizard admits as much, but then concedes himself to be "a good man." The Wizard is not good in either sense. He can be seen as a fascist dictator, who rules his land and people through fraud, fear, and intimidation.

Clearly, Baum wove a variety of strands into his text, but the obvious one—Populism—appears most promising. The economic and cultural turmoil in America at the turn of the century is apparent in Baum's symbols. The major forces within the nation concerned labor and the plight of the farmers. The western frontier had been settled, but the promised benefits remained largely illusionary to many scrabbling for a living in what was still described in many contemporary geography books as "The Great American Desert." While Baum was no political activist, he did express a desire during his newspaper career "to bear the stamp of our times." One theme of those hard economic times known to Baum was the plight of the common workers, farmer and labor. Populism promised a solution.

Dorothy, the meek and innocent, seeking guidance, represents the People–an Everyman/Woman. Dorothy's first companion is Scarecrow–a symbol of the farmer–with much common sense, who seeks brains because everyone knows how stupid the farmer is. Farmers are at the mercy of more powerful forces, who create them with straw and prop them up. Similarly, when scarecrows are not needed with crops safely harvested, the straw is removed and the hollow men no longer exist. Scarecrows are expendable, like farmers devoid of land. A brain will be sure to help things.

The Tin Woodman symbolizes industrialized labor, especially the de-humanized labor of the East–any one of Andrew Carnegie's steel-workers, for example. The more work produced and profits generated for the owners results in less wages. The hard-working Woodman, once human Nick Chopper, became a de-humanized man –again, perhaps one of Carnegie's workers. Hence, the desire for a heart to render human qualities.

The Cowardly Lion represents feckless William McKinley, whose Republican managers succeeded in convincing the industrial workers that their best interests lay with the GOP and not the resurgent Populists. McKinley was harmless and ineffectual, but as President put the nation on the gold standard that eliminated cheap dollars. As President, he was the supposed leader of the people, but he was a politician, who lacked any real convictions, he was seen as a tool of the trusts. Similarly, the putative King of the Beasts sought courage. The Lion proved to be brave enough, but did not believe in himself. Dorothy and her companions sought a solution to her problems following the Yellow Brick Road (gold in symbolic terms) of many elusive paths wearing the silver slippers (Free Silver was Bryan's cry. but free silver was illusory, too). Neither Dorothy nor her friends were aware of the magic contained in the silver slippers.

The Wizard, in the magical Emerald City, turns out to be nothing more than a "humbug," a fraud, a pompous windbag, a refugee from a circus balloon that went astray, who hails from Omaha, Nebraska (home of William Jenning Bryan). The Wizard calls himself a "good man," despite ordering Dorothy and her companions to kill the Witch of the West and deluding the citizens of the Emerald City. The Wizard makes the citizens build the city; it is no more green than any other. But the Wizard orders inhabitants and visitors to wear green-tinted glasses at all times. (Green for fertile fields, and for "greenbacks," perhaps.) The Wizard is a charlatan, the reader discovers. The people themselves are partially to blame, the Wizard explains, because they "make me do these things that they know can't be done." The iconoclastic lesson is that the people create leaders lacking real talent.

The once-esteemed leader, William Jennings Bryan, was lacking many qualities. The one-time Member of Congress, newspaper editor, native of Nebraska (in Omaha during the Populist convention that nominated Weaver), demonstrated many of the bogus credentials of the Wizard. Dorothy and her companions discover the Wizard is "a little man with a bald head and a wrinkled face." This is the aging Bryan, minus his political bluster mouthing empty promises. The people cannot put their faith in Wizards. Eventually, Dorothy solves her own problems. Baum's lesson is that the American people can do the same.

Baum lacked a literary agenda. *The Wonderful Wizard of Oz* was to be a one-time story. Baum had no intention of continuing the saga; four years elapsed before he was persuaded to write another. He wearied of Oz. Indeed, Baum wrote other fantasy stories, serialized in such magazines as *St. Nicholas* and the *Delineator*. Baum tried to end the Oz story, but was persuaded to bring his characters back again and again. He wrote eighteen Oz books, about one a year until his death in 1919. He used these books to expand his puns and jokes and parodies into lessons more clearly read. In *The Emerald City* Baum depicts an Oz reminiscent of More's *Utopia,* a refuge, perhaps, but with dark overtones of fascist control. Similarly, *The Marvelous Land of Oz* lays to rest any ideas that Baum was a feminist sympathizer.

Baum was a man of two worlds: one was the world of the practical newspaperman, the advertising salesman, the showman, the seeker of success who wrote more than thirty books. Baum was a pragmatist who used fantasy. He wrote as Floyd Akers (1908-11); Laura Bancroft (1906-11); John Estes Cooke (1907); Capt. Hugh Fitzgerald (1906-7); Suzanne Metcalf (1906); Schuyler Staunton (1905-6); and Edith Van Dyne (1906-19). These were not pseudonyms of a struggling author; Baum wrote as Edith Van Dyne until his death. None of these works beyond his Oz stories are remembered. Indeed, many of Baum's later Oz books lack vitality or show hasty writing. Most of what Baum wrote lacks literary merit or fails to interest successive generations; potboilers written for quick money, for he was often in debt with heavy expenses. The irony is that Oz was his pot of gold, but he constantly sought riches elsewhere.

L. Frank Baum had the fleeting genius to produce stories as charming as meadowlarks that could drift into dark woods with baleful visions, stories, whatever their lack of genuine literary merit, that remain timeless. Baum continued to seek success elsewhere: an Oz-like amusement park, motion pictures, and stage productions. All failed to make money.

The essential and elemental meaning of Oz, and a reason for its eternal success, apparently eluded Baum himself: the land of Oz remains Baum's enduring legacy for people of every age to explore.

SOURCES:

Brian Attebery, *The Fantasy Tradition in American Literature: From Irving to Le Guin* (Bloomington: University of Indiana Press, 1983).

Osmond Beckwith, "The Oddness of Oz," *Children's Literature* vol. 5 (Philadelphia: Temple University Press, 1976).

Neil Earle, *The Wonderful Wizard of Oz in American Popular Culture* (Lewistown, N.Y.: Edwin Mellin Press, 1993).

Martin Gardner and Russell B. Nye, *The Wizard of Oz and Who He Was* (East Lansing: University of Michigan Press, 1994).

Mark Evan Schwartz, *Oz Before the Rainbow* (Baltimore: Johns Hopkins University Press, 2000.)

3

Ida M. Tarbell

The Greatest Muckraker

Ida Tarbell was a muckraker, one of the best and the only woman. "Muckraker" was the name given by President Theodore Roosevelt in a Gridiron Club speech that derided journalists–the "lunatic fringe" TR detested–who exposed the seamy side of American society. Some of the most prominent included Ray Stannard Baker, who exposed corruption in labor unions; Lincoln Steffens, who revealed "the shame of the cities" and municipal graft; Frank Norris, who attacked the practices of the railroads; and David Graham Phillips, who wrote of the "treason of the Senate," the article that finally goaded Roosevelt's ire. The man with the muck rake, from Bunyan's *Pilgrim's Progress,* was used by Roosevelt as a harsh pejorative for those journalists. The muckrakers adopted the term as a proud badge of courageous journalism.

In many respects, however, Ida Tarbell's journalistic credentials and accomplishments outweigh them all. The muckrakers–America's first investigative reporters before that term was coined–gathered facts, figures,

Ida M. Tarbell: Chronology

1857   born, November 5, Erie, Pennsylvania

1870   school in Titusville, Penn.

1880   graduates from Allegheny College, Meadville, Penn.

1882   teacher at Poland Union Seminary, Poland, Ohio

1883   recieves M.A. from Allegheny College; joins editorial staff
       of *The Chautauquan,* rises to Managing Editor

1890   studies at the Sorbonne; research on Madame Roland;
       freelances for *Scribner's Magazine*

1893   returns to U.S. to work for *McClure's Magazine*

1895-
1896   magazine serial features published as *A Short Life of
       Napoleon* and *The Early Life of Abraham Lincoln;*
       coauthor of *Madame Roland: A Biographical Study*

1897   managing editor of *McClure's*

1902   serialization of expose articles becomes *History of the
       Standard Oil Company,* ushering in the muckraking era

1906   leaves *McClure's* over policy differences and with Ray
       Stannard Baker, Lincoln Steffens and Finley Peter Dunne
       buys *The American Magazine*

1907   *He Knew Lincoln*

1909   *Father Abraham* (Lincoln stories)

and statistics to present hard, well-reasoned case studies of unlawful business and wayward government. Tarbell gathered and included fact-laden data to her writing, like a Gradgrind acolyte from Dickens' *Hard Times*. Her searing factual indictment of John D. Rockefeller, *A History of the Standard Oil Company,* published in 1904, remains in print, a major contribution to American journalism.

Ida Minerva Tarbell (1857-1944) was born in Erie County, Pennsylvania. When oil was discovered in that region, her father began an oil tank business and the family prospered during the early boom years. The family moved to Titusville when Ida was in her early teens, but business growth was stunted when Standard Oil consolidated its holdings and absorbed many small businesses. The financial effects on the town and on her father marked Tarbell. Beyond the financial impact, Tarbell was also influenced by the subtle changes brought by industrialization. America's agrarian mileau was irretrievably altered–a pastoral back yard might house an oil derrick, or sylvan meadows be marred with a mine shaft. Tarbell also was influenced by moral Methodism and her inquiring inclination.

Early on, Tarbell developed an opposition to "privilege" and further determined that independence required a college education, a sense that grew out of the struggle for women's rights. Some of these advocates, with their personal and professional differences, left Tarbell with a permanent skepticism. Her model was Abigail Adams, a competent and capable woman without a need for more rights. Tarbell demonstrated a singular bent for personal independence from the outset of her career. She attended Allegheny College in Meadville, Pennsylvania, the only female in the 1880 graduating class. For two years she taught four languages and mathematics at the Poland (Ohio) Union

1911   *The Tariff in Our Times;* editor, *Selections from the Letters, Speeches and State Papers of Abraham Lincoln*

1912   *The Business of Being a Woman*

1915   *Ways of Woman;* ends association with *American Magazine*

1917   Women's Committee on National Defense

1919   Joins *Red Cross Magazine* in Paris; *The Rising of the Tide*

1920   *In Lincoln's Chair* (stories); free-lance wrier

1921   *Boy Scout's Life of Lincoln*

1922   *He Knew Lincoln and Other Billy Brown Stories; Peacemakers–Blessed and Otherwise*

1924   *In the Footsteps of the Lincolns*

1925   *Life of Elbert H. Gary: The Story of Steel*

1927   *A Reporter for Lincoln: The Story of Henry E. Wing*

1932   *Owen D. Young: A New Type of Industrial Leader*

1936   *The Nationalizing of Business, 1878-1898*

1939   *All in the Day's Work: An Autobiography*

1943   consulting editor, *Letter Magazine*

1944   dies January 6, Bridgeport, Conn.

Seminary; teaching was not her professional goal.

After quitting that grinding routine, Tarbell met and was hired by the editor of *The Chautauquan*. Before the days of the Chautauqua Institute, the New York lake area had been a center for Christian-related activities and its magazine, published in Meadville, was popular and well-read with a circulation of 50,000. Beginning in 1883, Tarbell served as a researcher and fact checker with a number of editorial duties, including some writing, although neither she nor her editor considered her a writer. In her methodical manner, Tarbell learned every aspect of magazine production.

Over the next seven years, she rose to managing editor, but left in 1890 (citing ill health, but probably because she was not promoted to editor), to pursue biographical research and study at the College de France, in Paris. Tarbell supported herself with free-lance work for American newspapers, published fiction for *Scribner's Magazine,* and articles for *McClure's Magazine,* competing with *Collier's Weekly* and the *Saturday Evening Post* as one of America's most popular mass circulation publications.

Editor Samuel S. McClure wrote in a 1903 editorial that American society was being corrupted by "capitalists, workingmen, politicians and citizens" who broke the law and "lawyers, judges, churches and colleges" who failed to uphold the law. McClure, impressed with Tarbell's writing, offered her a full-time post in 1894; it was a turning point for Tarbell. Her first assignment, a biography of Napoleon, led to a book, *A Short Life of Napoleon Bonaparte* (1905). Her serialized biography of Abraham Lincoln for *McClure's* was published as *The Early Life of Abraham Lincoln* (1896). Appointed associate editor in 1896, Tarbell then began extensive research on Standard Oil.

Her research was thorough; publication began in

McClure's in November 1902 and ran in nine install-
ments through July 1903. The concluding eight install-
ments beginning in December 1903 ran at irregular
intervals through October 1904. Tarbell had the ability
to describe the chicaneries and deceptions of big business that enabled the average reader to understand its
intricacies. Moreover, her scholarship, research, and
documentation from court transcripts and congressional
testimony penetrated the secrecy so prized by
Rockefeller and Standard Oil's management. Tarbell
provided factual evidence for her indictments.

Bias and prejudice motivated Tarbell, some charged.
Critics claimed that she sought to "get even" with
Rockefeller and Standard Oil for wrecking her father's
business and for blighting the rural idyll of her childhood environment. Perhaps those charges are valid.
Tarbell surely was motivated by ideals of social justice,
her outrage of privilege, and her moral sense of
Christian correctness. No one, however, could contest
the array of implacable facts that Tarbell marshalled in
her unrelenting account of the practices by Standard
Oil–and the railroads–many of which were unlawful,
illegal, or unquestionably unethical. Tarbell simply told
the truth.

Tarbell motivated public opinion. By 1911 the
Federal government won its case before the Supreme
Court to dissolve Standard Oil. Tarbell, convinced that
privilege was curbed, ceased her attacks on big business.
She continued to attack Rockefeller personally, however,
comparing him to a Machiavellian prince without scru-
ples. Rockefeller sought to change his image through the
wizardry of Edward Bernays' public relations activities,
while readers made Tarbell an international celebrity.

Following *McClure's* triumph with the Standard Oil
series, which vitalized mass media, differences between
the staff and editor Sam McClure drove several to leave.

Tarbell, Baker, Steffens and others purchased the *American Magazine.* One of her editorial colleagues, Willa Cather, remained with McClure and eventually was the ghostwriter for his autobiography.

For her first assignment for her new magazine, Tarbell undertook a history of the protective tariff, a subject as arcane to most readers today as it was then. The series ran from December 1906 through June 1907, resumed in November 1909 and concluded in June 1911. *The Tariff in Our Times* was published later that year, linking the tariff to the rise of big business. Tariffs, Tarbell wrote, protected business to the detriment of workers and consumers. The issue for Tarbell was national morals, a betrayal of the American Dream. This book, that prompted a reexamination of American policy, is another of Tarbell's notable contributions to muckraking journalism.

The movement for womens' suffrage drew her attention. Tarbell's factual history, "The American Woman" ran in the *American* from November 1909 to May 1910 and is one reason why Tarbell is no hero to feminists. Tarbell did not portray women as oppressed or downtrodden; in her view they were essentially co-equal, if lacking the vote. Further, woman's place was in the home. She followed this series with another conservative view in the *American Magazine,* "The Business of Being Woman," in 1912 and another in 1913 for the *Ladies' Home Journal* titled "The Ways of Women," none of which endeared her to the feminists. Tarbell felt that having the vote diminished women's moral force. Her views, honest and opinionated, were met with criticism and undoubtedly account today for Tarbell's absence from the pantheon of feminine icons, despite her journalistic achievements.

Tarbell next reexamined big business in a popular series that concluded in September 1915, "The Golden

Rule in Business" showed the better aspects of an American business that was well-regulated, safety-conscious, and humanitarian toward its workers. This work marked Tarbell's final contribution to the *American Magazine.* The magazine was sold and became a traditional, noncontroversial escapist magazine. The staff disbursed and Tarbell began a career as a lecturer for the Chautauqua circuit, extolling benevolent business. Tarbell became an apologist for big business.

At fifty-eight in 1915, Tarbell lectured and declined an invitation from President Woodrow Wilson to serve on the Tariff Commission. She maintained that she was unqualified, but more important, thought serving on a presidential commission would jeopardize her credentials as a journalist. She had met Wilson during an interview for *Collier's Weekly,* and they developed a mutual admiration. A pacifist, Tarbell had been working on an article, "The Case Against War," which she abandoned when America entered the war. In 1917 she accepted Wilson's appointment to the Women's Committee that worked closely with the (all-male) Council of Defense.

Her largely unsuccessful novel, *The Rising of the Tide,* was a telling of the American Dream that attempted to bridge the early American vision with the needs for a lasting peace. After the Armistice, she returned to Paris to take a post with the *Red Cross Magazine* and travelled extensively working on European relief. She returned to the United States and the Chautauqua circuit, exhorting support for Wilson's plan to join the League of Nations. Disillusioned with that defeat, Tarbell covered the 1921-22 Washington Disarmament Conference for the McClure Syndicate. The results of the Conference were similarly disappointing to Tarbell and her articles foresaw the coming conflict of World War II. Ironically, she saw hope for Mussolini, the

Italian dictator, because of his "efficiency."

In 1921 McClure attempted to resurrect his magazine and persuaded Tarbell to continue her history of Standard Oil, but the effort failed. Instead, McClure assigned Tarbell to undertake a biography of Elbert H. Gary, president of United States Steel. Her *Life of Elbert H. Gary: The Story of Steel* was serialized and published in 1925. But the effort to revive the magazine venture failed. New owner Hearst Publications failed as well and in 1929 *McClure's* was absorbed by what remained of H. L. Mencken's *Smart Set* and retitled *The New Smart Set,* with a bland fare of diets, fashions and cosmetics. *McClure's* muckraking disappeared forever and the new magazine itself expired a year later. Muckraking ended when magazines prospered with heavy advertising and broad readership. Advertisers have a low tolerance for controversy. Muckraking ended not with reform, legislation, and regulation, but when magazines became respectable. Tarbell continued undaunted.

Tarbell lauded Gary as the epitome of enlightened business, and her long-touted credentials were questioned. Some critics accused her of "selling out" and being an enemy of labor. She was, instead, an admirer of management; steel was a "good trust" where oil was not. Tarbell liked and admired Gary. Her thesis was exonerated when the government finally lost its case against steel. The liberal press castigated Tarbell. Unlike the other muckrakers, Tarbell was not for toppling the establishment; she sought reform and sincerely believed that Gary personified that movement.

In 1931 Tarbell turned to another business figure, Owen D. Young, chairman of General Electric. Following the usual formula, serialization began in the *American Magazine,* beginning in October 1931, but the story was never completed. Macmillan published *Owen D. Young: A New Type of Industrial Leader* in 1932. This was another laudatory salute to enlightened management that typified the stewardship theory, a Methodist tenet that Tarbell embraced. Young's service to the nation and abroad made him a leading candidate for the 1928 and 1932 Democratic presidential nomination. Tarbell certainly hoped so, for she had little admiration for Franklin Roosevelt or the New Deal. Tarbell roundly castigated women for their failure to support Alfred E. Smith. Women's lack of morality and their prejudice, Tarbell felt, demonstrated that having the vote did not ennoble the electorate. Simply put, Tarbell no longer spoke for the majority; the times had passed her by. If the views of the people changed, Tarbell's had not.

In 1936 Tarbell's last major work appeared, *The Nationalizing of Business: 1878-1898,* as part of a twelve-volume series *A History of American Life.* This panoramic view of the sweeping changes in business was not Tarbell's metier; she preferred the specific investigation, not academic analysis. For the last eight years of her life Tarbell continued to write articles–for the *New York Times,* the *Herald Tribune,* the *New Yorker, Cosmopolitan, Scribner's* and others–on topics such as old age, the joy of flying, the effectiveness of charities, the urban poor, and other issues. She lectured briefly at Allegheny College. In 1939 Tarbell published an autobiography, *All in the Day's Work,* that revealed little of her personal life. She never married and provided support for her brothers and sisters; she lived frugally in her later New England years.

Like most of the early twentieth-century muckrakers, Tarbell was virtually forgotten. Unlike Steffens, who hired Edward Bernays, the public relations pioneer, to publicize his memoirs, Tarbell's role faded to a mythic memory. She remained active, despite increasing problems with Parkinson's disease, until her death in 1944.

When the flame of most muckrakers faltered, Tarbell

did not. Through her long career she continued to seek reform and wrote of issues that required attention and regulation: the tariff, rogue businesses, factory inefficiency, working conditions, and other social issues

Tarbell wrote with unmistakable motivation, sometimes malicious, perhaps. But her facts were scrupulously accurate. She was no liberal; she fails the mythic stereotype of the muckraker. She maintained a vision of a better America. She knew how to "spin" before the term became known. Her profile of Rockefeller in *McClure's* of July-August 1905, arouses hostility. The illustrations of Rockefeller in her *History of Standard Oil* are unflattering, the Rockefeller quotes uniformly unsympathetic. The analysis is coldly analytical, however. Her writing was not without editorial direction. Tarbell had an agenda and drove home that thesis time and again: that the practices of Standard Oil were illegal and immoral. The courts proved her correct.

Tarbell remained unyielding. Her dismissal of feminist demands and her interpretation of woman's role was unpopular, and she recognized that. The tactics of activist women offended her sense of propriety and she said so. Tarbell fought for the principle that woman were equal, but with a distinct role. She never altered her view. Feminists never forgave her. Similarly, Tarbell felt that labor differed from management, and each had a distinct role. Liberals never forgave her that view.

Moral values and traditions were important to Tarbell; her elemental cultural basis–Protestant, white, Anglo-Saxon–was vital, in her opinion, for the well-being of America. Today's politically correct would decry that sentiment and undoubtedly deny Tarbell that ingredient, so essential to her interpretation. Her critics––academic historians–may argue that examinations of business, government, and institutions must be free from moral judgment. Tarbell disagreed. Her moral compass never wavered and her professional standards remained rigid.

Whatever her faults (and they were many); despite her perspective (and it was narrow); and however prejudicial her agenda (and it was biased), Ida M. Tarbell emerges as the greatest muckraker of them all; her contribution to American journalism was monumental.

SOURCES:

Kathleen Brady, *Ida Tarbell: Portrait of a Muckraker* (New York: Seaview/Putnam, 1984).

Louis Filler, *The Muckrakers: Crusaders for American Liberalism* (Chicago: Gateway/Regnary, 1968).

Robert C. Kochersberger Jr., ed., *More Than a Muckraker: Ida Tarbell's Lifetime in Journalism* (Knoxville: University of Tennessee Press, 1994).

Mary E. Tomkins, *Ida M. Tarbell* (New York: Twayne, 1974).

SELECTED BOOKS BY TARBELL:

All in the Day's Work (New York: Macmillan, 1939).

He Knew Lincoln (New York: Doubleday, Page & Co., 1939)

The History of the Standard Oil Company 2 vols. (New York: Macmillan, 1904). Reissued in one vol., 1963 (Gloucester, Mass.: Peter Smith).

The Life of Elbert H. Gary: The Story of Steel (New York: Appleton & Co., 1925).

Owen D. Young: A New Type of Industrial Leader (New York: Macmillan, 1932).

4

Howard Garis

Columnist as Storyteller

For much of the twentieth century an integral element of American newspapers was the continuing story. That feature disappeared by mid-century. The serialized story is a rarity today. Book serials were long a staple–Stephen Crane's *The Red Badge of Courage* first appeared as a newspaper serial. Radio and later television prompted their disappearance, as did the gradual demise of afternoon newspapers. Narrative gave way to puzzles or vocabulary-builders or other features. Many of the stories were romances written for adult readers, but not all. Conspicuously absent today are stories for children once a staple of newspapers. Parents would often read stories to their children before the evening dinner hour or before bedtime. One of the longest-lived and most popular story-column through the first six decades of the century was "Uncle Wiggily," written by Howard Garis. He was a newspaperman, but also a prolific author as well. His creation, Uncle Wiggily, remains one of journalism's best-known and beloved children characters.

Howard Garis: Chronology

1873   born April 25, Binghampton, New York

1889   baggage handler for Erie, Lackawanna Rail Road, Newark, N.J.

1896   joins Newark *Evening News,* reporter

1902   *With Force and Arms* (novel)

1904   *Isle of Black Fire* and *The White Crystals;* establishes boys' adventure formula

1908   leaves full-time employment for book writing with Stratemeyer syndicate as "Clarence Young"–the Motor Boys, the Smith Boys, and the Racer Boys.

1910   begins "Uncle Wiggily" column for the *Evening News* and as "Victor Appleton" begins the Tom Swift books.

1912   *Uncle Wiggily's Adventures* becomes a best-seller

1962   dies November 5, Amherst, Mass.

1965   posthumous *Uncle Wiggily Stories*

Howard Roger Garis (1873-1962) carried forward into the twentieth century the tradition of newspaper-man-as-story-teller. The immortal fame–and income–of L. Frank Baum, brought about by his popular Oz books, eluded Garis. Both men were prolific writers and produced works under a number of pseudonyms, Garis is perhaps best known as Victor Appleton, creator of the Tom Swift books. Garis was also the author of the Motor Boys and Baseball Joe series, among others–nearly 150 books were published under his own name; nearly as many were written under various pseudonyms.

Garis was born in Binghampton, New York, the son of a railroad telegrapher, whose job required frequent moves. Consequently, Garis' education was spotty. At sixteen he was employed as a baggage handler in Newark, New Jersey, for the Erie, Lackawanna Rail Road. His attempts to write–several novels, poems, and stories–met with rejection. *Arthur's Magazine* finally accepted a poetry offering for which he was rewarded with a subscription.

Eventually, after a few more local publications, Garis managed to land a job with the Newark *Evening News*. That career lasted twelve years. During the day Garis worked as a reporter–competent, but undistinguished–and in the evening, to add to his income, he wrote books. An adult novel, *With Force and Arms* (1902), sold poorly. He turned to juveniles and Lippincott accepted *The Isle of Black Fire* (1904), followed by *The White Crystals,* published by Little, Brown the same year. Garis was paid a flat fee of $100.

Garis' children's books attracted the attention of the Stratemeyer Syndicate: the "Bed Time" animal stories (more than seventeen were published by A. L. Burt) and the Charles and Arabella Chick stories–Charlie Chick was the adventurous and inquiring chicken hero.

Edward Stratemeyer, the author of the widely popu-

lar "Rover Boys" series, persuaded Garis to write under
a pseudonym. Garis greatly resisted initially; the decision was to frustrate him to the end of his career. The
eventual agreement enabled Garis to remain with the
Evening News, and also write a series of books, to be
named, outlined and owned outright by Stratemeyer.
The formula was simple: thirty chapters of seven pages,
at a flat fee of $100 with no royalties. Garis agreed to
remain anonymous and claim no ownership or attempt
future use of the pseudonym. The arrangement was a
satisfactory deal for Garis, a better deal for Stratemeyer.

Garis wrote his first book for Stratemeyer as
Clarence Young, author of *The Motor Boys or, Chums
Through Thick and Thin* (Cupples and Leon, 1904). The
Motor Boys proved to be a popular series: eighteen vol-
umes appeared through 1924. Young [Garis] also wrote
books about Jack Ranger, Dick Hamilton, the Smith
Boys, the Racer Boys, the Venture Boys, the Mystery
Boys, the Island Boys–all rollicking adventure yarns
with lots of fast-paced action and little plot.

Drawing from his newspaper background, Garis also
wrote of the adventures of Larry Dexter, the imagined
exploits of a boy newspaper reporter–and produced
some twenty-two Dexter books in all over six years.
Then came his most popular hero, Tom Swift.

Victor Appleton was born with publication of *Tom
Swift and His Motor Cycle* (Grosett & Dunlap, 1910). In
all, Garis wrote thirty-seven Tom Swift books (the Swift
series continues) as Victor Appleton through 1935. Tom
Swift was an inventer; his electric car was capable of
100 mph speeds and could run all day–this was in 1910
and its performance eludes today's engineers. Swift
appealed to boys and was an extremely popular figure.

In 1913, writing as Marion Davidson, Garis produced the first two of his Camp Fire Girl series, *The
Camp Fire Girls on the Ice* and *The Camp Fire Girls, or*

the Secret of an Old Mill (R. F. Fenno). Garis' "Curleytops" series included girls, but most of his work was aimed at young males.

Garis began his most-enduring series, "Uncle Wiggily" as a column for the Newark *Evening News* at the request of his editor in 1910, although Garis left full-time employment for the newspaper in 1908. (Meanwhile Garis' wife, Lillian C. MacNamara, was also writing for the Stratemeyer Syndicate as Laura Lee Hope, producing the "Bobbsey Twins" series.) The first Uncle Wiggily column appeared in the *Evening News* January 30, 1910. These stories featured a rabbit and were aimed at young readers. Garis continued to produce six "Uncle Wiggily" columns a week for the next fifty years.

The adventures of the old gentleman rabbit attired in a top hat, vest, and trousers, who lived in the Hollow Stump Bungalow, encountered daily a series of adventures that contained a good-humored message of behavior—with Neddie and Beckie Stubtail ("two nice bears"), Nurse Jane Fuzzy Wuzzy and a host of other charming friends—was an instant delight. The *News* widely syndicated the adventures to newspapers across the country.

The first book, *Uncle Wiggily's Adventures* (1912), was a best-seller. A board game featuring Uncle Wiggily, devised and marketed by Garis, was widely popular. Either A. L. Burt or Charles E. Graham & Co. published most of the Uncle Wiggily books: the Bedtime stories, the Uncle Wiggily picture books (illustrated by Louis Wisa with Lang Campbell's cover drawings), and *Uncle Wiggily's Story Book*. More than fifty of these books recounted the adventures of Uncle Wiggily.

Garis continued to produce other adventure series: "Nick and Neddie," the caveboy "Tam" series, the "Venture Boys" series, the "Buddy" series that ended in 1941, and the "Teddy" series that ended in 1947. Uncle

Wiggily endured. These were the last books that Garis
produced, compiled from his columns. After his death in
1962, Grosset & Dunlap published his last collection in
1965, *Uncle Wiggily Stories.*

If it appear that Garis was underpaid, and no doubt
he was, his $100 flat fee (upped to $125, when the Tom
Swift books proved to be widely popular) was equal to at
least $1,000 measurd by today's purchasing power.
Garis' prolific production of three hundred books would
in modern revenue equal $300,000, an average equiva-
lent today to $60,000 annually. That income was aug-
mented by the games and other items. Garis was no literary figure; his was popular fare. Like L. Frank Baum's
Oz books, none of Garis' Tom Swift or Uncle Wiggily
books were acceptable in respectable public libraries. In
order to read Garis' books, people had to purchase them
or buy the newspapers that recounted Uncle Wiggily's
daily adventures.

Howard Garis' work did not attain the fame of A. A.
Milne's *Winnie the Pooh,* or equal the grace of Kenneth
Grahame's *The Wind in the Willows,* or contain the sub-
tleties of Lewis Carroll's *Alice in Wonderland.* Nor did
Uncle Wiggily ever surpass Beatrix Potter's *Peter Rabbit*
and her other delightful inventions. None of these products of Britain were found in a daily newspaper, however, and were more expensive to own. Collectively, in
sales, Garis surpassed them all.

Garis' contribution was uniquely American. For the
most part, his prose, formula written and predicable,
nevertheless, contains an innocent charm that is evident
through every page. The moral lessons in each of Garis'
books portray a uniquely American outlook–with audac-
ity, courage, optimism–always with an element of
humor. These books were read with affection by millions
of readers, young and old. Nor should it be forgotten that
these columns were written under a newspaperman's

deadline on a daily basis.

Howard Garis' contribution to American journalism endured for the better part of the twentieth century. No one will place his work near the front rank of literary journalism; indeed, Garis has been dismissed as a "hack writer." Perhaps that charge is valid. Nevertheless, American publishers, who today wonder why young people no longer read newspapers, might look back into their files and examine that ingredient, long provided by Howard Garis, that once prompted young people to eagerly explore the pages of a daily newspaper.

SOURCES:

Sam Castan, "The Wonderful World of Uncle Wiggily," *Look* 26 (3 July 1962); 76-78.

Dictionary of Literary Biography, Vol. 22: American Writers for Children, John Cech, ed. (Gainesville: University of Florida: Gale Research, 1983).

Roger Garis, *My Father Was Uncle Wiggily* (New York: McGraw-Hill, 1966).

S. K. Overbeck, "Longears & Co.," *Newsweek* 68 (7 November 1966); 114 115.

SELECTED BOOKS BY GARIS:

Buddy on the Farm (New York: Cupples & Leon, 1929).

Dick Hamilton's Cadet Days (New York: (New York: Grosset & Dunlap, 1910).

Larry Dexter, Reporter (New York: Chatterton-Peck, 1907).

Rick and Ruddy Afloat (Springfield, Mass.: Milton Bradley, 1922).

Rocket Riders Across the Ice (New York: A. L. Burt, 1933).

The Camp Fire Girls on the Ice, as Marion Davidson (New York: R. F. Fenno, 1913).

The Curlytops in the Woods (New York: Cupples & Leon, 1923).

The Motor Boys Across the Plains, as Clarence Young (New York: Cupples & Leon, 1907).

The Venture Boys Afloat; Or, The Wreck of the Fausta (New York: Harper, 1917).

Tom Swift and His Airship, as Victor Appleton (New York: Grosset & Dunlap, 1910).

Tom Swift and His Planet Stone, as Victor Appleton (New York: Grosset & Dunlap, 1935).

Uncle Wiggily Stories (New York: Grosset & Dunlap, 1965).

Uncle Wiggily and Neddie and Beckie Stubtail (New York: A. L. Burt Co., 1914).

5

Edward W. Bok

Editor for Women

Edward Bok, for thirty years, editor of the *Ladies' Home Journal* until he voluntarily relinquished that post in 1919, was a major force in American journalism in the early years of the twentieth century. His influence exceeded mere editorial control of a publication. When he left its editorship, the *Journal* had a circulation of one and three-quarter million subscribers and was one of the most-influential magazines in America. Bok, who immigrated to the United States in 1870, was self-taught and became an editor of considerable acumen, but he was a master at advertising and promotion as well. Bok described himself as an "editor and publicist." In his efforts to build circulation and readership for his magazine, he was a reformer. He was no muckraker, but Bok's endeavors to expose the patent-medicine frauds put him into the front rank of crusading editors who sought change in American life.

Edward William Bok (1863-1930) was born in the Netherlands, and emigrated with his family to America in 1870 as a boy of seven. He was educated for a brief

Edward W. Bok: Chronology

1863 born, October 9, Helder, Netherlands

1870 family immigrated to United States

1876 left school, employed as office boy for Western
Union Telegraph Company

1882 Henry Holt & Co., stenographer; contributed articles to
Brooklyn *Eagle*

1884 Charles Scribner's Sons, stenographer; becomes editor
of *The Brooklyn Magazine*

1886 created and founded The Bok Syndicate

1889 becomes editor of *The Ladies' Home Journal*

1912 *The Edward Bok Book of Self-Knowledge*

1917 YMCA National War Work Council

1919 resigns as editor, *Ladies' Home Journal*

1920 *The Americanization of Edward Bok;* awarded
Pulitzer prize for autobiography

1922 establishes Mountain Lake Sanctuary, Lake
Wales, Florida (Bok Singing Tower)

1930 dies, January 9, Mountain Lake

time in the public schools of Brooklyn, New York, and held odd-jobs until he left school for good in 1876 to work for the Western Union Telegraph Company as an office boy, where his father was employed as a translator. One of his contacts at Western Union was financer Jay Gould, and based on the information he learned as a stenographer, Bok's market speculations based on Gould's information earned a good deal of money. This practice is outlawed today, of course, as "insider trading," but was legitimate, if unethical, at the time. It ended when Gould became aware of his sharp-eared stenographer, who passed on the tips to friends.

As part of his self-education process, Bok methodically studied an encyclopedia, focusing on successful men. Whenever he encountered a question, he took a direct approach. Bok wrote letters–to the President, ex-Presidents, famous generals, Mary Todd Lincoln. Amazingly, many people answered. Bok's collection become the object of media attention and Bok exploited his practice and managed to visit and become well-acquainted with many of his respondents.

In one instance, Bok wrote to the publisher of a cigarette card with photos of famous people, suggesting that a description be attached. Subsequently, the president of Knapp Lithographic Company (American Lithograph Company) offered Bok ten dollars each for short biographies of 100 people. He earned his first $1,000 and farmed out the second and third 100 biographies to friends (at five dollars each). Bok experienced his first beginnings as an editor.

Bok extended his journalistic activities by submitting theatrical reviews to the *Brooklyn Eagle*. He made the novice's mistake once of writing a review of a performance that had been canceled, but won forgiveness from his editor. Bok saw further opportunity in the theater programs distributed to patrons and proceeded to work a deal with advertisers to fund printing and production; the venture returned a healthy profit. With his partner, Bok took on the job of reporting church news for a publication that won wide acceptance and eventually became the *Brooklyn Magazine*. Bok showed innovative enterprise and a capacity for hard work.

In 1882, he took a job with Henry Holt & Company as a stenographer. Two years later he joined another publishing firm, Charles Scribner's Sons, again as a stenographer. That same year he became editor of *The Brooklyn Magazine* and a part-owner. He and his partner sold the magazine, which became in 1887 the *American Magazine* and eventually, *Cosmopolitan*.

Lacking any editorial duties, Bok in 1886 created and founded The Bok Syndicate, one of the early such enterprises in America. The idea occurred to Bok, sending newspapers interesting features from his *Brooklyn Magazine,* that perhaps he was supplying newspapers with free material that they would be happy to buy. He began his new enterprise with a weekly article by the Rev. Henry Ward Beecher, a famous Brooklyn church leader, whom Bok had met through his autograph pursuits. Bok was certain that newspapers would wish to publish a feature from Beecher and paid Beecher $250 per article, a handsome fee for that time. Within months Bok had more than forty subscribers.

While at Holt, Bok observed that few people were interested in books and in an effort to increase recognition, wrote a newsy, chatty feature about books. He began to supply more newspapers with a literary column. "Bok's Literary Leaves" started in the New York *Star* that eventually won acceptance in a number of newspapers across the country.

Bok observed that few women read newspapers and most editors made little effort to appeal to womens' interests. Bok produced reading matter that addressed women. He hired Ella Wheeler Wilcox and other women writers to assemble a page on women's topics. The "Bok Pages" won quick favor with a number of newspapers that further increased his syndicate success. This was a part-time activity for the industrious Bok.

Later, when he moved to Scribner's, he was placed in charge of advertising, with his colleague Frank N. Doubleday, for the newly established *Scribner's Magazine.* Bok produced startling stories for the press related to the then-best seller, *The Lady and the Tiger.* Bok had the knack of getting the attention of the press. Bok pursued advertising for the *Book Buyer* and the *Presbyterian Review.* Writing advertising copy, with its tight requirements for maximum information, appealed to Bok. He examined the relationship of illustrations to type. He studied typography, layout and the intricacies of advertisements. Bok was methodical in whatever task he undertook. He was an early advocate of "white space" in era where the tendency was to fill all available space with type. His efforts to publicize Andrew Carnegie's book *Triumphant Democracy* brought praise from the author; he used the successful device of employing well-known celebrities in his ads.

Through his "Literary Letters," now syndicated to forty-three newspapers, Cyrus H.K. Curtis, owner and publisher of the *Ladies' Home Journal,* became acquainted with Bok's writing and promotional talent.

Ladies' Home Journal was founded in 1883 in the wave of prosperity for magazines that lasted until the 1890s. The *Journal* grew from a woman's department called "Women and Home" in Curtis' *Tribune and Farmer,* edited by Curtis's wife. She continued as editor of the *Journal,* an unpretentious, cheaply-printed magazine with appeal for middle-class women. It was a prosperous enterprise; from its initial 25,000 circulation it had reached 440,000 by 1889. Curtis offered the post of

editor to Bok, who left New York and Scribner's to
become editor of the *Ladies' Home Journal,* based in
Philadelphia, in October 1889. He stayed for the next
thirty years.

Bok, a bachelor, would appear to be an odd choice for
editorship of a woman's magazine. He had fixed ideas
about women: they drew conclusions from something he
identified as "instinct," rather than reasoning or logic;
they possessed a "sensitivity" which raised them above
selfishness; he idealized women, inferring them to be
something both less and more than they actually were.
He listened closely to his mother's advice. Bok possessed
all the classic stereotypes concerning women. Bok himself suffered all the stereotypes of a man editing a
woman's magazine and became an object of ridicule.
Even his close friend Eugene Field offended Bok with
humorous comments in his popular column.

Bok was a success, however. If Bok clearly believed
that the editor should be a male, he was equally clear
that women of experience should serve as assistants, but
the direction and guidance must come from a man. He
brought innovation and change to the *Journal.* He personalized the magazine–the aloof and distant editor was
not Bok's ideal. To involve readers, an editor heeded
advice; he wanted to play a significant role in bettering
people's lives, to be a beneficial and needed segment in
everyday issues. Bok included his readers as advisors
with prizes for suggesting stories and features.

He instituted an advice column pertinent to the
needs of young women who had difficulty talking to their
mother. He wrote the first himself, "Side Talks with
Girls." The intimacy of the responses drove him to
employ Isabel A. Mallon to write the column as "Ruth
Ashmore" and Mallon continued to write and to answer
more than 100,000 letters for the next sixteen years. Bok
then began a column that appealed to the spiritual

needs of "mature" women. Bok employed Margaret Bottome to write a "Heart to Heart" column that became as equally popular as "Side Talks for Girls." He secured the services of the New York *Evening Sun's* "Woman About Town" editor for the *Journal.* Bok encouraged his readers to write to the *Journal* on all conceivable subjects, and readers obliged by the thousands.

To sell his magazine, Bok hit upon the idea of offering free scholarships for subscriptions. With enough subscriptions sold, an enterprising reader could obtain free room and board, free tuition, and a free piano. Initially, the plan was for women's colleges–primarily music–but came to include male colleges as well. By the time Bok left the editorship, 1,455 scholarships were awarded.

In the early years of the twentieth century, with the cooperation of physicians from the Babies' Hospital of New York, Bok instituted advice columns for baby care through a column. Care and direction for infants and children for the first two years were provided by the *Journal* through personal letters and correspondence, as well. Women looked to the *Journal* for modern advice on these ancient concerns, and this became a major source of its power and success.

Bok moved to improve the literary quality of the *Journal,* but he first moved to secure women's participation and interest. He instituted a series "Unknown Wives of Well-Known Men," written by these unknowns married to the famous. Bok broadened this circle with another series, "Clever Daughters of Clever Men." These ploys attracted famous names and more readers. Bok also managed to acquire the services of the best-known writers by the simple expediency of buying book rights. By this means Bok acquired future works by popular authors William Dean Howells and Rudyard Kipling. He snared William Gladstone through the device of inducing Mrs. Gladstone to write for him a series of articles

"From a Mother's Life." Civil War general William Tecumseh Sherman and Theodore Roosevelt were among the magazines' famous contributors. Howells was paid $10,000 for an article that Bok spent $50,000 advertising. Annual advertising costs frequently exceeded $300,000 annually. Bok wrote all of the advertising personally and did so until he left the magazine.

By the early 1900s *Journal* circulation soared to 750,000, despite the fact that subscription costs had doubled. Curtis was now president of a corporation, The Curtis Publishing Company; Bok was vice-president. (Two years after he was appointed editor, Bok married Curtis' only daughter.) The organization picked up some struggling periodicals–*Country Life* (subsequently sold to Doubleday & Page) and the *Saturday Evening Post*. Another of Bok's projects to improve America was launched with a series of modestly-priced home plans–a project Bok had hoped to use in *Country Life*. The "Ladies' Home Journal" homes were built by the thousands and helped improve America's landscape. Bok next undertook to do the same thing for America's interiors. Through the use of expansive promotion and full, four-color photo reproductions in the *Journal,* Bok promoted a number of exhibitions and sold 10,000 sets of room exterior photos.

Bok, through his magazine, took on the task of elevating American tastes–improving the furniture in the rooms of the houses he had had designed; decorating the exteriors with tasteful gardens and plants; even a campaign to redesign Pullman Company railroad coaches. Initially, Pullman ignored Bok, but month after month and page after page of lavish photos finally had an effect: the rail cars were converted more to Bok's taste. Bok also waged a campaign to bring the proper works of art to the American home; the Great Masters were printed and distributed widely to elevate the taste of

America's middle-class. Circulation soared. Bok was an editor with a dual mission: to sell magazines and shape America's taste.

Bok through his magazine waged a campaign to eliminate unsightly billboards from the landscape, but with only slight success. Bok did succed in eliminating a garish sign that obscured much of the natural beauty of Niagara Falls. Many advertisers retaliated by withholding advertising from the *Journal,* but, backed by Curtis, Bok held firm. His campaign to prohibit billboards was only a partial success, Bok attacked cities directly for generally poor conditions with a magazine series called simply "Dirty Cities." He won improvement in several– Lynn, Mass.; Trenton, N.J.; New Haven, Conn.; Atlanta; Cincinnati; and the magazine's home city, Philadelphia. A number of the cities took action to avoid adverse publicity in the *Journal*. Bok's campaign was aesthetic. He did not attack filthy slums, poor housing, or over-crowding. Bok wanted things to appear neat and tidy.

Bok was a do-gooder who thought he knew what was best. He involved himself in the agendas of women's clubs. Their programs were too superficial, in his opinion. He scoffed that "the Victorian poets could be disposed of in one afternoon" or that a women's group would have the temerity to feel that its treatment of German literature could be "adequately treated" in one session with "able papers." Bok's articles stirred women to anger; a number called for his resignation. One group advocated boycotting the *Journal*. Bok responded with legal action under the Sherman Act. The "little Dutch boy," as Bok referred to himself, brought his blunderbuss to bear on a fly. Women readers of a certain economic level never forgave him.

Bok also erred with his stand on suffrage. He tried informal polls and straw-votes among selected readers. The results were "overwhelming" in their opposition or "indifferent" to the subject. Bok then undertook a personal "thoughtful investigation" of the subject of the vote for woman from the point of view of "what is best for womanhood." Bok concluded that "American women were not ready to exercise the privilege [of voting] intelligently and that their mental attitude was against it."

To counter the outcry of protest, Bok filled the *Journal* with articles by people who sought to protect the sanctity of womanhood by masking her from full citizenship, such as former President Grover Cleveland, former Harvard president Charles William Eliot, Lyman Abbott, the well-known minister and Rudyard Kipling, who weighed-in with his poem, "The Female of the Species." Bok felt that the needs of the Great War reconciled these differences, but his views regarding the limits of women's intelligence never waned.

His experience with efforts to change American women's views of fashion confirmed Bok's view that woman lacked intellectual stamina. Through the pages of the *Ladies' 'Home Journal,* Bok ran a number of articles, accompanied with lavish photographs, to convince readers that Paris fashions were no better than domestic products. Under the slogan "American Fashions for American Women" Bok ordered designs and fashions, to little avail. Bok concluded that "the feminine nature" mitigated his efforts to inculcate patriotism and buy fashions from home and not abroad. Similarly, when his efforts to effect legislation to halt the importation of aigrette feathers failed, Bok felt women were selfish and vain and swayed by emotion. Women toppled from Bok's pedestal. Undaunted, however, Bok took his campaign directly to state legislatures and the National Audubon Society to secure protection laws.

Before Bok became its editor, the *Ladies' Home Journal* had refused patent medicine advertisements (as well as tobacco and liquor) under Curtis. As editor, Bok pursued the evils of these products. He exposed the fraud of Lydia Pinkham's patent medicine. One effort failed. He published a list of twenty-seven patent medicines with their harmful ingredients. He erred in one instance and Curtis Publishing lost a suit for $200,000. Undaunted, In 1904, Bok engaged Mark Sullivan to expose the fraudulent use of the mails. Sullivan produced an article that Bok felt was too "legalistic." Bok, however, persuaded Norman Hapgood, editor of *Collier's Weekly* to run it. The *Journal* was never a muckraking magazine, like *McClure's* or *Everybody's,* for example. With the patent medicine campaign, *Collier's Weekly,* with Sullivan and Samuel Hopkins Adams, led the fight for the Food and Drug Act reforms. Bok was a crusader, not a muckraker. Bok's close friend, President Theodore Roosevelt, came to attack the writers for reform and labelled them "muckrakers."

In 1906–at a time when the subject was not discussed–Bok undertook an education campaign in the *Journal's* pages explaining the threat of venereal disease. In the face of the storm of protest that came with Bok's editorials and 75,000 canceled subscriptions, Bok prevailed in his campaign. He published supporting articles by Jane Addams, Cardinal Gibbons, president Eliot, of Harvard, and others. From these articles, Curtis published, at cost, a series of books explaining the perils of venereal diseases, known as the Edward Bok Books, that sold in the tens of thousands. Another health measure that Bok pursued in the *Journal* was the danger in the then prevalent public drinking cup and community towels. Bok's magazine was responsible for the wave of legislation outlawing these unsanitary devices.

Bok turned his attention to civic issues. The *Journal* waged a campaign to curb drawing water from Niagara Falls. Bok, after prudently going to President Roosevelt to secure his agreement. moved a letter-writing campaign to electric power stations in Canada and the United States. Bok, observing the campaigns by *Life* magazine and the *Chicago Tribune,* to stop the carnage from July 4th fireworks, undertook a campaign in the pages of the *Journal.* He succeeded in effecting legislation in city after city. He then began a campaign to institute day nurseries for the children of working mothers that met with widespread success. Bok's efforts in these campaigns in the first decade of the 1900s succeeded in pushing the circulation of the *Journal* to one and three-quarter million copies a month.

Bok enthusiastically used his magazine during World War I as a propaganda instrument for the government. Bok decided to ignore the fighting front–other publications would do that–and concentrate on "keeping up morale" at home. Bok conferred directly with President Woodrow Wilson. Told that recruiting for the Navy would be the first priority, Bok commissioned Under Secretary of the Navy, Franklin D. Roosevelt to write a recruiting article for the *Journal.* He hired former President William Howard Taft as editor of the *Journal's* Red Cross column.

The Food Administration's first public policy, written by Herbert Hoover, appeared in the *Journal.* The Department of Agriculture published its guides for gardens in the *Journal.* Bok's magazine, he reported with pride, "became the semi-official mouthpiece of all the various government war bureaus." Bok was appointed to the National War Work Council of the YMCA and served as the major link to Washington and London. Before stepping down as editor, Bok worked to promote the program of the Federal Bureau of Americanization.

Bok rounded out a full thirty years as editor of one of the most powerful magazines in America in 1919. He wrote his autobiography, *The Americanization of Edward Bok,* for which he was awarded a Pulitzer Prize in 1920. Wealthy, he turned to philanthropic educational activities, and fulfilled, he wrote a number of books in his leisure. He died in Mountain Lake, Florida, January 9, 1930; his "Singing Tower" is a tourist attraction.

Bok saw himself as a competent, hard-working and exacting editor. Americans, in his opinion, fell short of initiative, education, and ambition. To the end of his career, Bok remained critical of work that failed to measure up to his standards. He continued to do much of the research at the *Journal,* but never found anyone who could match his thoroughness. His credo was that anyone who worked hard and studied could become a success and be wealthy (he thoughtfully ommitted the technique of marrying the boss' daughter, however). Bok's contribution to journalism was significant and he did his utmost to raise the cultural taste of his vast army of readers. Bok was close to his readers, intellectually and emotionally, a vital ingredient in any good editor. Most of all, Bok was an uneven idealist whose reach sometimes exceeded his grasp, but he shaped American ideas and ideals in the early years of the twentieth century.

SOURCES:

Edward Bok, *The Americanization of Edward Bok: An Autobiography* (New York: (Scribner's and Sons, 1920/Philadelphia: The American Foundation, 1965).

Frank Luther Mott, *A History of American Magazines* (Cambridge: Cambride University Press, 1957).

SELECTED BOOKS BY BOK:

A Dutch Boy Fifty Years After (New York: Charles Scribner's, 1927).

A Man from Maine: A Biography of Cyrus H. Curtis (New York: Charles Scribner's, 1923).

Before He Is Twenty (New York: F. H. Revell, 1894).

Her Brother's Letters [published anonymously] (New York; Moffatt, Yard and Co., 1906).

Successward (New York: Doubleday, McClure & Co., 1890).

The Edward Bok Book of Self-Knowledge (New York: F. H. Revell, 1912).

The Young Man in Business (New York: L. C. Page and Co., 1900).

Why I Believe in Poverty (Boston: Houghton Mifflin Co., 1915).

Twice Thirty (New York: Charles Scribner's Sons, 1925).

6

Franklin P. Adams

Literate Columnist

Newspaper columns flourished in Chicago at the beginning of the twentieth century. Finley Peter Dunne's creation, Mr. Dooley, began in the Chicago *Times* and later the *Evening Post*. By 1900 Dunne had departed for New York and a larger audience. Eugene Field's "Sharps and Flats," with verse and poetry was featured in the Chicago *Daily News* and internationally known. George Ade's popular "Stories of the Streets and of the Town" ran in the Chicago *Record*. The *Chicago Tribune* carried an advice column by publisher Joseph Medill for farmers about planting and ploughing. Bert Leston Taylor (B.L.T.), began his popular column, a "Line o' Type or Two" in 1901, for the *Journal*, but was lured away by James Keely, of the *Tribune* to "personalize" the newspaper.

Readers appreciate the journalistic power of a newspaper column. Publishers surely do. A popular columnist can attract and hold thousands of readers. Outstanding columnists are rare assets, however. Relatively few individuals have the talent and ability to

Franklin P. Adams: Chronology

1881	born, November 15, Chicago, Illinois
1900	University of Michigan (one year)
1902	*In Cupid's Court* (verse)
1903	Chicago *Journal,* weather column
1904	New York *Evening Mail,* column "Always in Good Humor"
1909	failed musical comedy, "Lo," with O. Henry
1914	New York *Tribune,* begins "The Conning Tower"
1918	commissioned with AEF, works on *Stars and Stripes*
1922	joins New York *World*
1931	*World* folds, rejoins *Herald Tribune*
1936	leaves *Herald Tribune,* writes free-lance tennis column for the *New Yorker*
1938	joins New York *Evening Post;* joins NBC radio program "Information, Please"
1941	leaves New York *Post,* last newspaper position
1948	leaves television version of "Information, Please"
1960	dies, March 23, New York City

produce commentary on a continuous basis that is lively, clever, timely, and literate.

Chicago's newspapers provided an inspiring array of talent. One of America's best columnists, Franklin P. Adams (who signed his column with his initials FPA), began in Chicago in those early years. Adams gained fame with verse, puns, humor, comments about his friends and a made-up "diary." written in a column. Modern readers with less time and attentiveness no longer have a liking for poetry and often lack the literary credentials to appreciate allusions.

Franklin Pierce Adams–F.P.A. (1881-1960)–was one of the best-known newspaper figures in America in the 1920s and 1930s. His column, "The Conning Tower," in Joseph Pulitzer's New York *World,* was one of the most read op-ed page features in that newspaper.

Adams was born November 15, 1881, in Chicago, of modest background; his father was in the dry goods trade. Young Adams attained grades good enough to qualify him for high school at the Armour Institute and managed to attend one year at the University of Michigan, in Ann Arbor, before failing family finances caused him to withdraw. In 1901, he worked for the Transatlantic Insurance Company.

Later that year, Adams called on George Ade to sell him a policy. Ade was a popular humorist with the Chicago *Record;* his collected columns, *Fables in Slang,* was one of Adams' favorite books. Adams aspired to be a newspaper columnist, He admired B.L.T. (Bert Leston Taylor), who wrote "A Line o' Type or Two," for the *Chicago Tribune,* a column that combined humor, verse, parodies, news items, and contributed poems. Adams began submitting items to B.L.T. and some were printed. He continued to sell insurance, but more of his contributions met acceptance. Adams self-published a volume of his poems, *In Cupid's Court.*

By 1903, on the strength of that slim volume and the work he had done for B.L.T., Adams landed a job, with Ade's help, writing a light-hearted weather column with the Chicago *Journal*. His contributions on the entertainment scene won him a job as occasional drama critic. He inherited a column, "A Little about Everything," that was a success and clearly imitative of B.L.T.'s formula. Adams had wit, imagination, and ambition. His wife-to-be, one of the Floradora girls in the touring company, returned to Brooklyn and Adams determined to try prospects in the East. Adams left for New York City with hope, love and ambition, but more important, a letter of recommendation from his Chicago editor to the managing editor of the New York *Evening Mail*. The letter landed him a job.

When he joined the *Mail* in 1904, Adams began with a by-lined column, "Local News," which quickly became "A Line or Two in Jest," a shameless copy of his idol B.L.T., as was the format and content. The column quickly became "A Manhattan Bargain Counter" and finally, and permanently, "Always in Good Humor."

His column was a success, with poems, drolleries, puns and talk of the theater. Adams was an avid baseball fan and continued to root for his beloved Chicago Cubs. In 1910, he wrote a poem priasing the double-play combination of the Cub infield that became widely popular. It begins—

> *These are the saddest of possible words:*
> *"Tinker to Evers to Chance."*
> *Trio of bear cubs, and fleeter than birds,*
> *Tinker and Evers and Chance.*

The poem has entered the lexicon of baseball lore as much as "Casey at the Bat." Factually, the Cub trio was not that amazing as a double-play combination, but the baseball poem swept the nation.

With his rising popularity, Adams was rewarded with another special column that ran as a Saturday feature, "The Gotham Gazette." A parody of rural newspapers with features real and imagined and its success was assured when William Allen White, legendary editor of the Emporia (Kansas) *Gazette,* wrote to congratulate Adams and wish him well. The column ran until 1922.

Adams built a rapport with readers and contributors and helped young and struggling aspirants, like poet Louis Untermeyer, music critic Deems Taylor and a then-unknown Walter Lippmann. The well-known and famous figures of music and stage regularly competed to place items in his column. Adams' annual dinner to award an engraved gold watch for the year's best contribution became an event in New York. One year, he presented a young man newly graduated from Harvard, unknown to anyone and with no notable background, except that Adams had heard he was very funny. Robert Benchley gave a recitation on the "History of the Watch Industry," a sketch that made Benchley known in New York newspaper circles.

In 1909, Adams tried playwriting with O. Henry (William Sydney Porter) and they collaborated on a musical comedy. LO (after Alexander Pope's "Lo, the poor Indian!..."); the company closed after several performances in the mid-West. Adams entered that effort in his *Who's Who* listing for forty-four years.

Adams began "The Diary of Our Own Samuel Pepys" in 1911 and the inserts in his column–commenting on current events written in the style of Pepys–became a staple of his column for more than twenty years. These commentaries were published in book form in 1935, and proved quite popular.

When T.E. Niles, the editor who had hired him, retired, Adams' loyalty faded and he left the *Evening*

Mail. His successor for "Always in Good Humor" was George S. Kaufman, who had been a frequent contributor. Adams joined the New York *Tribune* in January 1914 to continue his column with its large following and a promise as managing editor for a new Sunday section. Adams' column had a new name, "The Conning Tower." He continued his usual routine of being around town, talking to people who counted, reading his voluminous mail for reader contributions, and composing his verse; Adams was diligent. He managed to produce the *Tribune's* Sunday magazine feature and hired Robert Benchley as an assistant with contributors such as George S. Kaufman, Walter Lippmann, and artist Rea Irvin, among other notables.

With the outbreak of war, Adams pulled strings to get a commission with the American Expeditionary Force (AEF) in France, and joined *Stars and Stripes,* a newspaper for the troops. His light style was unsuitable for the military newspaper, but FPA met and worked with people who were to remain close friends for years: Harold Ross, Adolph Ochs, Mark Watson, Steven Early, Alexander Woollcott, and Grantland Rice.

Adams returned to civilian life and "The Conning Tower" in January 1919, just in time to witness baseball's Black Sox scandal, Babe Ruth's coming to New York, and Prohibition. With the Twenties just around the corner, Adams was on the scene to witness the gaudiest era in American history–and his fame soared. It was the time of the Algonquin Round Table, a luncheon group of the New York literati and theater people, who met in the hotel's Rose Room. And FPA chronicled every witticism, every wisecrack and *bon mot.* His column was read by everyone who counted. Busy with a daily column–the column always came first–Adams usually met only on Saturday, but he was an avid participant of the fabled poker sessions. Participants included Heywood

Broun, Harold Ross, George S. Kaufman, Harpo Marx, Raoul Fleischmann, and Herbert Bayard Swope. Stakes were enormous and FPA was a terrible poker player with a gambling addiction; Adams lost a lot of money. He won, and lost, several hundred shares of stock in Ross' fledgling magazine, the *New Yorker,* to which he contributed an article for its initial issue.

Swope, editor of the New York *World,* gathered some of the best writing talent in America to make his great newspaper even better. The people Swope brought to the *World* reads like a *Who's Who* in newspapering: Walter Lippmann, Frank Cobb, James M. Cain, Allan Nevins, Maxwell Anderson, Arthur Krock, O. Henry, Alexander Woollcott, Heywood Broun, Gene Fowler, Deems Taylor, and Robert Benchley, among others. Swope scooped up FPA in January 1922, with a promise of freedom of action and a lot more money. Adams' old boss at the *Tribune,* publisher Ogden Reid, was displeased with Adams' departure.

In 1931, the *World* collapsed through penny-pinching and mismanagement (Swope left in disgust in 1929) and every staffer was fired. The wreckage became the *World-Telegram.* Adams took a deep salary cut and returned home. The *Trib* had become the *Herald Tribune* and feelings were bitter on both sides. This was in the height of the Depression, however, and Adams had a job that paid him $25,000 (one-quarter-of-a-million dollars measured in today's purchasing power). The hard times in America saw little evidence in "The Conning Tower." Adams was, for the most part, insulated from the harsh facts of life (although he did lose his entire savings in the 1929 Wall Street crash). He held a high-paying job, but became active in the formation of the Newspaper Guild and was elected New York president (Broun was national president). Many newspaper workers were unemployed or earned less than $3,000. Nevertheless, Adams went on writing what he knew best in his column–light, topical gossip and humor. Readership began falling off, at a time when newspapers lost 40 percent of their circulation. Consequently, when Reid, who was still angry over Adams' early defection, offered a contract renewal with a $3,000 pay cut, Adams refused and was out of work.

Adams filled in time writing, mainly a tennis column (he was an expert player), for the *New Yorker*. But not until 1938, almost two years, did he manage to return to newspaper work with the New York *Evening Post*. But a new career beckoned. In May 1938, FPA began the inaugural program of radio's "Information, Please" on NBC. He was a success and so was the program, which later moved to CBS and lasted until 1948. His job at the *Evening Post* ended quietly in 1941 and FPA's journalism career came to a close.

Adams and "Information, Please" failed to make the transition to television, partly because the beginnings of his deterioration from Alzheimer's disease were apparent. Homeless and broke, Adams spent his last years living at the Players Club, sustained by a make-work stipend from old friend Harold Ross. Adams died in March 1960.

Adams was the consummate columnist, well-known and well liked, a *bon vivant* with a public reputation for a quick wit and ready quip, who wrote of the people and events of his time with verve and grace. His poems and verse, light and frothy, are apt to be unappreciated–and little understood–by contemporary readers, nevertheless, FPA was the last, and one of the best, to provide readers with a literate, humorous view of a world beyond their own.

SOURCES:

Sally Ashley, *F.P.A.: The Life and Times of Franklin Pierce Adams* (New York: Beufort, 1986).

Robert E. Drennan, ed. *The Algonquin Wits* (Secaucus, N.J.: Citadel Press, 1968).

James R. Gaines. *Wit's End: Days and Nights of the Algonquin Round Table* (New York: Harcourt, Brace Jovanovich, 1977).

SELECTED BOOKS BY ADAMS:

By and Large (Garden City: Doubleday, Page and Co., 1914).

Christopher Columbus and Other Patriots (New York: Viking Press, 1931).

The Conning Tower Book (New York: Macy-Massius, 1926).

In Cupid's Court ((Evanston: W.S. Lord, 1902).

The Diary of Our Own Samuel Pepys (New York: Simon and Schuster, 1935).

F.P.A. Book of Quotations (New York: Funk and Wagnells, 1952).

Half a Loaf (Garden City: Doubleday, Page and Co., 1927).

Innocent Merriment (New York: McGraw-Hill, 1942).

In Other Words (Garden City: Doubleday, Page and Co., 1912).

The Melancholy Lute (New York: Viking Press, 1936).

Overset (Garden City: Doubleday, Page and Co., 1922).

Something Else Again (Garden City: Doubleday, Page and Co., 1920).

So Much Velvet (Garden City: Doubleday, Page and Co., 1924).

Toboganning on Parnassus (Garden City: Doubleday, Page and Co., 1911).

Weights and Measures (Garden City: Doubleday, Page and Co., 1922).

7

Don Marquis

That Damned Cockroach

Christopher Morley, a columnist and author of wide popularity in the 1930s, described Don Marquis as a notable successor to Mark Twain. Both were born in a hamlet near a Big River, both worked in a print shop and moved from city to city, and both wrote first books about a boy, using Middle American dialect, employing grotesque humor and parables too blunt for intellectuals to perceive. Also, both were newspapermen with little formal training, whose writings were known to millions of readers. If Marquis was no Twain, he was one of America's best-known and favorite columnists, who left a lasting literary legacy–Archy, the cockroach.

Donald Robert Perry Marquis (1878-1937) was a man of multiple talents: short story writer, dramatist, screen writer, poet, novelist and essayist for national magazines, such as *Collier's Weekly* and the *Saturday Evening Post*. But newspapers brought him major fame–from his columns, "The Sun Dial," in the New York *Sun,* and later "The Lantern," in the New York *Herald Tribune.* And when Marquis is remembered, it

Don Marquis: Chronology

1878   born, July 29, Walnut, Illinois

1899   odd jobs, including a column for local newspaper

1894   Knox College, Galesburg, Ill., for several months

1900   brief work at the Census Bureau, Washington

1902   newspapers in Washington, D.C. and Philadelphia;
        works for Atlanta *News* and Atlanta *Journal*

1907   editorial post with *Uncle Remus's Magazine*

1909   free-lance work in New York City

1912   joins New York *Evening Sun* and begins "Sun Dial"
        column; *Danny's Own Story* (novel)

1916   *The Cruise of the Jasper B.;* archy and mehitabel appear
        March 29 in "Sun Dial"

1917   *Hermione and Her Little Group of Serious Thinkers* (verse)

1919   *Prefaces* (humorous sketches)

1921   *Carter and Other People* (stories); *The Old Soak* (humor);
        Noah an' Jonah an' Cap'n John Smith (poetry)

1922   joins New York *Herald Tribune,* column becomes "The
        Lantern"; Broadway play, "The Old Soak"; *Sonnets to a
        Red-Haired Lady* and *Famous Love Affairs* (poetry); *The
        Revolt of the Oyster* (short stories)

is for his antic creations–Archy, the typewriting cock-roach and his caustic accomplice, the cat Mehitabel. These creations "belong to an era," E. B. White observed, "but remain timeless."

If journalistic immortality exists, Archy and Mehitabel paved the way for Marquis. Late in his career, Marquis lamented that he would be remembered only as the creator of "a goddamn cockroach." Well, part-ly. Mehitabel, too, illustratively brought to life by artist George Herriman, creator of "Krazy Kat," is an integral part of Marquis' heritage.

Marquis maintained that he was born during an eclipse, in Walnut Grove, Illinois, July 29, 1878. If that is so, none of his biographers documented the fact, but it shows that Marquis' imagination lent drama to any story. In 1898, he attended Knox College in Galesburg, Illinois, for one semester. Marquis' college career was brief because he lacked funds and failed to win a football scholarship. A series of jobs–school teacher and railroad section hand–finally led him to a local newspaper. He wrote a column with poetry, politics, and stories. The outlandish tall tale was popular fare for newspaper columnists of that era. He read and was influenced by the columnists of nearby Chicago newspapers: Eugene Field's "Sharps and Flats" and George Ade's "Stories of the Streets and of the Town" provided inspiration. But an editorial he wrote led to a job with the Bureau of the Census, in Washington. He left that position (acquired through political influence) for unexplained "political reasons" and in 1900, Marquis was looking for work.

Marquis managed to pick up some newspaper jobs in Washington, seeking a column, before moving on briefly to Philadelphia. Unsuccessful, he moved to Atlanta. By 1902, he found a position with the Atlanta *News,* where he could write whatever he wished as a general assign-ment reporter. Marquis wrote occasional columns, but

1924   *The Old Soak's History of the World* (humor); *The Dark Hours* (drama); *The Awakening and Other Poems; Hermione and Her Little Group of Serious Thinkers*

1925   gives up daily column

1927   *Archy and Mehitabel; The Almost Perfect State;* Broadway play, "Out of the Sea"

1928   *Love Sonnets of a Caveman* (poetry); *When the Turtle Sings and Other Unusual Tales* (stories); brief career as Hollywood screenwriter

1929   *A Variety of People* (stories)

1930   *Off the Arm* (novel); "Everything's Jake" (play)

1932   Broadway play "The Dark Hours"

1933   *Archy's Life of Mehitabel;* play "Master of the Revels"

1934   *Chapters for the Orthodox* (humor)

1935   *Archy Does His Part*

1936   *Sun Dial Times*

1937   *The Old Soak; Old Soak Hail and Farewell;* dies December 29, New York City

was not paid for these contributions. Later, he moved to the Atlanta *Journal.* In 1907, he joined the staff of *Uncle Remus's Magazine,* as associate editor under the editorship of Joel Chandler Harris. After Harris' death a year later, the magazine lost circulation and a pay cut prompted Marquis to seek opportunity elsewhere. By this time Marquis had married a free-lance writer, Reina Melcher, and developed a close and lasting friendship with a local sportswriter, Grantland Rice.

At his wife's urging, Marquis decided to try his fortune in New York and managed to pick up free-lance work from the New York *American* and later, the New York *Herald.* They both continued to submit work to *Uncle Remus's Magazine,* managing a precarious living. This and later free-lance work for the *American* and the *Brooklyn Eagle* continued until 1912, when Marquis landed a full time position with the New York *Sun* to produce a daily column.

With the appearance of the "Sun Dial" in the New York *Evening Sun,* Marquis was able to use his many literary talents as a poet, a reporter, satirist, parodist, teller of tall tales, and humorist to fill a column with commentary on the fads and politics of the times. Unlike FPA's "Conning Tower," where Adams relied on a host of contributors, Marquis produced his prose and poetry virtually solo. Moreover, in an era of the personalized column, Marquis quickly proved to be one of the best in the business.

From the outset, Marquis spun out comic characters—the Old Soak, Hermione, Captain Peter Fitzhurse and a dozen other colorful creations. Unlike Heywood Broun, for example, who could type out a column in less than a half-hour, Marquis labored to produce his daily quota, usually two full columns.

Finally, on March 29, 1916, Marquis' unpaid collaborator appeared. Simply put, Archy was a gigantic cockroach of literary talent who inhabited the *Sun* news room. At night, Archy, with a convenient piece of typing paper placed in the platen, would hurl himself head foremost at the typewriter keyboard and slowly produce a message, often profound. Unable to move the shift key, everything was typed in lower case with little punctuation. Often the lines were short and helped to fill up the column. If Archy signed himself "archy," Marquis invariably employed the correct capitalization in his comment to and about the cockroach.

Archy, vain, self-pitying, cynical, constantly shifting from humility to pride, observed all aspects of the human condition and allowed Marquis to give opinion freely and without restraint. Moreover, Archy's comments, sometimes in verse, served to fill up the columns with its short lines of copy. Archy was soon joined by Mehitabel, a cat. Mehitabel, vain, hoydenish, self centered, a free spirit and totally unreliable, produced another voice of opportunity for Marquis, and another source of copy. Each is a persona of Marquis that the reader comes to know–Mehitabel is selfish and uncomplicated; Archy, who gradually reveals a complex make-up, has the soul of a poet. Indeed, Archy was, it was discovered, a poet in another life. Each creature, however, is portrayed with humor that endures to the present day. For example, even when Archy confronts and complains about the policies of President Franklin Roosevelt's New Deal, Archy's cynical political commentary holds its own in the contemporary arena.

Marquis was a multi-talented man who maintained a love-hate relationship with his newspaper column. After success at the *Sun,* he sought release from his contract to produce a daily column and moved to the New York *Herald Tribune* in 1922. His column, renamed "The Lantern," retained its format; Archy and Mehitabel and all of Marquis' other characters came along.

His books include *Danny's Own Story* (1912, a novel); *The Cruise of the Jasper B.* (1916, a novel); a collection of sketches from his column–*Hermione and Her Little Group of Serious Thinkers* (1917), *Prefaces* (1919) and a play, "The Old Soak" (1921). Based on a character in his columns, "The Old Soak" enjoyed a successful Broadway run and was made into a motion picture, starring Wallace Beery. A later play, "Out of the Sea" (1927), had a brief New York run. Marquis ended his newspaper column in 1925, when he bought out his contract in order to devote his time to other work and more efficient means of making money. Producing a column was agony for Marquis, who came to see his efforts as "a twenty-three inch grave" (the length of his column), in which he buried himself. Marquis, who had lacked financial resources beyond his writing, was the sole support of his two sisters and a family with illness; income was a constant need. Marquis derived ample financial reward from the theater and motion pictures.

Hollywood beckoned, but Marquis' career as a screenwriter was sporadic at best. He enjoyed much more success as a weekly free-lance writer, featuring Archy's adventures mostly, for *Collier's,* and as an author. He published other works of humor, drama, and poetry but his notable successes were with the series of books featuring Archy: *Archy and Mehitabel* (1927), *Archy's Life of Mehitabel* (1927), and *Archy Does His Part* (1935).

Marquis' religious beliefs are apparent in much of his work. A convert to Catholicism, Marquis flirted with spiritualism and was a believer in the occult. Archy's conversations with Shakespeare and Johnson are recounted; reincarnation was not to be ruled out. His 1932 drama of the Crucifixion, "The Dark Hours," was not a success, financial or literary. Marquis invested his own money in its production, invariably a serious error for a playwright. Shortly before its opening, Marquis suf-

fered a stroke. His health had not been good since a
1929 heart attack in Hollywood. He again suffered a
stroke in 1936 that left him unable to speak. Marquis
died in December 1937. His personal life was full of
tragedy–his child died at an early age, his two wives
died, and Marquis had troubles with alcohol; none of
these travails were mentioned in his public work.

Marquis was an artist of merit whose career as a
newspaper columnist marked an epoch in American
journalism; he brought the humor column to its finest
heights, especially as a personal vehicle. His literary
work, aside from the Archy and Mehitabel saga, is out of
print and is likely to be available only on library
shelves. Marquis was a newspaperman who reached for
the stars. The fortune he sought eluded him, however,
and his fame has faded. Nevertheless, Marquis and his
"goddamn cockroach" remain as a rich journalistic legacy, uniquely American.

SOURCES:

Edward Anthony, *O Rare Don Marquis* (Garden City:
    Doubleday, 1962).

Lynn Lee, *Don Marquis* (Boston: Twayne, 1981).

Thomas Masson, *Our American Humorists* (Freeport: Books
    for Libraries Press, 1966).

Christopher Morley, "A Successor to Mark Twain," and "O
    Rare Don Marquis," in *Letters of Askance* (Philadelphia: J.
    B. Lippincott, 1939).

E. B. White, "Don Marquis," *Second Tree from the Corner*
    (New York: Harper and Bros./Perennial, 1954).

SELECTED BOOKS BY MARQUIS:

The Almost Perfect State (Garden City: Doubleday, Page & Co., 1927)

The Best of Don Marquis, Christopher Morley, ed. (Garden City: Doubleday & Co., 1946).

Chapters for the Orthodox (Garden City: Doubleday, Doran & Co., 1934).

The Cruise of the Jasper B. (New York: D. Appleton & Co., 1916).

Danny's Own Story (Garden City: Doubleday, Page & Co., 1912).

The Dark Hours (New York: Doubleday, Page & Co., 1924).

Hermione and Her Little Group of Serious Thinkers (New York: D. Appleton & Co., 1916).

The Lives and Times of Archy and Mehitabel (Garden City: Doubleday & Co., 1950).

Love Sonnets of a Caveman and Other Poems (New York; Doubleday, Doran & Co., 1928).

Noah an' Jonah an' Cap'n John Smith (New York: D. Appleton & Co., 1921).

The Old Soak (New York: Sun Dial Press, 1937).

Old Soak and Hail and Farewell (Garden City:Doubleday, Doran & Co./Sun Dial Press, 1937).

Old Soak's History of the World (Garden City: Sun Dial Press, 1937).

Revolt of the Oyster (New York: Doubleday, Page & Co., 1922)

Sun Dial Time (Garden City: Doubleday, Doran & Co., 1936).

8

George S. Schuyler

Black Press Iconoclast

In the early years of the twentieth century, American society was deeply divided–black and white–so far as race was concerned. After the Civil War and passage of the Thirteenth, Fourteenth, and Fifteenth Amendments to the Constitution–to free the slaves, confer citizenship, and grant black male suffrage–a society increasingly divisive constrained blacks. In the South, state Jim Crow laws restricted black activities. After the 1895 Supreme Court decision, the United States followed guidelines laid down in Plessy v. Ferguson. "Separate but equal" facilities for blacks became the law of the land. Under increasingly restrictive legislation, black-white social contact, schools, and other institutions, were assuredly separate, but hardly equal. This status remained fixed under federal and state laws until the 1955 Brown v. Board of Education decision mandated equal facilities.

By the outset of the twentieth century, three major movements vied for the means to improve black status in America. One was the "back to Africa" plan of Marcus

George S. Schuyler: Chronology

1895   born, February 25, Providence, Rhode Island

1912   enlists in U.S. Army, 25th Infantry Division

1923   columnist, "Shafts and Darts," for the *Messenger;* served
        as assistant editor through 1928

1925   Joins Pittsburgh *Courier;* columnist, "Views and Reviews"
        (1925-1966); editorial writer (1942-1944); associate editor
        (1942-1964); New York editor (1944-1960); international
        correspondent (1931-1961)

1927   "Our White Folks," the *American Mercury*

1930   begins Young Negroes' Cooperative League

1931   *Black No More;* series on Liberian slave trade, New York
        Post; Slaves Today: A Story of Liberia

1937   business manager for the *Crisis*

1943   associate editor, the *African*

1947   *Red Drive in the Colonies*

1949   WLIB radio, "Negro World," and "The Editors Speak"
        (through 1964)

1961   joins John Birch Society, contributor to *American
        Opinion*

1964   contributor to Manchester, N.H. *Union Leader*

1982   dies August 31, New York

Garvey (not unlike Abraham Lincoln's idea) for a black homeland. Garvey's followers, the Universal Negro Improvement Association (UNIA), published the *Negro World,* had their own flag, and their own nobility. Blacks "who pretended to be white" disturbed black newspaperman George S. Schuyler, who characterized Garvey as a "fascist leader," backed by a "few racist idiots." Garvey's indictment for fraud eroded his credibility and support for the UNIA waned.

A less radical movement for accommodation with white America was begun by Frederick Douglass in the nineteenth century. Douglass spread his ideas through his newspaper, the *New National Era.* After Douglass died in 1895, his role as national leader passed to Booker T. Washington. He advocated that blacks accept an agrarian economy with a separate-but-equal role and won favor from the white power elite. Schuyler termed the idea "nonsense."

Newspapers played a significant role in black communities. At the beginning of the century, the visibility of the black press was negligible to whites, but the black audience numbered eight million, approximately double since the end of the Civil War. This was a formidable market and the growth of black enterprises–physicians, teachers, clergymen, business, professional and shopkeepers–followed divided lines. That development was endorsed by Washington, who headed the Tuskegee Institute, in Alabama. Washington advocated hard work, to earn right to full admission to white society. "Nonsense," again scoffed Schuyler.

A reformist-integrationist move was championed by W. E. B. DuBois, who advocated a more militant movement with aggressive activities for blacks to enter into the mainstream of American life. DuBois, founder of the NAACP (National Association for the Advancement of Colored People) and co editor of its journal, the *Crisis,* was an active voice in black-white relations. Schuyler, a conservative, decried violence and militant actions.

Basically, the black press was divided in its advocacy for one or the other of these approaches. The ideas and techniques for reaching these goals occupied the attention of most black writers. Except for George Schuyler, who opposed each of these approaches. Every camp was a target for his criticism. He used invective, parody, and satire to castigate opponents–black or white. For example, Schuyler mocked black newspaper advertisements for skin whiteners and hair straighteners alongside editorials extolling black pride. He described himself as an iconoclast, with no apologies. Like most iconoclasts of any race, in any society, his career was (self described) "stormy and lonely."

George S. Schuyler (1895-1977), born February 25, 1895, in Providence, Rhode Island, grew up in Syracuse, New York. His father, chef in a local hotel, was described by Schuyler as "an aristocrat in the colored community." After his father's death, Schuyler's mother remarried in 1898, and his step-father was a cook for the New York Central Railroad. George Schuyler's family was black, but thorough Yankees. For generations, the Schuylers were freemen. None were descended from slaves and they looked down on anyone who had been in servitude. Schuyler was taught to regard Southern blacks as "illiterate, ignorant, ill-bred, and amoral." His family lived among whites and shared the same prejudices as native whites toward Southern blacks and equally disdained European immigrants–people on a par with the traffic from Dixie. Schuyler's early teachings were traditionally conservative, and he held to that view lifelong.

His mother introduced him to books before he began school and he was "one of three or four colored children" attending the city schools. He did well, but at seventeen enlisted in the Army. He served from 1912 to 1919–in

Seattle, Hawaii, Japan, and the Philippines–with the Twenty-fifth Infantry Division, a black elite unit with high standards and a distinguished history.

Schuyler instructed troops in English and geography. The Army acquainted Schuyler with the discrimination of "black" blacks by the lighter skinned and the excesses of drinking and gambling–practices he deplored. He later wrote of these years a decade later. During the army years, Schuyler developed his journalistic skills writing for regimental publications–the *Service* and the *Daily Dope* and occasional articles for the Honolulu *Commercial Appeal.* Schuyler was accepted to Officer's Candidate School and the high school dropout lacking a college degree won a commission, one of 629 who finished in a class of 1,200. He was discharged in 1919 as a first lieutenant, and returned to New York. A former army colleague help him land a temporary civil service position processing military prisoners. When that work ended, Schuyler found odd jobs–drug store clerk, delivery man, brass factory hand, and dishwasher–the last experience he used as an article, "Memoirs of a Pearl Diver," for H.L. Mencken's *American Mercury.* In 1921 he returned to Syracuse briefly, joined the Socialist Party, and became active in party recruitment and meetings. Back in New York in 1922, he worked briefly as a railroad hand and at other odd jobs.

He met A. Philip Randolph, leader of the Friends of Negro Socialism and co-editor of the *Messenger,* a monthly journal of "Scientific Socialism." Given a clerical job by Randolph, he learned something of the publication routine and eventually submitted an article to the *World Tomorrow* that told of the difficulties of finding work, "From Job to Job." In 1923 an article in the *Messenger* led to a job and he was given a monthly page "Shafts and Darts: A Page of Calumny and Satire," at a salary of fifteen dollars a week. He stayed with the

Messenger, rising to associate editor, through 1928.

In 1925 Schuyler was invited to write a column, "Views and Reviews"–for three dollars a week–for the Pittsburgh *Courier,* the second-largest circulation black newspaper in America; his column continued until 1966. From 1931 to 1961, he was the *Courier's* international correspondent; from 1942 through 1964, he served as editorial writer and associate editor; and was the *Courier's* New York editor from 1944 through 1960.

Schuyler became increasingly political. He detested the hypocrisy of the Socialists and despised the racist policies of the Communists, and used his column to say so. An assignment took him across the country from November 1925 to July 1926 to write observations on the Negro South. He now earned fifty dollars a week (that included travel and expenses). Schuyler visited every city of 5,000 or more in thirteen states. He found that "white hatred for the Negro was a myth," that treatment of blacks varied considerably from community to community, and that stereotypes abounded on all sides. This work provided an early example of Schuyler's thorough investigative reporting.

That series for the *Courier* and a piece in the *Nation,* "The Negro Art Hokum," ridiculed "the current gabble about a distinctive Negro art and literature," helped to make Schuyler a celebrity. Schuyler ridiculed the idea of a separate black literature and unique art, and continued this view to the end of his days.

Randolph organized the Brotherhood of Sleeping Car Porters and Schuyler was one of its speakers at a founding meeting. At this time he was offered the job of writing editorials for the *Courier*–a post he held for thirty-eight years. Schuyler wrote also for the black show business journal the *Interstate Tattler,* and influential publications–the *Nation,* the *New Masses, Ebony,* and *Topaz.* His lead article for the *American Mercury* in December

1927, "Our White Folks," delighted Mencken and a number of readers. Mencken's *Mercury* was the preeminent critical journal of its time and Schuyler its leading contributor in the last six years of Mencken's editorship.

The *Mercury* article led to a testimonial dinner from the influential black community and a speaking tour. When the *Messenger* folded in July 1928, Schuyler landed a Chicago-based job editing a newspaper-magazine filler, the *Illustrated Feature,* published by W.B. Ziff. Other Schuyler publications included a *Little Blue Book,* published by E. Haldeman-Julius, and articles for the *Modern Quarterly,* an avant-garde magazine. Schuyler helped organize the Young Negroes' Cooperative League for retail selling with white merchants in New York. Schuyler held fast to his belief that cooperatives were a solution to black economic prosperity and the door to equality with whites.

In 1930 Schuyler, with prospects for a book, visited Liberia to investigate the alleged slave trade. Charges that looked substantial held that high officials, from the president on down, were involved. Schuyler's findings were to be published in the New York *Evening Post.* In January 1931, Schuyler began his investigations. His findings created a sensation when he disclosed that slavery was a government-backed enterprise and that blacks were the culpable participants, not whites. Moreover, blacks used slaves throughout the economy. Garvey followers and black nationalists were furious. Schuyler's six-part series in the *Post* was also printed in several other leading white newspapers–the *Washington Post,* the Buffalo *Express,* and the Philadelphia *Public Ledger*–a first for a black journalist.

Schuyler's *Black No More* (1931) won praise from black and white critics. W.E.B. DuBois described it as "a satire, rollicking keen, good-natured criticism of the Negro problem," even though DuBois was one of the leaders caricatured. The book contained humor, but "good-natured" it was not. Schuyler's book of the African slave trade, *Slaves Today: A Story of Liberia* and another article for the *American Mercury,* "Uncle Sam's Black Stepchild," created controversy. Schuyler attacked black hypocrisy, and especially the American black press for turning a blind eye to the slave trade practiced by supposed "brothers."

In the early 1930s Schuyler went to war against the Communist Party, a group he distrusted and felt exploited American blacks for selfish gains. No good could come from the "black-belt"–a scheme the Communists advocated whereby a separate land area inside the United States would be set aside for blacks–whites would be dispossessed of land and property and excluded. This idea of a "49th state" was advocated by the *Daily Worker,* the American based Communist-voice newspaper. "Gullible blacks," Schuyler wrote, "should know that success would not flow from Red-backed schemes."

When the Scotsboro incident broke in March 1931, the Communists deposed the NAACP and led their cause. Nine blacks were accused of raping two white women on a freight train near Scotsboro, Alabama. The Communists used this episode to push for the "black-belt" concept and Schuyler's outspoken opposition caused friction within the black community. Similarly, his April 1932 article in the *American Mercury,* "Black Americans Begin to Doubt," an attack on the black churches, also aroused opposition. The church remains a bulwark in black social and political life. Church leaders are sacrosanct. No icon remained unscathed from Schuyler. His attacks on futile black economic boycotts also came under fire. Schuyler was attacked by editors of the Chicago *Defender,* a leading liberal black newspaper, and by William M. Jones, managing editor of the powerful Baltimore *Afro-American* newspapers. Jones, Schuyler said, was a "Red."

Schuyler used intemperate language, exemplified by his commentary in a 1935 *Crisis* column:

> Whenever the Aframericans, flailed unduly by poverty, prejudice and proscription, yammers aloud for succor...we have been periodically afflicted with the Back-to-Africa dervishes...to the advent of the infantile paralysis of Garveyism; the high pressure Group Economy salesmen who view segregation through rose-colored spectacles....The shamans rattle their shells and toss their gri-gri bags for a season, charm a moron minority with their bombastic amphigories... then hock their wardrobes and hold off their landladies until they glimpse another vision of cash.

In 1937 Schuyler, assigned by the *Courier* to survey effects of the industrial labor union drive on blacks, travelled through forty-two cities and seventeen states. He found that infiltration by the Communists did not benefit black workers–or whites.

By 1939 Schuyler was warning his *Courier* readers about the suspected link between Fascist Germany and the Communist Soviet Union. And through much of the 1940s and the 1950s, Schuyler wrote extensively about the continuing Communist conspiracy in the United States. His theme was not politically correct; it was unpopular to attack World War II ally Soviet Russia, but Schuyler persisted in his theme. He wrote for the *African,* a magazine where he served as associate editor, the *New Leader* and *Negro Digest* on the Communist threat to America.

In 1944 *Courier* management asked Schuyler to become New York editor and in 1947, he became a contributing editor to *Plain Talk,* an anti-communist magazine. When W.E.B. DuBois joined the Communist-backed *New Masses,* Schuyler broke with him. Schuyler attacked his opponents–DuBois and singer Paul Robeson among them–as "deluded lame brains" and lost even more friends. But he was being printed in such publications as *Reader's Digest* and the *Christian Science Monitor*. His anti Communist support prompted Schuyler to describe Senator Joseph R. McCarthy as "well-intentioned" and a "great American." McCarthy conducted one of America's great witch-hunts searching for largely imaginary Communists in the State Department. But McCarthy's anti-communism stand made an ally of Schuyler. International issues dominated Schuyler's attention; he warned incessantly of the Red Menace in China, Cuba, and Latin America.

Radio offered Schuyler an outlet in 1949 when New York station WLIB signed him to a weekly broadcast, "The Negro World" and later a guest-panel program, "The Editors Speak," which continued for the next fifteen years. His initial program began with the Communist threat in the Caribbean, and the "Red Menace" continued to be a constant theme.

The issue was not one of color for Schuyler, but his comments became increasing abstract to a black community, relatively indifferent to Communism but deeply concerned with race relations. In September 1960, management of the *Courier* relieved Schuyler as New York editor, after seventeen years, without any notification, verbal or written. They simply named a successor and neglected to inform Schuyler. He remained an associate editor, however.

Schuyler dismissed "the so-called Negro Revolution and the insane antics identified with it" and continued to deplore sit-ins, civil rights demonstrations, and marches because these protests were instigated by professional "agitators." Schuyler sincerely felt civil disobedience created enemies for blacks, whatever the gains. Schuyler became a John Birch member and wrote for their publication, *American Opinion,* where conservative, anti-communist views were welcome.

He opposed the "constructive demonstrations" of Dr. Martin Luther King Jr. and his denounciation of King's award of the Nobel Peace prize in 1964 was not printed in the *Courier.* The attack found a place in William Loeb's Manchester, (N.H.) *Union Leader.* This publisher and his newspaper was one of the most scurrilous in America, resorting to name-calling of minority groups and other devices to inflame readers. The same month Schuyler wrote his last editorial for the *Courier,* and the *Union Leader* became his outlet. The notoriety of the King attack brought Schuyler a contract with NANA (North American Newspaper Alliance). The *Crisis* editorialized that Schuyler had gone "too far."

Schuyler died in New York, August 31, 1977, at the age of 82, still following his own independent and iconoclastic ideas: that individuals count; that race is a "superstition"; no separate black "culture" exists; and despite color lines, black and white can come together with a shared heritage.

George Schuyler helped build the Pittsburgh *Courier* into the largest and most-powerful voice in black America and it offered him a convenient forum to express his often-unpopular opinions. That is asking a great deal of any newspaper. Unquestionably, Schuyler consistently went too far–his outspoken, opinionated, caustic comments frequently made enemies. Schuyler was among the first to say "black is beautiful"; that many problems could be solved if the Constitution was simply enforced; that out-moded laws restricting voting, inter-racial marriage, segregated education, housing, and union quotas should be abolished. He constantly urged education, hard work, and cooperative efforts as solutions to the race issue. He mocked schemes for separatism and correctly saw that "isms" were not the answer, and said so.

Schuyler deplored "white do-gooders and dreamers" as well as "black apologists and agitators" for their easy reasons for the hapless situation of crime, drugs, and other social evils often offered as excuses for failure. Nor were government handouts the answer; these were devices to continue the status quo. He termed these "messages of mass disparagement." Schuyler's iconoclastic conservatism was shunned by leaders, black and white. He said–and wrote extensively–opinions that others did not wish to hear.

Black No More is a classic that rivals Mark Twain in its biting satire of race relations, humor steeped in acid. Mencken described Schuyler as a man of "intelligence, independence, and courage" and one of America's best columnists. Few newspapermen, black or white, left such a rich heritage of achievement to American journalism.

SOURCES:

Michael Peplow, George S. Schuyler (Boston: Twayne, 1980).

George S. Schuyler, *Black and Conservative: The Autobiography of George Schuyler* (New York: Arlington House, 1966).

Clint C. Wilson II, *Black Journalists in Paradox: Historical Perspectives and Current Dilemmas* (New York: Greenville Press, 1991).

Roland E. Wolseley, *The Black Press, USA* (Ames: Iowa State University Press, 1990).

SELECTED BOOKS BY SCHUYLER:

Black and Conservative (New York: Arlington House, 1966).

Black No More (New York: Macauley, 1931).

9

Ring Lardner

Sportswriting as Literature

Newspaperman and columnist Ring Lardner, an author of uncommon merit, is virtually ignored by serious critics as H. L. Mencken gloomily predicted. Of Lardner, Mencken wrote in the 1920s: "no other American of his generation, sober or gay, wrote better." Lardner captured, with a perceptive eye and caustic word, the buffoonery of classic Americans–ballplayers, the middle class moron–with humor and savage analysis of character. He is usually dismissed as a minor American writer. Many of the people he wrote about have disappeared from the American scene, but he depicted the time and place of the vulgate America as no other of his time.

A contemporary of Franklin P. Adams and Eugene Field, Lardner won his initial fame as a newspaper columnist in Chicago, writing primarily about baseball. Unlike those two, however, Lardner's humor contains a savage and satirical edge. Lardner was a superb writer whose work demands recognition, if not as literature, certainly as an example of America's finest journalism.

Ring Lardner: Chronology

1885   born, Niles, Michigan, March 6

1901-
1902   office boy for McCormick Harvester Co.; freight "hustler"
        for Michigan Central Railroad; fails out of Armour Institute

1905   meter reader for Niles Gas Co.; musical comedy
        "Zanzibar"; reporter for South Bend (Indiana) *Times*

1907   sportswriter for the *Chicago Inter-Ocean;* baseball
        reporter for the Chicago *Examiner*

1908   sportswriter for the Chicago *Tribune*

1910-
1911   managing editor of the *Sporting News;* sports editor for
        the Boston *Herald;* copy reader for the Chicago *American*

1912   baseball writer for Chicago *Examiner,* writes as
        "Roy Clarkson"

1913   rejoins Chicago *Tribune* to write column "In the Wake of
        the News" for the next six years

1914   first stories in the *Saturday Evening Post*

1915   "Jack Keefe" stories in *Saturday Evening Post;* "Fred
        Gross" stories in *Redbook; Bib Ballads*

1917   *Gullible's Travels, Etc.;* war correspondent for *Collier's*

1918   *Treat 'Em Rough*

1919   *The Real Dope; Own Your Own Home; Regular Fellas I
        Have Met;* begins weekly column for Bell Syndicate

Ringgold Wilmer Lardner (1885-1933) was born on March 6, 1885, in Niles, Michigan, of wealthy parents and was tutored at home. His education was a classic liberal curriculum that included Greek and Latin. After graduation from high school, he worked briefly in Chicago for McCormick International Harvester and a real estate firm, neither job lasted a month. He returned to Niles and worked as a freight agent for the Michigan Central Railroad.

In 1902, Lardner attempted a course of study at the Armour Institute in Chicago but failed after a year and returned home to work as a clerk for the Niles Gas Company. He participated in local theatricals and wrote words and music for "Zanzibar," a local musical success. He began his journalism career as a reporter for the South Bend (Ind.) *Times* in 1905. At a salary of $12 weekly, Lardner was a general assignment reporter, who covered baseball as well. An indifferent reporter, Lardner was a good baseball writer who understood the fine points of the game.

In 1907, Lardner met Hugh S. Fullerton, a sports writer for the Chicago *Examiner,* who had earned a local reputation for correctly predicting the outcome of the 1906 World Series, a home town event where the favored Cubs lost to the "Hitless Wonders" White Sox. Fullerton took a liking to Lardner, partly because of his writing ability, partly because he knew the technical points of the game, and partly because Lardner was a formidable drinking companion. Through Fullerton's assistance, Lardner left small-town South Bend to become a sports reporter in Chicago for the *Inter-Ocean,* earning $18.50 a week.

Lardner was given the donkey work, covering high school sports, but more important, he met people who influenced his work. Charles Dryden, a fellow sports writer, helped Lardner develop his writing style. His

1920   *Young Immigrants*

1921   *The Big Town; Symptoms of Being 35*

1924   *How to Write Short Stories [With Samples];* contributes
        sketches to Ziegfeld's "Follies"

1925   *What Of It?*

1926   *The Love Nest and Other Stories*

1927   *The Story of a Wonder Man;* ended Bell Syndication

1929   *Round Up;* successful play with George S. Kaufman,
        "June Moon"

1930   Failed play with George M. Cohan, "Elmer the Great";
        begins column with New York *Telegraph;* signs with Bell
        Syndicate

1931   autobiographical series for the *Saturday Evening Post*

1932   new Busher series for the *Saturday Evening Post*

1933   *Lose With a Smile;* radio columns for the *New Yorker;*
        dies September 25, New York City

1934   *First and Last*

contacts and good work led to an offer from William Randolph Hearst's *Examiner* at $25 a week for a sports department desk job writing heads. Later he was assigned to cover the White Sox, where he wrote as "Roy Clarkson." In that era, writers came and went frequently and it was convenient for the newspaper to have staff members write by the same name. Lardner travelled with the team and came to know the players well. The ball players' arcane vocabulary found its way into Lardner's reporting and columns.

Lardner did well enough to be invited to join the *Chicago Tribune* in 1908, at a $10-a-week raise to $35, when his friend Dryden left that newspaper and recommended Lardner as his replacement. The *Tribune* was the city's largest, and best, newspaper. Harvey Woodruff was sports editor and Hugh E. Keough's column, "In the Wake of the News," was widely read. Lardner, as baseball writer, would cover both Chicago teams, the Cubs and the White Sox. Lardner favored the Cubs, the world champions, who, if not as zany as the Sox, supplied him with better copy.

The White Sox, however, supplied him with a songwriting partner when he revisited that early experience from "Zanzibar." Lardner and Guy Harris (Doc) White, a good 19-game winning pitcher, teamed to produce songs in 1910 and 1911. Their salute to baseball, "It's A Wonderful Game," however, failed to displace the 1908 hit, "Take Me Out to the Ball Game." Lardner spent considerable free time trying to promote his songs.

The two years that Lardner worked for the *Tribune* enabled him to develop his writing style, inventive and humorous. In addition to the game coverage, Lardner wrote columns of commentary–"Notes of the Cubs," or "Notes of the White Sox," where he was able to insert trivial comments that were sometimes humorous, always perceptive, and often whimsical. In the winter

Lardner covered college football games, but his principal interest lay clearly with baseball and increasingly his writing reflected that interest.

Lardner bounced around from job to job, still focusing on baseball. In 1910 he resigned from the *Tribune* and began work in St. Louis as managing editor of *The Sporting News* for $50 weekly. Lardner proved to be no editor; the job lasted only two months. Rather than return to Chicago and the *Tribune,* which held his job open, Lardner joined the Boston *American* for $45 a week, a respectable salary at that time. At this point Lardner married and he and his bride set up housekeeping. The marriage was successful, the job less so. Lardner chose to leave the *American* after covering the Giant-Athletics World Series when management fired two of his newspaper friends.

Lardner returned to Chicago and the best job he could find–baseball writers are not in great demand during the off-season–was copyreader for the Chicago *American,* another Hearst newspaper. In February 1912, he rejoined the *Examiner* with his old friend Dryden, to cover the Cubs. The next year Lardner returned to the *Tribune,* (again on Fullerton's recommendation) to write the popular daily variety column, "In the Wake of the News." It was an important assignment and a change of pace; he was given a three month trial at $50 a week. He was successful and conducted the column for the next six years. Here Lardner began to produce the dialect and cadence of the players' voices, often using real players in his vignettes. "In the Wake of the News" provided Lardner with opportunity to find his own voice and provided the foundation for future writing.

After unsuccessfully trying to write free-lance pieces for Chicago newspapers, Lardner sent one of his baseball stories to the *Saturday Evening Post* in 1914. The editor wanted more. From an initial $250 payment, the fee for

his stories reached $1,250 each (Lardner was then earn-
ing $75 weekly at the *Tribune*). These stories were pub-
lished in book form as *You Know Me Al*. Lardner, who
was hoping to make a move to New York, wrote his old
colleague from Chicago, Franklin P. Adams. But
Lardner's salary at the *Tribune* was raised to $200, per-
suading him to remain in Chicago.

Lardner continued to submit stories to the *Saturday
Evening Post* and other popular magazines–*Collier's
Weekly, Redbook, McClure's,* the *American,* and one of
his greatest stories, "Champion," for *Metropolitan*. His
Post stories were published as *Gullible's Travels, Etc.* In
1917, Lardner was assigned to cover the war in Europe
and the activities of America's soldiers in the AEF in a
series of "Reporter's Diaries" for *Collier's* magazine. He
also continued his column for the *Tribune*. His song writing career was revived when the black song-and-dance
man Bert Williams, star of the 1917 Ziegfeld "Follies"
used one of his contributions. From his *Collier* series
came a book, *My Four Weeks in France,* but he was home
in time to cover the World Series between the Giants
and the winning White Sox. He also sold another of his
songs, performed by Nora Bayes, "Prohibition Blues."
Lardner resigned from the *Tribune* to write a weekly column for John N. Wheeler's Bell Syndicate, an association that was to last for half-a-dozen years, and earn
Lardner $30,000 a year.

Lardner was greatly disillusioned with the "Black
Sox" World Series scandal in 1919; his ball players were
no longer humorous "rubes" or the sports heroes of a
more innocent time, and this episode contributed to
Lardner's cynicism. Increasingly, his writing turned to
general fiction and theatrical writing. Lardner wrote
more musical lyrics for Nora Bayes, Bert Williams, and
Marilyn Miller and contributed material to several of
Florenz Ziegfeld's "Follies." Lardner continued his Bell

Syndicate work until 1927. His humor, however, became more deadly and bitter, his parodies more satirical as he focused his writing on the "little guy," who was often a boob, and the gaucheries of the middle-class. Lardner's misogynist humor had a bite savage at times.

In these years Lardner published a half-dozen books, including *Big Town* and *How to Write Short Stories*. When the *Saturday Evening Post* rejected his "The Golden Honeymoon," one of his best, Lardner sent his material to *Liberty* magazine (for $3,500 a story) and *Cosmopolitan*. He collaborated with George M. Cohan on "Elmer, the Great," which failed as a play but was more successful as a motion picture–once in a version starring Jack Oakie and later with Joe E. Brown. "Champion" later became a starring vehicle for Kirk Douglas. Lardner's stage drama with Robert E. Sherwood was unsuccessful, but he had better luck with co-author George S. Kaufman and "June Moon," a long-running Broadway comedy.

Lardner returned to journalism in 1930 to write four columns weekly for the New York *Telegraph,* at a $50,000-a-year salary. But the job ended after a few brief months. In his last years–he was suffering from tuberculosis–Lardner continued, with less success, to write for the *Saturday Evening Post,* and an autobiographical series for the Bell Syndicate. In his last major writing project, Lardner proposed a series of radio criticisms to his friend, Harold Ross for the *New Yorker.* (Lardner was a member of the Algonquin Circle, but confined himself to the poker sessions.) Confined for long periods to a hospital bed, Lardner had many free hours to listen to radio, day and night, and his *New Yorker* essays became a trail blazing crusade into early radio criticism. Lardner, a moralist at heart, carried on a futile campaign to clean up radio's dialogues and music of smutty language. Ironically, the print journalist believed that radio needed a censor. Ill as he was, it was some of the best work Lardner did. He died in September 1933, of a heart attack and complications from drinking.

In 1924 H.L. Mencken suggested a parallel between Mark Twain and Ring Lardner. Twain, Mencken reminded readers of the *American Mercury,* remained long unrecognized for his literary merit and was seen as little more than a comic writer whose background was journalism and who lacked literary credentials. The average book critic, Mencken wrote, dismissed Lardner because the reviewer "belongs to the white collar class of labor, and shares its prejudices."

Lardner all the same wrote with a savagery that targeted ordinary people as morons and boors. His literary credentials continue to be questioned, even though recognized writers–Virginia Woolf, Edmund Wilson, F. Scott Fitzgerald and H.L. Mencken–praised his work. Several of his more than two-dozen published books remain in print. For the most part, Lardner's journalism legacy is neglected and, however significant his literary accomplishments, he saw himself as a newspaperman. Indifference and inattention to Lardner's work belies the legacy that he left to journalism. Lardner was a savage and perceptive writer who had the ability to make us laugh at ourselves, when people could still do so. Lardner transcended mere sports writing; in his hands that world is a metaphor for our own. The scorn of "literary" critics (to which Lardner mutually subscribed) who dismiss Ring Lardner as a "mere newspaperman" (which Lardner would heartily endorse) should be a badge of nobility to any aspiring journalist.

SOURCES:

Matthew J. Bruccoli and Richard Layman, *Ring Lardner: A Descriptive Biography* (Pittsburgh: University of Pittsburgh Press, 1976).

Donald Elder, *Ring Lardner* (Garden City: Doubleday & Co., 1956).

Ring Lardner, *The Story of a Wonder Man: Being the Autobiography of Ring Lardner* (New York: Charles Scribner's Sons, 1927).

Walter B. Patrick, *Ring Lardner* (New York: Twayne, 1963).

Jonathan Yardley, *RING: A Biography of Ring Lardner* (New York: Random House, 1972).

SELECTED BOOKS BY LARDNER:

First and Last (New York: Scribner's, 1934).

Ring Around the Bases (New York: Charles Scribner's Sons, 1992).

Ring Lardner Reader, George Geisner, ed. (New York: Charles Scribner's Sons, 1963).

Shut Up, He Explained Babette Rosmond and Henry Morgan, eds. (New York: Scribner's, 1962).

The Annotated Baseball Stories of Ring W. Lardner, George W. Hilton, ed. (Stanford: Stanford University Press, 1963).

The Love Nest and Other Stories (New York: Scribner's 1926).

You Know Me Al (New York: Dover, 1995).

10

Edmund Duffy

Tiger on a Rampage

The past century may be remembered as the "Golden Age" of the American newspaper editorial cartoon. Beginning with Benjamin Franklin's "Unite or Die" engraving exhorting the English colonists to take arms against the French, through Thomas Nast's 1860s *Harper's* magazine art that helped jail Tammany Boss William Marcy Tweed, cartoons played a central role in imparting messages that could be understood by even the illiterate. From that rich heritage, the editorial cartoon was a basic staple of American newspapers.

By the end of the twentieth century, however, editorial cartoons appear in fewer newspapers and less than 150 retain their own cartoonist. First, fewer newspapers exist in America–basically, one-city newspapers prevail, even in the major cities of the nation that once enjoyed as many as a dozen newspapers. Second, cost-cutting has eroded the staff and cartoonists are no longer considered essential. Most newspapers rely now on syndicated art. Cartoonists have become an endangered species in American journalism.

Edmund Duffy: Chronology

1899   born, Jersey City, N.J.

1916   leaves high school, Art Students' League

1918   Armistice Day illustration, New York *Tribune*

1922   illustrator, theatrical and sports, Brooklyn *Eagle*

1923   editorial cartoonist, New York *Leader*

1924   *Leader* folds, returns to *Eagle*

1924   September, joins Baltimore *Sun,* for ninety-day trial

1925   Scopes trial with H. L. Mencken

1931   Pulitzer Prize for "An Old Struggle Still Going On"

1934   Pulitzer Prize for "California Points with Pride"

1940   Pulitzer Prize for "The Outstretched Hand"

1948   June, leaves *Sunpapers*

1949   January, joins *Saturday Evening Post*

1956   March, leaves *Saturday Evening Post;* April, joins Long
         Island *Newsday*; November, leaves *Newsday*

1959   November, joins *Washington Post*

1960   Herblock returns, leaves *Washington Post*

1962   dies September 12, New York City

A number of editorial cartoonists made notable contributions through the 1900s. At the outset of the century, several contributed memorable work. No Pulitzer prize–a recognition of excellence–was awarded for editorial cartooning until 1922, but cartoons were an essential journalistic element long before prizes were awarded. A number of cartoonists are absent from that roll. The rules required newspaper publication, hence, artists like John Sloan were ineligible; other artists whose work appeared primarily in magazines are excluded. Art Young, for example, was a voice of violent protest, whose work appeared in the *Masses* and the *New Masses* after his work was banned from the popular press. Young was indicted under the Sedition Act of 1918, but his cartoons remained inflammatory. Young's work was printed in newspapers until he began to espouse a Socialist view. Boardman Robinson, another powerful voice of Socialism, whose work also appeared in the *Masses, New Masses,* and *Metropolitan,* held brief appointments with the Baltimore *Sun.* These cartoonists held social views anathama to popular taste.

Other cartoonists were similarly shunned. Robert Minor was another excellent cartoonist in the early years of the century whose work was ignored by the Pulitzer committee. Minor worked for Joseph Pulitzer's St. Louis *Post-Dispatch* and the New York *World.* When Minor refused to draw pro-war cartoons for the *World,* he was fired; subsequently, his work appeared in the Socialist *Masses.*

The early years of the century saw work by other excellent artists who played a role in American public opinion. Clifford Berryman joined the *Washington Post* in 1896 and his 1902 cartoon, "Drawing the Line in Mississippi" depicted President Theodore Roosevelt sparing the life of a bear cub. That cub became the famous "Teddy Bear," a symbol that captured the nation's fancy and endures to this day. For more than fifty years, the bear cub was a constant element in a Berryman cartoon. He joined the Washington *Evening Star* in 1907 and worked there until he died at his desk in 1949. Berryman was awarded a Pulitzer prize in 1944. President Harry Truman described Cliff Berryman as a great "cartoonist without malice." Another notable cartoonist without malice was John T. McCutcheon, "the first man of Chicago," who spent a decade at the Chicago *Daily Record* before joining the *Chicago Tribune* in 1903. He spent the next forty-three years there and was awarded a Pulitzer prize in 1932. McCutcheon is remembered for his gentle depictions of everyday life, but his 1932 Pulitzer award was for an atypically bitter commentary on the Great Depression. McCutcheon produced his classic cartoon, "Injun Summer," in 1907 that was reprinted annually by the *Tribune* for more than four decades.

A more "political" commentator, Nelson Harding began with the *Brooklyn Eagle* in 1903 and continued with that newspaper until 1929, when he joined the New York *Journal* where he worked until his death in 1945. Harding is the only recipient of back-to-back Pulitzer prizes, in 1927 and 1928. Harding also contributed a perceptive political opinion column that ran on the *Eagle's* front page.

Although his work was political, Jay N. ("Ding") Darling, of the Des Moines (Iowa) *Register* was another midwestern cartoonist known for gentle, folksy drawings. Through the mid-1950s, Ding was one of the best-known cartoonists in America. His work was syndicated through the New York *Herald Tribune* and he enjoyed a national reputation as a conservationist. Ding's cartoons depicted an America that had already disappeared, a rural, small town environment already old-fashioned by the early years of the century. For fifty years Ding reminded America of its rural heritage and held to a conservative moral compass. Ding Darling won two Pulitzer prizes, in 1924 and 1943, but his most famous cartoon was drawn in 1919, "The Long, Long Trail," on the death of Theodore Roosevelt. Another midwesterner shared fame with Darling–Daniel Fitzpatrick.

Fitzpatrick began his career in the early 1900s with the Chicago *Daily News,* but found a permanent niche with the St. Louis *Post-Dispatch,* where he served until his retirement in 1958. His was a long career that rivaled Ding's; he too won recognition with two Pulitzer prizes in 1926 and 1955. Like McCutcheon and Ding, Fitzpatrick was an institution in midwest America. Unlike these two, however, his work was somber and solemn. His powerful black crayon work resembled somewhat that of his predecessor, Robert Minor. His focus was often local in rooting out corruption in city politics. St. Louis and Kansas City, Fitzpatrick showed, could be as corrupt and crooked as big cities in the East. In one area, however, Fitzpatrick's work was distinctive–during the World War II years Fitzpatrick's depiction of the Nazi war machine was unsurpassed in its ferocity. Fitzpatrick's drawings of a brutal, malevolent, mechanized swastika made his work a social force.

Rollin Kirby must be remembered as one of the outstanding cartoonists of American journalism. After study at New York's Art Students' League, he travelled to Paris to study with James McNeill Whistler, but gave up a career in academic art. In 1913 he joined the editorial page of the New York *World,* with virtually free rein. His targets were the enemies of the liberal *World.* Kirby lacerated the United States Senate and its opposition to the League of Nations, the evils of Tammany Hall, the lunacy of the Ku Klux Klan, and the improbable ideals of the Scopes trial. His most famous creation was Mr. Dry, symbol of the Prohibitionist. Kirby is one of the few cartoonists, beyond Nast–with the Republican elephant, the Democratic donkey, and the Tammany Tiger–who can be credited with creation of a universal symbol. Kirby won three of the first ten Pulitzer prizes awarded for cartooning, a feat unmatched until Edmund Duffy won his third in 1940.

Three modern era cartoonists deserve mention as significant influences on editorial cartooning in America in the later years of the twentieth century. Herblock who has reigned at the *Washington Post* for more than fifty years, has made a monumental contribution. Herblock followed Kirby and Duffy to be honored with three Pulitzer prizes–in 1942, 1954, and 1979. The *Post* gives Herblock a space to fill on its editorial page, without direction or prior approval; he is one of the few cartoonists who have enjoyed this signal honor.

Bill Mauldin, the youngest to do so, won a Pulitzer prize in 1945 for his syndicated wartime cartoons "Up Front." Unique in that he worked not in a newsroom, but in the European theater of operations, Mauldin captured the genuine GI for an American audience with a blunt, distinctive pen-and-ink drawings. His pictorial message was true reporting. After the war, Mauldin returned for a brief stint with the short-lived New York *Star,* then succeeded Daniel Fitzpatrick at the St. Louis *Post-Dispatch,* where he won another Pulitzer in 1959. He ended his career with the Chicago *Sun-Times.*

Pat Oliphant, who at the end of the century was America's most widely-syndicated editorial cartoonist, is not affiliated with a newspaper. A native of Australia, he began his American career in 1964 with the Denver *Post* and won a Pulitzer prize in 1967, then moved to the Washington *Evening Star* until that paper folded. Since that time his cartoons have been syndicated by United Features–to more than 500 newspapers at the latest count. Oliphant consciously tries to do with art what

H. L. Mencken did in print–to outrage, arouse, and attack any group, regardless of race, creed, color, or political persuasion. He generally succeeds. Unlike most cartoonists, who are generally beloved, Oliphant has an army of enemies, primarily of people whose pomposity has been punctured with his stiletto thrusts. Mencken may have admired Oliphant, but as a matter of record, Mencken discovered one of the greatest cartoonists in American journalism.

Edmund Duffy (1899-1962), a cartoonist of outstanding merit, made a major contribution to American journalism during his career. Arguably, any one of the others mentioned could be nominated, but if one individual can best typify the highest qualities of art and journalistic integrity, Edmund Duffy meets that criteria.

Duffy, born in Jersey City, was a grade-school drop-out, and a product of the Art Students' League, tutored by John Sloan and Boardman Robinson. Robert Benchley gave Duffy his first job–a page in the New York *Tribune* illustrating the events of Armistice Day. He joined the *Brooklyn Eagle* as a general illustrator for the theatrical page and built a life-long interest in the legitimate theater. After a brief episode as editorial artist for the worker-owned New York *Leader*–the job lasted only three months–Duffy returned to the *Eagle*. Chances of becoming its editorial cartoonist, however, were remote, because Nelson Harding had been established there since 1903.

Duffy's connection with the theater and Benchley led him into contact with the Algonquin group, the famous circle of literary wits that boasted of people like Heywood Broun, Harold Ross, Alexander Woollcott, Dorothy Parker and others. Reportedly, Duffy drew a cartoon that depicted the luminaries arrayed as knights around a round table–hence, the name Round Table.

Benchley and Boardman Robinson introduced

Duffy's work to H.L. Mencken, the author and critic known in New York as editor of the *Smart Set* and the *American Mercury*. Mencken, however, was a newspaperman and an influential member of the Baltimore *Sunpapers*. Robinson had worked with Mencken on the Baltimore *Evening Sun* covering the 1921 Washington Naval Disarmament Conference. The morning newspaper, the *Sun,* was looking for an editorial cartoonist; its editorial page had been using Ding's syndicated work. The *Sun,* under Mencken's prodding, aspired to be a front-rank newspaper. Publisher Paul Patterson agreed to take on Duffy for a ninety-day trial period in 1924. Duffy stayed for the next quarter-century.

Duffy, presumably on board to tout the *Sun's* Democratic candidate John W. Davis, practically ignored the candidate—the most conservative Democrat to be nominated in the twentieth century. Duffy began to lambast the Ku Klux Klan, President Cal Coolidge, the "soft-soap" foreign policy of the GOP, and the failure of the United States to join the League of Nations. Mencken, who liked nothing more than "to stir up the animals," was delighted with his find. It was a startling departure for the *Sun;* its once folksy editorial page of gentle humor became a battleground.

Mencken was pleased with Duffy's work, especially those targets that coincided with Mencken's aims. When the Scopes trial began in Dayton, Tennessee, in 1925, Mencken included Duffy as part of the *Sunpapers'* team that covered the trial. The "Monkey Trial" pitted scientific theories of evolution against Fundamentalist teaching in public schools and created international interest. The *Sunpapers'* coverage with Mencken's copy and Edmund Duffy's cartoons created a sensation. Duffy's art displayed his contempt for the religious bigotry and bias; he won national attention through his powerful artwork that ran on the front page.

Duffy had earned a reputation as a fiercely independent artist, who drew cartoons that reflected his view. A colleague wrote: "If Duffy don't believe it, Duffy don't draw it." The *Sun* learned this lesson when Mencken was reprimanded editorially by that newspaper during the "Hatrack" episode that involved Mencken and the *American Mercury.* Duffy's cartoon space on the same editorial page supported Mencken. Duffy had his view; the newspaper had its view. Professionally, Gerald W. Johnson, a *Sunpapers* colleague, wrote: "Duffy was regarded with the uneasy delight that a zoo keeper has in a particularly fine Bengal tiger...everybody shuddered to think what would happen if he went on a rampage."

Rampage Duffy did when a lynch mob murdered a black suspect on Maryland's Eastern Shore. His powerful, satiric cartoon, "Maryland, My Maryland!," incited street riots and *Sunpaper* trucks were burned. Duffy won his first Pulitzer prize in 1931 for a cartoon showing the Communist attack on religion. He won again in 1934 for an anti-lynching cartoon, "California Points with Pride." Duffy, denied national syndication under the *Sunpapers'* policy, nevertheless, gained increasing national stature. His targets were the rise of Nazism in Germany, militant fascism in Italy, the menace of Japanese imperialism in the Far East and unrest in shaky South America. No one portrayed these topics more often than Duffy. He also regularly attacked the Ku Klux Klan, a powerful political force in the 1930s, and Prohibition. Like many other American cartoonists, Duffy freely adopted Rollin Kirby's "Mr. Dry," and his art clearly reflected his admiration of Kirby.

Duffy's third Pulitzer prize in 1940 attacked Hitler as a bloody ogre, with broken treaties and oppressed "minorities." Nazi race prejudice and banditry were staples of Duffy's art in the pre-war era. With that award, Duffy became the only cartoonist, other than Kirby, to win three Pulitzer prizes. (Kirby reached that goal in seven years, Duffy in nine.) They shared that distinction for the next four decades.

After a quarter-century Duffy drew his last cartoon for the *Sun* in 1948–typically, a cartoon backing underdog President Harry Truman (his newspaper supported Republican Thomas E. Dewey). Duffy kept his distance from *Sun* editorial policy–he would go on "vacation" when he disagreed with the newspaper's stand. That stance led to his departure from the *Sun* in 1948; Mencken had retired and was no longer around to shield his one-time protegé from publisher Patterson, who disliked Duffy.

Duffy joined the *Saturday Evening Post,* a national magazine reaching millions of readers. This move from daily journalism removed Duffy from further consideration for future Pulitzer awards, but gave him a vast national audience. His independent view prevailed. The *Post,* traditionally conservative, stated that a Duffy cartoon "is an editorial in itself." So it was that when the magazine and Duffy differed, his cartoons simply disappeared. If editor Ben Hibbs disagreed with a Duffy cartoon, it did not run. It was an uneasy arrangement–a strong Republican publication that featured the work of an outspoken liberal–but the *Saturday Evening Post* boasted the best editorial cartoonist in America. That partnership lasted until June 1956, when Duffy quietly left the chore of preparing cartoons weeks in advance to return to the hectic deadline of a daily newspaper.

Richard Clurman, an editor with an ambitious Long Island daily, saw opportunity to snag Duffy for his tabloid *Newsday.* The newspaper was struggling for recognition and a national reputation. Edmund Duffy, the only cartoonists honored with three Pulitzer prizes, would add stature to the ambitious newspaper. Duffy worked primarily from his New York apartment and delivered his cartoons on topics of his choosing. Publisher Alicia Patterson Guggenheim had other ideas, however. Like many owners, Alicia, as she was called, often wanted her ideas displayed on the editorial page, and expected her cartoonist to draw what she directed. Duffy listened and went ahead with his views. Duffy was simply being Duffy–independent and determined to present his view. Patterson was happy to have an editorial cartoonist of Duffy's stature, but most unhappy to have a hired hand who refused to do her bidding. However excellent the cartoon and provocative the topic, publisher Patterson found fault. Duffy, for his part, saw *Newsday* as a "hick paper" with pretensions of grandeur. Expectedly, the marriage came to a quiet end. Duffy did not leave, he was not terminated; he simply failed to come back. *Newsday* found a house artist who would draw as directed. Duffy, however, found a first-rank newspaper who gave him the latitude he needed.

The *Washington Post* beckoned in 1959. Its regular cartoonist, Herblock (Herbert Block), had a massive heart attack and Duffy was summoned by publisher Philip L. Graham to fill in during his absence. No direction here: "Duffy can draw as he likes," Graham stated. That is precisely what Duffy had always done. For the rest of that year Duffy produced excellent work, undirected and free from control. Herblock returned and Duffy's last cartoon drawn on deadline for a daily newspaper appeared January 1, 1960.

In the later years Duffy was ill with the cancer that finally claimed him in 1962, moreover, his eyes were failing. His art grew less crisp and reverted to his early techniques of dark, black masses. Journalism lost a towering influence with the departure of Duffy, his statements were stark; no lettering or text littered his powerful art. Duffy, a serious artist of somber subjects in a serious time, was a man of purpose described as a "good hater" of sham and pomposity. H. L. Mencken, one of America's foremost critics, never lavish with praise, described Edmund Duffy as a "genius." Journalism in America was poorer without Edmund Duffy.

Duffy's contribution was singular; he established the standard, seldom achieved, that an editorial cartoonist does not draw by direction. Publishers viewed cartoonists—and many do still—as hired hands who illustrate the opinion of the newspaper's proprietor. Publishers who would not dare tell a reporter or columnist what to write have seldom hesitated to direct a cartoonist what to draw. Duffy did not tolerate it; he would "take a vacation" rather than appear to support a candidate or cause he did not believe in. Publishers have the right not to publish; Duffy established a precedent that cartoonists have the same right. He paved the way for cartoonists like Herblock, who enjoys editorial freedom: the publishers of the *Washington Post* do not see his cartoons before they appear. Paul Conrad enjoys somewhat of the same freedom, although the *Los Angeles Times* moved his cartoons from the editorial page to the op-ed page. Pat Oliphant, whose cartoons are syndicated, enjoys the best of both worlds. If a client objects to an offering, Oliphant simply cancels further submissions. Lamentably, few other cartoonists today enjoy the freedom that Duffy sought to establish. Most bow to their employers' demands and remain employed.

Today the trend is for cartoons to be less confrontational, less offensive, and to include a gag or humorous approach. Newspaper publishers dislike controversy and many modern cartoonists follow newspaper policy without question. Modern ideas of sensitivity are responsible, too, for the watering-down. Increasingly, various groups are offended by cartoons that poke fun or puncture their pomposity. Rather than arouse protest by vocal groups, sensitive subjects are ignored. Consequently, editorial cartoons are often feeble efforts of fun and tend to resemble art from the comic page. Journalism has eroded, with less bite. Overall, however, cartoons, once powerful weapons of outrage and attack, are bland and blunted. The legacy of Edmund Duffy demonstrates that once newspaper editorial cartoonists led the way into controversy with courage and conviction, an element largely absent in modern newspapers.

SOURCES:

Editors of the Foreign Policy Association, *A Cartoon History of United States Foreign Policy: 1776-1976* (New York: Wm. Morrow, 1975).

Herbert Block, *Herblock: A Cartoonist's Life* (New York: Macmillan, 1993).

Albert Christ-Joiner, *Boardman Robinson* (Chicago: University of Chicago Press, 1946).

Paul Conrad, *Drawn and Quartered* (New York: Abrahams, 1985).

Roger A. Fischer, *Them Damned Pictures: Explorations in American Political Cartoon Art* (North Haven: Archon, 1996).

Daniel R. Fitzpatrick, *As I Saw It* (New York: Simon and Schuster, 1953).

S. L. Harrison, *The Editorial Art of Edmund Duffy* (Cranbury: Fairleigh Dickinson University Press, 1998).

Gerald W. Johnson, *The Lines Are Drawn* (Philadelphia: J. B. Lippincott, 1958).

Kevin Kallaugher [KAL], *KALtoons: Political Cartoons from the Baltimore Sun* (Baltimore: Chatsworth Press, 1992).

Rollin Kirby, *Highlights: A Cartoon History of the Nineteen Twenties* (New York: Payson, 1931).

David L. Lendt, *Ding: The Life of Jay Norwood Darling* (Ames: Iowa State University Press, 1989).

Jeff MacNelly, *MacNelly: The Pulitzer Prize Winning Cartoonist* (Richmond: Westover, 1972).

Bill Mauldin, *A Sort of a Saga* (New York: Wm. Sloan Assoc., 1949).

Linda Mullins, *The Teddy Bear Man: Theodore Roosevelt and Clifford Berryman* (Cumberland: Hobby House Press, 1987).

Stephen Hess and Sandy Northrop, *Drawn and Quartered: The History of American Political Cartoons* (Montgomery: Elliott & Clark, 1996).

Pat Oliphant, *Ban This Book* (Kansas City: Andrews and McMeel, 1972).

Art Young, *Art Young: His Life and Times* (New York: Sheridan House, 1939).

11

Ernest Hemingway

Mythic Journalist

Despite acclaim as one of twentieth-century America's foremost novelists, Ernest Hemingway inflated his modest newspaper beginnings. A notorious self-promoter, Hemingway often referred to that brief portion of his career with pride, and expanded its meagre reality with hyperbole. Consequently, a myth of Hemingway as intrepid reporter and newspaperman, lingers in legend, a pseudo-image that exists even, or perhaps especially, in newsrooms.

Although Hemingway began his career writing for newspapers, and worked for several, he was not a good reporter. He lost several jobs because of this failing. One episode in particular–his coverage of the 1935 Florida hurricane–demonstrates that point. Throughout his career, Hemingway undertook a number of journalistic assignments–he reported briefly on the Spanish Civil War for NANA (North American Newspaper Alliance), where he was fired for faking stories and lifting material from other correspondents. He investigated military conditions in China for Ralph Ingersoll's New York

Ernest Hemingway: Chronology

1899   born July 31, Oak Park, Illinois

1917   joins Kansas City *Star*

1918   American Field Service, Italy

1920   writes advertising copy; joins *Cooperative Commonwealth;* freelances for Toronto *Star*

1923   *Three Stories and Ten Poems*

1924   resigns from *Star;* writes for *The Quarter, The Dial*

1925   *The Sun Also Rises; In Our Time*

1929   *A Farewell to Arms*

1932   *Death in the Afternoon*

1935   *Green Hills of Africa;* covers Labor Day hurricane in Florida Keys for *New Masses*

1937   NANA correspondent, Spanish Civil War

1941   reports on Far East for New York *PM*

1944   war correspondent for *Collier's*

1951   freelance articles for *Look* (through 1956)

1952   *The Old Man and the Sea*

1954   Nobel Prize for Literature

1956   death by suicide, July 2, Ketchum, Idaho

newspaper *PM,* and reported the Chinese army could handle the Japanese, with no awareness of the internal strife clearly evident. Hemingway filed dispatches on the European war for several magazines–*Esquire, Collier's Weekly,* and *Look,* and was unaware of the decision to allow the French forces to take Paris. Beyond his earned reputation as an outstanding novelist, Hemingway throughout his lifetime cultivated a dubious reputation on the thinnest of evidence as an astute military strategist, war correspondent, and seasoned newspaperman. Consequently, that myth lingers. Hemingway remains an inspiration still in countless class rooms in America as the epitome of a newspaperman who made good. That Hemingway is a myth. Myths are lovely legends, largely bereft of fact.

Ernest Hemingway (1899-1961) was born in Oak Park, Illinois, in 1899 into an upper-income family. His father was a doctor. Hemingway attended the local high school and had journalistic aspirations. He wrote for the school's literary magazine *Tabula* and its weekly newspaper *Trapeze,* averaging a story a week with most modeled on the style of his idol, Ring Lardner. He rejected college and chose newspaper work.

Hemingway bragged about his early beginnings in 1917 as a cub reporter with the Kansas City *Star.* He seldom noted that, with slim credentials, he was taken aboard largely through his uncle's influence and because the staff was depleted of more-qualified men by the wartime manpower shortage. His short apprenticeship lasted six months before he left for war adventures.

After wartime service as a volunteer ambulance driver in Italy, Hemingway resumed newspaper work in 1920. Well-connected friends helped land him with the Toronto *Star,* where the staff was highly impressed by Hemingway's inflated accounts of his Kansas City experience. Hyperbole was a life-long Hemingway trait; he has been described as "a romantic liar for whom the line between fact and fiction was thinner than a hair." This quality aided his Toronto human-interest stories, modelled after his early writing hero, Ring Lardner. His slice-of-life newspaper columns contain kernels of fact flavored with invention. Like that of H.L. Mencken and Mark Twain, Hemingway's work included a fair amount of "stretchers" to spice up a story. Hemingway was fired from the Toronto *Star* in 1923 for poor reporting, not for poor writing. He wrote excellent "color" but was lax with facts. He continued to submit free-lance stories to the *Star* until 1923, a number of which were rejected. Later in life, after he gained fame as a novelist, his reporting was still not up to accurate standards. Hemingway's reporting was creative, not factual; during the Spanish Civil War, his dispatches–colorful and creative–lacked facts and lagged behind the opposition, particularly the *New York Times.* He was fired by NANA after he was caught in several instances of filing stories with material lifted from the competition.

In 1921 Hemingway returned to Paris to begin a career as a novelist. He became part of the literary circle with such people as Gertrude Stein, Ford Madox Ford, and Ezra Pound. His first book, *Three Stories and Ten Poems* was published in 1923, followed in 1925 by *In Our Time,* a short story collection that made him known in America. Hemingway's characters captured the imagination of the twenties generation; he was one of the prominent voices of the "lost generation." The appearance in 1926 of *The Sun Also Rises* solidified Hemingway as one of the preeminent novelists of the time. His 1929 novel of the Italian war, *A Farewell to Arms,* established Hemingway into the front rank of American literary work. He virtually abandoned his journalistic work, with minor excursions from time to time, prompted when money was short.

In 1935, Hemingway lived in Key West, enjoying the critical and commercial success of his novels, and writing occasional magazine articles. He was working on his newest book and indulging from time to time in deep sea fishing aboard his black, 40-foot yacht *Pilar*. The country was deep in the economic hardships of the Great Depression. The adventure of the Great War was over; the jazz era had faded and harsh realities of unemployment, hunger, and homelessness confronted millions of Americans. Many writers and intellectuals sought explanations or solutions for the financial crisis. But Hemingway's writings displayed little public concern for these issues. The rough handling of the so-called "bonus army" that marched on Washington and was fired on by the Army may have angered Hemingway, but not enough to write of that abuse. Journalistically, Hemingway took little notice of President Herbert Hoover's failed programs or the efforts of President Franklin Delano Roosevelt's New Deal to solve the nation's economic troubles. Hemingway disliked Roosevelt and his policies, as a matter of fact.

The leftist, Communist-supported magazine *New Masses* provided a continuing voice of protest, however, with regular and relentless attacks on FDR and his policies. Hemingway avoided the camp of the writers of the left, who were baffled, angry, and scornful over his refusal to join their ranks. Hemingway professed an ignorance of economics and said that "all the state has ever meant to me is unjust taxation....I believe in the absolute minimum of government."

Saturday evening before Labor Day 1935, Hemingway relaxed with a drink after his writing chores. The local paper reported a tropical storm somewhere off the Bahamas and he made certain that *Pilar* was securely berthed. The forecast held no prediction of a hurricane for the Florida Keys. Key West experienced only heavy rains, and no winds exceeded 45 knots. Tuesday's local paper reported a few downed trees (one in Hemingway's walled front yard), but no real damage. Miami's press reported that a mild tropical storm was expected west of the city by mid-day. A hurricane, in fact, had already struck the mid-Keys the night before.

The Key West *Citizen* reported "Great Loss of Life" in the middle Keys on Wednesday. The next day an Associated Press dispatch in the *Citizen* reported that the loss of life from the hurricane–unnamed in those days–"may reach thousands." Loss of life was feared, from winds and flood waters over the low-lying islands. In those days the Keys were inhabited by few permanent residents but concern was expressed for the safety of workers in several government work camps.

One of FDR's New Deal solutions created jobs for the hapless veterans of the "bonus army." Under auspices of the Federal Emergency Reconstruction Administration, several hundred veterans were put to work building a highway in the Keys under a state program, funded with Federal money. The bonus veterans were feared to be victims of the storm.

One who knew this, and sensed the political implications of the story, was Joseph North, *New Masses* editor. North was the "political watch-dog" of the magazine, who made certain that copy conformed to the Communist line. As soon as communication was established with the mainland, North, who was sure Hemingway would do the story, wired him to look into it for an on-the scene report on the veterans.

Clearly an anti-fascist, Hemingway was no Communist. While the *New Masses* was outspokenly anti-fascist, it was also publicly pro-Communist. Moreover, Hemingway openly disliked the magazine, particularly after a critical review. North's invitation enabled Hemingway to visit the scene of the disaster as a working reporter. Hemingway disliked government and Roosevelt; the disaster provided opportunity for North and Hemingway to join forces against a common opponent. The job promised ready money; Hemingway was short of cash.

All of these factors helped motivate Hemingway to undertake a news assignment with a slant. North, with a political ax to grind, saw opportunity to attack Roosevelt. Before any details were known, Hemingway's bias toward government promised a less than even-handed approach. By September 5, four days after the hurricane hit, Hemingway was on assignment to cover one of the biggest news stories in years: Florida's worst hurricane since 1926 and one of the most powerful ever recorded to hit North America.

The *Miami Herald* and the *New York Times* contained broad coverage and the nation's press carried wire service stories. Roosevelt dispatched full military aid on Tuesday. Facts were hard to come by, as Hemingway discovered. Reports of the death count varied enormously, according to the sources. Headlines in Thursday's *Times* described 200 deaths, 181 of these veterans. The *Miami Herald* reported that the death toll was 115 with many missing. Hemingway fretted that the Red Cross "steadily played down the number" of deaths, beginning with forty-six and by September 7, listed the dead as 446. But, he wrote, "the number of veterans dead and missing alone numbers 442," neglecting to cite a source. The roster for the veterans was available on the scene, in Matecumbe, where Hemingway was reporting; he never did account for the actual number of veterans involved.

The devastation was staggering, as contemporary newspaper photographs show. Wind and water had stripped the land; bodies littered the shorelines and were entangled in branches of the few trees that remained standing; bodies were buried in the dunes and floating in off-shore waters. Hemingway, for all his concern over the fate of the veterans, was callous toward other possible victims: "It is not necessary to go into the deaths of the civilians [sic] and their families since they were there of their own free will....knew the hazards involved." Hemingway apparently held the belief that the veterans were not "civilians," evidently confusing the FERA program with the better-known CCC, which had a para-military status. Another factual lapse for the newsman.

Hemingway devoted the greater portion of his story to graphic descriptions of the bodies, comparing the irony of death in the dunes to death on the battlefield. His writing, colorful and emotional, was short on facts. Repeatedly, Hemingway asks: Why did these men die? Who was responsible? Why were not the weather advisories more precise in predicting the path of the storm? Hemingway wanted someone to blame.

Although Hemingway's 2,800-word piece was billed by the *New Masses* as a "first-hand report on the Florida Hurricane," it was not a news report. It was a polemic. Hemingway wrote a long editorial. He asks "who sent nearly a thousand war veterans...to live in frame shacks on the Florida Keys in hurricane months?" He asks "who sent them down there?" Hemingway neither answers the questions nor apparently seriously sought to find out.

To be sure, there was much confusion, initially. But by the time Hemingway arrived on the scene, help had mobilized, cleanup was underway with Federal and national guardsmen, victims had been hospitalized, and rosters examined for the missing. Facts were available that Hemingway simply missed, or ignored.

The following facts, according to the contemporary press, were known during Hemingway's visit to the storm site (the newsman had missed them all):

Many veterans died, but not the 440-odd that Hemingway reported, nor the 700-1000 he later described to Maxwell Perkins, his editor at Scribner's. Total deaths, veterans and residents, did not exceed 400.

One thousand veterans were not involved. Far less than one thousand veterans were in the camps. Three work camps–on Windley Key, and Upper and Lower Matecumbe Keys–housed 700 workers, including administration and other support officials.

The veterans' work camps were under FERA jurisdiction and state operated, not the CCC (Civilian Conservation Corps), a Federal project.

Accommodations were primitive, but the men were not living in "shacks." Administration buildings and mess halls were wooden structures with concrete foundations; a few men, waiting more permanent quarters, were in tents.

Hemingway asks "who sent them?" One correct answer is a program that provided work. He implies some kind of criminal motive in working through the hurricane season. If the rich vacationers and politicians, as Hemingway mentioned in his story, fled Florida during the hurricane months, residents lived and worked year round. The vets with jobs had reason to stay.

Hemingway mentions a drinking problem in passing. He neglects to mention, as do other first-hand accounts, that many surviving vets shirked rescue work to dig into dunes and debris looking for buried beer bottles.

Hemingway belabors the point that somehow the Weather Bureau should have known when and where the hurricane would strike. In those days the Weather Bureau's main office was in Jacksonville, some 400-plus miles north of Miami and the Keys. Reports of the whereabouts of the storm and its landfall were about as precise as was possible.

Officials planned rail evacuation of the workers. A relief train was ready noon Monday. Orders to move the train came too late, however. Hemingway   fails to answer his own question of why: "who advised against sending the relief train to evacuate the veterans until four-thirty o'clock on Monday...?" As an on-the-scene reporter, this is one fact he might well have nailed down. No one knew when the hurricane would hit, or where, or how intense it really was. Hemingway himself writes that his last check on the progress of the reported tropical storm on the Saturday before disclosed no predictions of a massive blow. Specifics were unavailable.

Florida Governor Dave Sholtz (who actually "sent" the vets to work) is quoted by several sources available to Hemingway as saying that there was "great carelessness somewhere." On-the-scene reporter Hemingway lacked any substantive quotes to provide answers to his emotional questions.

Later, the President turned the entire affair over to the Congress for investigation. Rep. John Rankin (D-Miss.) chaired the House Committee on War Veterans Legislation and issued a report a year later. The report confirmed that of 716 veterans involved, 121 died in the storm (along with 279 residents) and concluded that weather reports gave "adequate" warning. The question of why the relief train was delayed until mid-day Monday was attributed to "incompetence" with no named individual or agency held responsible.

Hemingway did not write a news story. His article contained color and drama–accusations lacking substance. Hemingway's copy lacked facts, it raised political charges to hector FDR. Hemingway's report, freighted with heavy political overtones, contained clear implications of manslaughter, if not murder. He wrote a political tract that delighted the editors and North. It was the political propaganda they sought, an emotional diatribe to embarrass the Administration.

If Hemingway's sense of realism deserted him, he always told a good story. A blend of reality and invention is an excellent quality for a novelist, not so admirable for a reliable reporter. Hemingway's stirring account of the aftermath of the 1935 hurricane lacked documentation. It was not a news story, not "truly." He once warned of reporters:

> ... they just have a romantic view of life. And almost all reporters are inaccurate. Have you ever noticed when you read something in the papers you truly know about that ninety percent of it is inaccurate? A lot of mistakes have to do with early deadlines, of course, the need to get something down in a hurry for the afternoon or morning editions. Often, there's just no time to check the accuracy of your sources, I know–I started out as a reporter for the Kansas City *Star.* But some of it comes from the reporter's conceit and the contempt for a reader's intelligence that only a truly conceited reporter can have. And a lot comes from laziness, or, to be more accurate, from fatigue.

Hemingway was not a good reporter. A vast gulf separates a newspaper reporter from one who writes for a newspaper. Even H. L. Mencken, a great newspaper man if ever there was one, modestly said "I was never a good reporter." Similarly, Stephen Crane, a first-rate novelist, was a poor newspaper reporter. Once, on assignment for the New York *Herald,* Crane returned with vivid crowd descriptions and color stories but neglected to describe the fire, its location, or its victims.

Hemingway's *New Masses* report lacked in-depth investigation, fact or details. The result was an emotional diatribe, without substantive support. Propaganda is not news reporting. The Communist publication *Internatsionalnaya Literatura* reprinted Hemingway's piece (apparently without his knowledge) as another

Marxist attack on the capitalistic system. Hemingway's reporting deficiencies included bias.

Hemingway, for all his fame as a writer of uncommon merit, was not a good newspaper reporter. But he made that claim throughout his lifetime. He was a creative writer, one of America's best, who served a brief apprenticeship in the newsroom with little distinction. Hemingway, the artist, endures with no need for the manufactured myth of Hemingway, the newsman.

Hemingway, however, was a major force in twentieth-century American journalism simply because he was Hemingway. A 1954 Nobel Prize laureate for literature, he exemplified the wonder and magic allure of newspapering for a generation of journalists. Myths are useful, even necessary, but the heretic and historian who question myth are unpopular. Nevertheless, accuracy and fact are essential requirements for legitimate journalism, elements Hemingway himself would concede are "truly" important.

SOURCES:

Daniel Aaron, *Writers on the Left: Episodes in American Literary Communism* (New York: Columbia University Press, 1992).

Carlos Baker, *Ernest Hemingway: A Life Story* (New York: Collier/Macmillan, 1988).

Charles A. Fenton, *The Apprenticeship of Ernest Hemingway* (New York: Viking Press, 1954.

S. L. Harrison, "Hemingway as Negligent Reporter: New Masses and the 1935 Florida Hurricane," 11:1 *American Journalism* (Winter 1994), 11-19.

J. F. Kobler, *Ernest Hemingway: Journalst and Artist*
(Ann Arbor: University of Michigan Press, 1985).

Kenneth S. Lynn, *Hemingway* (New York:
Fawcett/Columbine, 1987).

Stuart B. McIver, *Hemingway's Key West* (Sarasota:
Pineapple Press, 1993).

Sarah R. Shaber "Hemingway's Literary Journalism:
The Spanish Civil War Dispatches," *Journalism
Quarterly* 57:3 (Autumn 1980), 420-424; 535.

Edmund Wilson, "Letter to the Russians About
Hemingway," [1935], *The Shores of Light: A Literary
Chronicle of the Twenties and Thirties* (New York:
Farrar, Straus and Young, 1952).

SELECTED WORKS BY HEMINGWAY:

*By-Line: Ernest Hemingway: Selected Articles and
Dispatches of Four Decades.* Edited by William
White (New York: Touchstone/Simon & Schuster,
1998).

Ernest Hemingway: Cub Reporter. Edited by Matthew J.
Bruccoli (Pittsburgh: University of Pittsburgh, 1970).

"Old Newsman Writes," *Esquire* (December 1934),
pp. 25-26.

"Who Murdered the Vets?" 16 *New Masses* (September 17,
1935), 9-14.

Across the River and Into the Trees (New York: Scribner,
1950).

Death in the Afternoon (New York: Halcyon House, 1932).

A Farewell to Arms (New York: Scribner's Sons, 1929).

The Fifth Column (New York: Scribner, 1969).

For Whom the Bell Tolls (New York: C. Scribner's Sons, 1940).

Men Without Women (New York: Scribner, 1927).

A Movable Feast (New York: Bantam Books, 1965).

The Sun Also Rises (New York: C. Scribner's Sons, 1954).

To Have and Have Not (New York: C. Scribner's Sons, 1970).

12

Heywood Broun

Columnist as Crusader

In the 1920s and 1930s, when newspaper columnists were America's leading opinion-molders, Heywood Broun was one of the most-influential columnists in the nation–his liberal views were known across the country. As he later wrote, "I was really a newspaperman and not merely a columnist." Clearly more than "merely" a columnist, Broun was a legend in his time, and his contributions to journalism should not be neglected. Broun is remembered for his New York *World* column, "It Seems to Me." Here it was said, "he launched a crusade every hour" and readers–and there were millions–knew exactly what Broun thought. Broun can also be remembered as a founder of the Newspaper Guild. Broun should be remembered, however, with editor Herbert Bayard Swope, for his major contribution to modern journalism: the free thought column that may disagree with the newspaper in which it is published.

Heywood Campbell Broun (1888-1939) was born in Brooklyn Heights, of upper middle-class parents of Scots-German ancestry. He grew up in Manhattan in a

Heywood Broun: Chronology

1888   born, December 7, Brooklyn Heights, New York

1904   editor of the *Record,* Horace Mann School

1906   Harvard College, rejected three times by the *Crimson;* worked summers for New York *Sun* and *Morning Telegraph*

1910   failing academically, leaves Harvard and joins New York *Morning Telegraph,* fired for seeking a raise

1912   joins New York *Tribune* as copyreader, then sportswriter

1915   named *Tribune's* drama critic

1917   *Tribune* war correspondent covering A.E.F.; *Our Army at the Front; The A.E.F.: with General Pershing in France*

1919   named literary critic of the *Tribune,* begins column "Books and Things"

1921   *Seeing Things at Night;* joins New York *World* and begins column, "It Seems to Me"

1922   *Pieces of Hate and Other Enthusiasms; The Boy Grew Older*

1924   *Sitting on the World*

1926   *Gandle Follows His Nose*

1927   exiled from the *World,* writes for *Nation*

1928   returns to the *World* but is fired over conflict with column; joins New York *Telegram*

racially-mixed neighborhood and attended Horace Mann, a private school that prepared him for Harvard College. His classmates included Walter Lippmann, John Reed, Stuart Chase, and H. V. Kaltenborn, all destined to become journalists of national reputation.

Broun, who had been editor of his high school newspaper, sought a post on the Harvard *Crimson,* but was rejected three times. Denied journalistic activity, Broun ignored Lippmann's Socialist Club and Kaltenborn's Dramatic Club, and spent most of his time following the fortunes of the Boston Red Sox. English professor Charles Townsend Copeland advised Harvard's aspiring journalists to "get in, get wise, get out." Broun simply wanted in.

Through his father's influence, Broun worked during summer vacations at the New York *Morning Telegraph* and the *Sun.* Of the dozen or so New York City newspapers of that time, the *Telegraph* was probably the least respected, with quarters in an abandoned stable and a raffish staff. The *Telegraph* specialized in vaudeville, Broadway shows, scandals, and sports, horse racing especially. Sports editor was William B. Masterson, better known as "Bat," renowned for his reputation as the frontier marshall who tamed Dodge City.

After failing several senior courses, Broun left Harvard and joined the *Telegraph* as a $20-a-week reporter. Years later, Broun observed, "I went to a car barn instead of a school of journalism." Broun probably learned more over the summers than he would have acquired in a journalism diploma mill.

Broun did well and was raised to $28 weekly,, but lost his job when he sought another raise. He landed a job with the *Tribune* as a $25 a week copyreader then moved to sportswriting, covering John McGraw's Giants. Broun was a partisan rooter who loved the Giants and soon his stories earned a byline (when

1931   *Christians Only;* Broadway play, writes and produces a
        Broadway revue, "Shoot the Works," for Depression-era
        jobless

1933   helps organize Newspaper Guild, elected national
        president

1935   *It Seems to Me: 1925-1935*

1938   buys newspaper, Connecticut *Nutmeg,* lated renamed
        Broun's Nutmeg

1939   contract terminated by *World-Telegram;* signs with New
        York *Post;* after only one column, dies in New York,
        December 18

bylines were rare) and ranked with exemplary writers like the *Mail's* Grantland Rice and Damon Runyon, of the *Journal*. In 1915 Broun was named the *Tribune's* drama critic–his beat also included books and theater.

He met and married Ruth Hale, an ardent feminist who had strong newspaper experience at the Washington *Evening Star*, the Philadelphia *Ledger*, as drama critic for *Vogue* magazine, and as a reporter for the *New York Times*. Both were given assignments in 1917 to cover the A.E.F. in France after America's entry into World War I, Broun for the *Tribune*, Hale with the *Chicago Tribune's* Paris bureau.

Hale returned home after a short time to give birth to their son, Heywood Hale Broun. Broun put his brief six month stint to good use, writing two popular books–*Our Army at the Front* (Broun himself was never near the front) and *The AEF: With General Pershing and the American Forces*.

With General John J. Pershing only in the sense that both were in France, Broun was probably Pershing's least-favorite correspondent. Most of Broun's dispatches were highly critical of the Army and its mismanagement of logistics and supplies. Broun was no muckraker, merely a conscientious newsman with a legitimate story, but his criticism was not welcome. After his return, in 1919 Broun was named literary critic of the *Tribune*. He conducted the Book Page and wrote a three-times-a-week column, "Books and Things."

Lively commentary and controversial stances established Broun as a voice to be heard. He wrote Sunday theater pieces and covered major sports events. Books were not ignored. He liked Sinclair Lewis, he disliked F. Scott Fitzgerald and Eugene O'Neill, and said so. Increasingly, "things" occupied more of his columns–he found fault with the Harding Administration and sought clemency for Eugene V. Debs, the Socialist leader impris-

oned for opposing the war. His crusading was ably abet-
ted by his wife. Ruth Hale and Harold Ross' wife, June
Grant, organized the Lucy Stone League to fight for
women's rights and Broun supported the movement in
his column. He was one of only two men to join.

In this era, the New York *World* was the best newspaper in America and in 1921 Broun sought a job from
editor Herbert Bayard Swope, for more "freedom of
expression," Broun said. His column, "It Seems to Me,"
appeared on the op-ed page (a Swope invention). He
joined such illustrious writers as F.P.A. (Franklin Pierce
Adams), Deems Taylor, Alexander Woollcott, Frank
Sullivan, Laurence Stallings, Samuel Chotzinoff, and St.
John Ervine. Harvard classmate Walter Lippmann was
to become editorial page editor and another Swope
recruit, Arthur Krock, was also a staff member. Broun
was determined to make his name stand out in this
august company.

Broun and Hale shared a Manhattan house with
Grant, now with the *Times,* and Ross, who was attempt-
ing to continue the wartime success of the *Stars and
Stripes* with a magazine called *Home Sector* and was
preparing a prospectus for a venture to be called *The
New Yorker*. Broun's social life centered on a poker
group, drawn from a nucleus of wartime colleagues, populated with people like Ross, FPA, Woollcott (alumnus of
the *Stars and Stripes*), playwright Marc Connally, *Times*
drama critic George S. Kaufman, newsman Steve Early,
and two refugees from *Vogue,* now working for *Vanity
Fair*–Robert Benchley and Dorothy Parker with new-
comer Robert E. Sherwood. The Thanatopis Literary
[from the group in Lewis's *Main Street*] and Inside
Straight Poker Club gradually emerged into the luncheon group that came to be known as the Algonquin
Round Table. Others–by invitation only–would join from
time to time including Harpo Marx, Edna Ferber, Swope,

Grant, or Broadway producers and theater people. Broun was one of the stellar members in this group of America's leading celebrities.

With a salary of $25,000 annually, Broun was one of the highest-paid journalists of his time. His income was augmented with best-selling books: collections from his columns—*Pieces of Hate and Other Enthusiasms, Sitting On the World, It Seems to Me;* novels, *The Sun Field* and *Gandle Follows His Nose;* and perhaps his best literary effort, a collaboration with Margaret Leech, *Anthony Comstock: Roundsman of the Lord.* (Leech, wife of the *World's* publisher, would win two Pulitzer prizes for other works.) FPA made claim that Broun was "one of the great journalists of all time," and if that claim was overstated, it was clear that Broun was one of the brightest stars in the *World* galaxy.

His stand on the Sacco-Vanzetti case, however, directly opposed the *World's* editorial view, now led by Lippmann—there was little love lost between the former classmates. Anarchists Nicola Sacco and Bartolomeo Vanzetti had been convicted on suspect evidence of murder in Massachusetts. Liberals worldwide sought clemency from the death penalty. The *World,* speaking through Lippmann's editorials, sought commutation and a new trial. Broun, however, was intemperate in his denunciation of the governor and the three-man committee headed by Harvard president A. Lawrence Lowell. Broun's fiery columns created concern in *World* management, and publisher Ralph Pulitzer warned Broun "writers write and editors edit." Newspapers, however great and liberal, publish only what management wishes to have published.

The upshot was expected; the editorial board spiked his final two columns and, after explaining his position to readers, Broun resigned. The *World* stated that its star columnist had taken a "witch's Sabbatical." (The terminology was Swope's whimsy, but there was serious division within the *World's* editorial hierarchy.)

Under his contract Broun was restrained from writing for another newspaper for three years, so he chose to ply his trade for the *Nation*. Editor Oswald Garrison Villard gave him a weekly page for opinion and comment, without restrictions. To keep busy, Broun proposed to Harold Ross, and Ross agreed, that Broun write his own "Profile" for the *New Yorker*. Broun's "The Rabbit That Bit the Bulldog," one of only three autobiographical Profiles ever in that magazine, appeared in the *New Yorker* October 1, 1927, signed "R. A."

Exile ended in January 1928, after Swope convinced management that Broun's absence affected circulation. Broun returned, but kept his *Nation* connection where commentary was unfettered. This was a formula for conflict. Sure enough, when Broun confronted *World* policy on the issue of birth-control, the *World* fired Broun: "His disloyalty to this newspaper makes any further association impossible." The newspaper, Broun concluded in the *Nation,* "lacked courage." Management of the *World,* Broun remained firmly convinced, caved in to Roman Catholic pressure, from the church itself and the large number of Roman Catholic readers, that implacably opposed birth control.

Broun rejected an offer to write for the *Herald Tribune;* it was too much like the *World.* Roy Howard, proprietor of the Scripps-Howard chain, offered Broun $30,000 to write for the *Telegraph* and his syndicate. This salary, later raised to $40,000, put Broun into the company of columnists Walter Winchell and Dorothy Thompson, the highest-paid in the nation. More important, Broun was promised he could write without restriction on any topic he chose.

The economic crash of 1929 and the Great Depression with its accompanying social ills provided fodder for passionate columns. It hardly needs to be said that Broun was a fiery supporter of President Franklin D. Roosevelt and his liberal New Deal programs. Then Broun decided to run for Congress as a Socialist candidate. Despite glittering endorsements from many of his newspaper and Broadway pals, Broun finished a poor third, outvoted by more than three-to-one behind his Republican and Democratic rivals.

Early in 1931 the *World* was sold and absorbed by the *Telegram.* Broun's departure probably hastened the demise of the *World,* long in decline; he was responsible, it was estimated, for 50,000 lost circulation. In contrast, Broun was riding high. He collaborated with George Britt on a book dealing with anti-Semitism, *Christians Only.* This attack on a wide-spread social issue brought only tepid response. Americans needed jobs.

One effort to create jobs led to a Broun column campaign, "Give A Job Till June" that did little to generate work. Similarly, Broun's idea for a 1931 Broadway revue, "Shoot the Works," to create jobs for actors, singers, and dancers lasted only 89 performances, despite contributions from Irving Berlin, Ira Gershwin, E. B. White, and Peter Arno. Divorced in 1933 (Ruth Hale died in 1934), Broun married Connie Madison, a "Shoot the Works" member of the chorus.

The plight of newsmen out of work, including many from the defunct *World,* led Broun to work for unionization of newspapers. Newspaper publishers argued that reporters were professionals–hence, free from the protection of the New Deal's National Recovery Act. News people held themselves aloof from unions, despite the fact that the unionized pressmen and engravers, were better paid and protected than news staff. The compromise was to name the organization a Newspaper Guild, this had a more uplifting tone, a better ring than crass union; the euphemism did not win Lippmann over.

Broun led the way to an organization meeting in October 1933; FPA was elected vice-president in New York (Broun was elected president) and president of the national organization. The Guild movement succeeded, despite inroads by Communists. If Broun was aware of this element, he turned a pragmatic blind eye as a necessity of hard economic times. The Guild, was for Broun, the capstone of his career; it brought him no personal or economic rewards.

Broun found time to begin a weekly county newspaper, the Connecticut *Nutmeg,* where he indulged himself and his friends with a personalized effort that reflected idiosyncracies–Gene Tunney was sports editor.   The *Nutmeg* was to newspapers what a gentleman squire's farm is like, indulgent and cash consuming.   Ironically, it was a non-Guild enterprise.

Despite his column's popularity–FDR used one for a Christmas "fireside" chat–Roy Howard grew increasingly irritated by Broun's Guild activity and enthusiastic New Deal support. Howard brought in Westbrook Pegler to counter Broun's liberal stance, in order, it was explained, to give "balance" to the op-ed page. Pegler, once a respected sportswriter, was a rabid anti-New Dealer specializing in attacking Mrs. Roosevelt. Pegler's views were what Howard wanted in his newspapers.

Consequently when Broun's $49,000 contract came up for renewal in December, Howard took the opportunity to cut expenses and Broun from the payroll. Offers were few. The one-time open-ended $50,000 offer, with syndication, from Hearst was not proffered. Then Pegler took this opportunity to attack Broun publicly as a Communist and a liar. Broun could not believe that his friend and poker-playing crony had betrayed him, but Pegler had long been jealous of Broun's popularity. Many others envied and disliked Broun for his success, his wealth, his liberal causes and this was a good time to get even. Few of his former colleagues at the *World-Telegram* bothered to say goodbye–or thanks–to the man who had done so much to improve their jobs. Broun was deeply hurt.

Finally, the New York *Post* came through, with an offer one-quarter his previous salary. It was important, Broun thought, to keep your name before the public. He managed to produce one column. Broun contracted a cold that became pneumonia and he died suddenly December 18, 1939; Broun's life-long hypochondria and fear of colds proved valid.

Heywood Broun was more than a columnist, as he observed. He called himself a "newspaperman," with some pride. But he was more than that–he was a genuine crusader, a liberal voice for justice for those without justice; a voice for better wages and jobs for those who were unemployed or received less than an adequate wage, and he crusaded for family management in a hostile environment. Broun was a member of the privileged class who never forgot those who lacked the necessities of life. Broun was a crusader in a time where the American Dream had become a nightmare. He lent his considerable stature and influence to the formation of the Newspaper Guild and that may be his greatest monument. A non-Jew, he wrote of anti-Semitism when it was not popular to do so; he chronicled the rise of Comstockery in an era when literary and other censorship flourished.

Broun was more than a newspaperman; he was one of the most articulate and influential voices of the twentieth century, a newspaperman with a conscience that prompted him to lead liberal crusades whose causes he felt were just. Broun's regard for his fellow workers transcended class and status and often for his effort he was shunned and his motives questioned. Broun was a member of the privileged class, always well-off himself, who fought for the underdog. His courage, commitment, and compassion never failed. Herbert Bayard Swope remembered that Broun "left the world a better place."

SOURCES:

Dale Kramer, *Heywood Broun: A Biographical Portrait* (New York: A. A. Wyn/Current, 1949).

Richard O'Conner, *Heywood Broun: A Biography* (New York: G. P. Putnam's Sons, 1975).

SELECTED BOOKS BY BROUN:

The Boy Grew Older (New York: G. P. Putnam's Sons, 1922).

Christians Only: A Study in Prejudice, with George Britt (New York: Vanguard, 1931/Da Capo, 1972).

The Collected Edition of Heywood Broun, ed. by Heywood Hale Broun (New York: Harcourt, Brace and Co., 1941).

Gandle Follows His Nose (Philadelphia: Boni and Liveright, 1926).

It Seems To Me: 1925-1935 (New York: Harcourt, Brace and Co., 1935).

Pieces of Hate and Other Enthusiasms (New York: Geo. H. Doran Co., 1922).

Seeing Things at Night (New York: Harcourt, Brace and Co., 1921).

Sitting on the World (New York: G. P. Putnam's Sons, 1924).

13

Dorothy Thompson

America's Most Influential Woman

Once rated by American opinion polls as equal in influence to Eleanor Roosevelt, journalist Dorothy Thompson was a legend in her time. Her newspaper column "On the Record," her monthly column in the *Ladies' Home Journal,* and her NBC weekly radio broadcasts made Dorothy Thompson known to millions of readers and listeners for three decades. Her books, collections of her columns and radio commentaries, provide a unique insight and reflection of the history of those turbulent years. In her time, Thompson was one of the most-influential voices of American journalism. She was the prototype for the 1942 Katharine Hepburn-Spencer Tracy motion picture "Woman of the Year," an unflattering portrait.

Dorothy Thompson [1893-1961] was born in a middle-class family in Lancaster, New York, her father was a Methodist minister. She attended the Lewis Institute, a junior college, and Syracuse University, majoring in English and history. Her fiction writing efforts brought only rejections. Active in the feminist rights movement

Dorothy Thompson: Chronology

1893   born, Lancaster, New York

1914   graduates from Syracuse University

1917   publicity director for National Social Reform Unit;
         freelance work for New York *Sun, New York Times*

1920   covers World Zionist Convention for International News
         Service; publicity director for Red Cross, Paris

1921   unsalaried Vienna correspondent for Philadelphia
         Public Ledger

1922   Vienna bureau chief for *Public Ledger*

1928   *The New Russia;* resigns newspaper posts, freelances for
         Saturday Evening Post

1930   interviews Adolf Hitler for *Cosmopolitan*

1932   *I Saw Hitler!*

1936   begins column, "On the Record," for New York *Herald
         Tribune* (until 1941)

1937   NBC weekly radio program; begins column for *Ladies'
         Home Journal* (until 1957)

1938   *Dorothy Thompson's Political Guide*

1939   *Let the Record Speak*

1941   signs with Bell Syndicate and New York *Post*

1957   *The Courage to Be Happy*

1958   *Elderly Reflections;* retires from journalism

1961   dies January 30, Lisbon, Portugal

in college, Thompson became an organizer for women's suffrage in Buffalo.

In 1917 Thompson moved to New York but, unsuccessful in finding a newspaper job, she free-lanced and worked as a publicist for a Bible publishing group. Later, she became publicity director for the National Social Reform Unit to aid the urban poor. She continued to sell free-lance pieces to New York newspapers, such as the *Sun,* the *Times,* and the *Tribune.*

After the Armistice, armed with the vague assurance that her free lance pieces would be printed in the Buffalo *Evening News* and the New York *Post,* Thompson, with friend Barbara De Port, sailed for Paris in 1920 and opportunities there. Aboard ship were delegates to the World Zionist convention. Thompson took credit for the subsequent stories from that event, although De Port was the author. Lifelong, Thompson had a bent for self-promotion and a tendency to magnify her journalistic work.

A side trip to hunt up relatives in Ireland yielded interviews with Sein Fein rebels and when Earl Reeves, INS bureau chief, tipped her off to their news value, she managed to become a credentialed International News Service correspondent. She landed a publicity job in Paris with the Red Cross, where one of her coworkers was Rose Wilder Lane, daughter of Laura Ingalls Wilder (author of the *Little House* books). On advice of the bureau chief of the Chicago *Daily News,* Thompson left Paris for Vienna, a "second-rate" news city that promised opportunity. Here she managed to become a special correspondent for the Philadelphia *Public Ledger,* working at space rates, and continuing her publicity work for the Red Cross.

Thompson's Sunday supplement feature stories covered Viennese society, cafes, and people with a natural freshness, lacking any real news style, that editors

liked. Thompson covered the politics in similar fashion
and filed reams of copy. The sheer volume of stories com-
pelled the *Ledger* to make her a full correspondent, to
save money. Her career as a journalist improved when
she was named chief of the *Ledger's* bureau in Berlin,
the first woman to head an overseas news bureau.
Thompson did well as a reporter. She covered the hectic
time of German inflation and Hitler's rise. The Nazis did
not impress Thompson as a political threat; she visited
the Soviet Union to cover the tenth anniversary of the
revolution. Thompson's career was going well, her personal life was erratic.

In Vienna Thompson married Joseph Bard, a novelist, but by 1926 it was over. By 1928, Thompson met and
married another novelist Sinclair Lewis. She quit her job
to return to the United States with Lewis and wrote her
first book, *The New Russia,* and she found much to
admire in the post-revolution society.

In retirement Thompson's journalistic reputation
faded; she was becoming known as Mrs. Sinclair Lewis.
When Lewis was awarded the Nobel Prize for
Literature, Thompson accompanied him to Stockholm
with an assignment from the *Saturday Evening Post.*
She continued free lance assignments that ranged from
Prohibition to domestic and international politics for a
variety of journals. In 1931 she returned to Germany
and interviewed Hitler–Thompson was a poor prophet;
she saw little hope for Hitler as a leader–but wrote a
popular book *I Saw Hitler!,* condemning the Nazi leader
for his anti-Semitic programs. Thompson consistently
championed the Jews and Zionism.

Subsequently, when Thompson returned to Germany
in 1934 she was expelled. Her notoriety earned her a column for the *Herald Tribune,* in 1936 as a three-time
weekly alternative to Walter Lippmann for $10,000 a
year, plus syndication. Her column "On the Record"

appeared March 17, 1936, with liberal views that contrasted with Lipmann's well-argued prose. Within a year
Thompson's column appeared in 130 newspapers.

By 1937 Thompson had a press agent, Irving
Mansfield, and an NBC national weekly radio program.
In the same year Thompson began a column for the
Ladies' Home Journal, at $1,000 a month, that was to
run for twenty years. Her topics for the magazine were
lighter than her politically-laden newspaper fare. For
the *Journal* Thompson wrote of her family, her garden,
her home and kitchen. She wanted, she said, to be
known as a woman. *Time* magazine pronounced her one
of the most influential women in America. Her opinionated views appealed to many Americans–she dictated
her columns, hence her style was a natural, free-ranging
commentary. Short, choppy sentences, punctuated with
many exclamation marks, hammered her points like
ten-penny nails. To critics, her writing was like someone
bellowing in your ear. Thompson's writing was emotional, but left no doubts regarding her point of view. And
Thompson always had a view.

Thompson was a celebrity, but overbearing company.
One of the complaints friends noted, was Thompson's
tendency to talk incessantly; she dominated any conversation and answered her own questions. John Hersey,
Lewis' secretary in those years, likened her to a
Wagnerian Valkyrie. She was described by other friends
as a prima donna–charming, but a "monster."

Her books in this period, collections of her columns,
included *Dorothy Thompson's Political Guide* (1938) and
Let the Record Speak (1939). She was a leading voice
against the dangers of fascism–and for the New Deal. A
"Profile" in the *New Yorker* reported that between 1938
and 1940 more than sixty percent of her words dealt
with Hitler. She was well rewarded; *Time* reported that
her income in 1939 was $103,000.

Her effort with a Broadway play in 1940, "Another Sun," dealing with the plight of Jewish refugees, was a financial and dramatic failure, however. She lost $30,000 and all desire to attempt any further career in the theater. The critical failure, however, provided fodder for her columns in the *Journal* and the *Tribune* and served to draw attention to the plight of the Jews in Europe under Nazism.

Thompson's growing popularity–and Lewis' decline–led to the breakup of her second marriage. The pair were also at odds politically. By this time, Thompson had become an ardent convert to President Roosevelt's policies in opposing fascism. Lewis was a pacifist; certainly a non-interventionist. Thompson and the *Tribune* were also at odds over her bellicose views and her support of the New Deal. Her support was not confined to her columns; she appeared at FDR rallies and endorsed him on radio programs. Initially, Thompson had flirted with support for GOP presidential candidate Wendell Willkie, and the *Tribune* was unhappy when Thompson endorsed FDR's third term bid. The Republican *Tribune* let her go; despite being syndicated to 150 newspapers, her contract was not renewed in 1941. Thompson was immediately signed by the Bell Syndicate. Nationally her column reached an estimated eight million readers and she moved to the New York *Post,* a liberal newspaper.

After her divorce from Lewis in 1942, Thompson married Maxim Kopf, a painter. After the war, her support for a Jewish homeland in the British protectorate of Palestine was enhanced when she and Kopf visited there. But her strong opposition to Jewish terrorist activity in Palestine infuriated Zionist groups in America, and the publisher of the *Post.* Ironically, after years of avid and public support for the Jews, by 1945 Thompson was condemned for attacking Jewish terrorism. Thompson had exposed Charles Lindbergh for his pro-Nazi views; she had mocked the German-American Bund, and for years had espoused Jewish support. Now, she was accused by many, including columnist Walter Winchell, of being a pro-Arab propagandist. Her column was dropped by the *Post* in 1947. Her *Ladies' Home Journal* column continued, however now at $1,500, and her books included *The Courage to Be Happy* (1957) and *Elderly Reflections* (1958).

By the 1950s, Thompson was virtually forgotten; she spent her time traveling and lecturing, mostly at colleges and she still commanded a then-handsome fee of $1,000. Too many times, however, she was mistaken for Dorothy Parker by a new generation. Her writing had become erratic; deafness was a problem and after Kopf's death, she retired from journalism in 1958. In her later years, Thompson worked on a projected autobiography that was unfinished when she died in 1961, during a visit to Lisbon.

Dorothy Thompson was a dynamic combination of self-made talent, combined with calculated promotion, self-assurance, and ambition, who exerted a profound influence in pre-war American journalism. Thompson exuded greatness, but lacked an elusive human touch; her enemies outnumbered her friends. Those Jewish leaders, who should be indebted to Thompson, have forgotten her early, earnest efforts on their behalf. She was not a feminist, but her early work for women's rights are similarly ignored. Others have never forgiven Thompson for her supposed betrayal of Israel; she merely made the point that terrorism in the name of patriotism is terrorism. She was a leader of causes whose followers have forgotten her many contributions. Her influence helped to pave the way for a new generation of journalists.

SOURCES:

Margaret Case Harriman, "The 'It' Girl," *The New Yorker*
    (April 20, 27, 1940), 24-30, 23-29.

Peter Kurth, *American Cassandra: The Life of Dorothy
    Thompson* (Boston: Little, Brown and Co., 1990).

Donald A. Ritchie, "Dorothy Thompson: First Lady of
    American Journalism," *American Journalists: Getting the
    Story* (New York: Oxford University Press, 1998), 200-
    204.

Marion K. Sanders, *Dorothy Thompson: A Legend in Her Time*
    (Boston: Houghton Mifflin Co., 1973).

SELECTED BOOKS BY THOMPSON:

The Courage to Be Happy (Boston: Houghton Mifflin, 1957).

Dorothy Thompson's Political Guide (New York: Stackpole
    Sons, 1938).

I Saw Hitler! (New York: Farrar and Rhinehart, 1932).

Let the Record Speak (Boston: Houghton Mifflin, 1939).

The New Russia (New York: Henry Holt, 1928).

14

Henry R. Luce

Time, Life, and the American Century

The third decade of the 1900s saw the birth of an extraordinary group of magazines destined to play a major role in the development of American culture. With television little more than a dream, radio still in its infancy, and motion pictures silent, flickering images, print publication dominated the field of communication. In the 1920s Americans witnessed the emergence of the *Readers' Digest,* brainchild of the DeWitt Wallace's, a husband and wife team who provided a magazine based on abridged stories and features aimed at middle-class readers with little pretense of sophistication. Diametrically opposite emerged the urbane *New Yorker,* a cosmopolitan collection of satire and humor, created by an eccentric, self-described "hobo newsman," Harold Ross. Both magazines, after initial struggles for recognition, became staples with readers. Henry Luce, a Yale graduate of modest beginnings, but with uncommonly good connections, saw the need for a weekly news magazine capable of keeping Americans informed. Luce named his brainchild *Time the Weekly*

Henry R. Luce: Chronology

1898   born, April 3, Tengchow, China

1908   British boarding school, Chenfoo, China

1912   Hotchkiss preparatory school

1918   military training

1920   B.A., Yale College

1921   Oxford University; Chicago *Daily News,* reporter

1922   Baltimore *News,* reporter

1923   *Time* magazine; first three years business manager, then editor-in-chief

1924   published *Literary Review* magazine

1929   *Fortune* magazine; editor-in-chief

1931   "March of Time," CBS network radio program

1935   first movie short, *The March of Time*

1936   *Life* magazine; editor-in-chief

1954   *Sports Illustrated;* editor-in-chief

1954-
1964   Time Inc.; editorial chairman

1967   dies February 28, Phoenix, Arizona

News-Magazine and his publication grew to became an American institution and provide the foundation for a gobal media empire.

Henry R. Luce (1898-1967) was born in China; his parents were Presbyterian missionaries. Luce's early schooling came from his parents and later he attended a British-run boarding school. Young Luce read widely and early on harbored thoughts that he would like journalism because of its "possibilities for influencing good." His father, in a visit to the United States, became a close friend with Mrs. Cyrus McCormick, widow and heir of the founder of the International Harvester Co. Her generous gift of funds enabled Luce to attend the Hotchkiss School, in Connecticut, one of the best preparatory schools in America. He excelled in Greek and captained the Debating team, but even at that early age, Luce was remote, somber, and reticent. Luce was also editor-in-chief of the *Hotchkiss Literary Monthly* and assistant managing editor of the weekly newspaper, the *Record.* At Hotchkiss, his newspaper colleague, rival, and friend, was outgoing, gregarious, and talented Briton Hadden; both went on to Yale.

Luce's father paid $500 for college tuition, but Luce himself earned the remainder of his funds for Yale College with jobs; he managed student eating clubs and sales for a tailor. Both Luce and his friend Hadden competed for a place on the *Yale Daily News;* Hadden became chairman and Luce editor. In 1918 both men interrupted their college career with officer training at Camp Jackson, S.C., but the war ended before further military service disrupted their lives. They returned to Yale and the *Record,* agreeing that college students and most Americans were ill-informed about world events. Luce graduated from Yale in 1920, voted by his class as "most brilliant," Hadden was voted "most likely to succeed," and both men were tapped for Skull and Bones, most-prestigious of Yale's secret societies.

Luce furthered his education at Oxford for a year. (Hadden landed a job with the New York *World.*) Upon his return from England, Luce applied to the Chicago *Daily News* and won a $16-a-week job as legman-assistant for Ben Hecht, then busy with his popular column, "One Thousand and One Nights in Chicago." Later, through a lead from a fellow Yale man, Luce and Hadden landed work at the Baltimore *News.* In their after-hours the two worked on a prospectus for a weekly news magazine to be called *Time.*

In February 1922, Luce and Hadden began in earnest to launch their magazine. For the next eight months they raised capital, primarily using their Yale connections. Yale alumnus and Skull and Bones members purchased $86,000 of stock in the venture, a bit short of their goal of $100,000. The two decided to go forward. Fittingly, most of their new staff came from Yale people. Both Hadden and Luce saw themselves as editors, but one would have to be the business manager. They decided to serve on alternate years. On a coin toss, Luce lost and became so enmeshed with financial affairs that three years passed before he managed to assume the title of editor-in-chief. *Time* magazine began with 25,000 subscribers

Those three years, however, were sufficient for Hadden to stamp *Time* with his personality, his writing style, and his ability to coin new words that the public accepted. Most of the material came from the *New York Times*–the magazine could afford no wire service, and scant reference sources, and employed no reporters or correspondents. *Time* had a few rewrite men (women were hired only as researchers), and Hadden.

Hadden's style revolted the purists, but his trick, inverted sentences, compound words, and doubled adjectives used as barbed epithets delighted readers with their wit and irreverence. Hadden was the originator of what came to be called *Time*-style, a form of warped English imitated still. Under editor Hadden's tutelage, *Time* writers abjured "said:" people barked, snapped, croaked, opined, chuckled, gushed. Hadden used photographs to embarrass people and racy captions when photographs were wanting. He enlivened his pages with fabricated letters to employ ripostes already written. Hadden encouraged his writers to liven the fare lifted from the daily press with fictive or wholly imaginary details. Hadden, however, had an inquiring, if flamboyant, mind and was responsible for *Time's* first radio program, a quiz show to boost circulation, devoted to events in the latest issue of the magazine.

In 1924, the pair launched a new, short-lived venture, the *Literary Review* that lasted until 1927. Economics dictated a shift of operation to Cleveland, Ohio, but by 1927 the operation was back in New York City. Then in February 1929, Hadden died of a streptococcus infection. Luce managed to buy Hadden's stock and proceeded to build an empire.

Luce alone founded *Fortune* in 1929. Hadden, before his death, indicated no enthusiasm for a business publication and did little toward its creation. Luce spent two years in planning this enterprise for Time Inc. (no comma, by Luce edict). Three months before *Fortune's* debut as a paean of praise for the American corporation, Wall Street crashed with a thud, ushering in the Great Depression. Undaunted, Luce pressed forward with a quality publication priced at one dollar a copy and an initial subscription list of 30,000. Luce's goal, he said, was "to let the public know how business works" and *Fortune* would inform readers of the triumphs of business as well as its failures.

Well after the muckraking era, *Fortune* was exposing business sins like the embezzlement crimes of the

Swedish match king, Ivar Kreuger, the inner workings of the European munitions makers, and the devices of the DuPonts. United Fruit, U.S. Steel, and the Great Atlantic & Pacific Tea Co. were examined with iconoclastic scrutiny. Luce's editors penetrated the innermost secrets of Allied Chemical and Dye with information unknown to most of its stockholders. Within five years *Fortune* turned a profit of $500,000 and raised its price to $1.50. Critics from the political left and right attacked *Fortune;* similarly, praise came from across the political spectrum. More important, the magazine was being noticed and its editorial point of view made a difference. At this stage of his career, Luce was a firm supporter of the New Deal and President Franklin D. Roosevelt. Later, that view would change when he felt that government programs–Democratic programs specifically--for economic recovery and war preparedness were inadequate. By the 1940 campaign, Luce was an ardent supporter of Republican policies.

Luce indulged his interest in building and design, picking up *Architecture Forum* and *House & Home;* neither of these "hobby" magazine made money. Both were extinguised by Time Inc. in the 1960s.

"The March of Time," popular and effective movie shorts, began in 1930 as a radio program. Initially, the program was recorded and distributed free of charge to radio stations as a device to boost circulation. The authoritative voice of Westbrook Van Voorhis intoned "Time marches on!" and millions of listeners were convinced this was Truth. The series ran fifteen years, until 1945 on the CBS network, with *Time* and other advertisers making more money for Luce. In fact, Luce had little to do with the actual production. Later in 1935. the series began as motion picture shorts, produced by Louis de Rochemont, running every six weeks in motion picture theaters, again with narration by Van Voorhis under exclusive contract. Hollywood rewarded the series with a 1936 Academy Award Oscar for revolutionizing newsreels. The series totaled 257 dramatic and captivating episodes and ended in 1953, a victim of television.

In 1935 Luce acquired from Conde-Nast, for $85,000, the rights to the title *Life* for a new magazine he was planning; Luce spent six million dollars nurturing the project. The idea for a picture magazine came from his second wife, Clare Booth Brokaw, an editor of *Vanity Fair*. (Luce married Lila Holtz in 1923 and divorced in 1935 when he became enamored with Brokaw.) *Fortune* often used quality photographs and had talented staffers like Margaret Bourke-White and Walker Evans to capture the images of American business. *Life,* however, would alter the balance and importance. "Photoessays" (another new coinage) dominated the text, and the magazine's pictures portrayed America and the world.

The first issue of *Life* appeared November 23, 1936 and within a month was selling 500,000 copies a week (at ten cents a copy), double the expectations; within a year circulation exceeded a million. By 1939 *Life's* circulation reached two million; a decade later, its readership reached twenty-one percent of the entire population of the United States.

Life was an institution in the United States, a magazine, indeed, of world significance. The magazine was the element in the Luce publishing conglomerate that made his "big little business" into a "little big business" that became an empire. *Life* was like a Broadway show, Luce once observed, that would eventually come to an end. The weekly edition ceased December 29, 1972, (a monthly version, much reduced in scope, exists) and an institution ended in America.

More than seven million readers (when America had a population of 150 million) looked at life as defined by Luce. Causes for its demise are easily identified: shrinkage of advertising pages; skimpy issues because of reduced ad pages discouraged readers to renew subscriptions; added mail and distribution costs–ironically, increased circulation mostly added to cost, rather than prompt advertisers to its pages. At bottom, television that drained away advertising dollars, killed *Life;* television, with its more immediate and vivid pictures replaced the print media in popularity. *Life's* credo was for mankind "to see and be instructed." Television provided ample ability to see, but rarely the words, however, to enlighten the audiences it entertained.

No high-minded purpose like those that propelled *Time, Life,* and *Fortune* was behind *Sports Illustrated,* Luce's 1955 creation. Kindly, one might observe that *Sports Illustrated* took sports out of the locker room into the living room. "Muscles," as Time Inc. people called it, was created to cater to America's growing leisure class, with money and time to spend. Luce in this instance, had no compelling "uplift" motive nor any interest in sports, but he recognized a potential and lucrative market. In one editorial meeting, Luce suggested that the magazine would fulfill the Socratic idea that the unexamined life is not worth living. That was, Luce said, the "philosophical justification." Luce needed a "cause."

Sports Illustrated lost twenty-three million dollars during its first five years, but after that rocky start, went on to become another plump cash cow in the growing Luce enterprises.

Luce was the driving force behind his magazines– *Time, Life,* and *Fortune*–and even *Sports Illustrated* and he devoted long and inventive effort to their content. To be sure, he hired delegates–talented and well-paid–but Luce edited, shaped, and initiated stories, ideas, and concepts; and if he did not create, Luce set the tone for innovative essays in prose and photojournalism unequaled in American journalism.

In later years, Luce conceded that many of *Time's* notorious literary mannerisms "went too far." Reform was helped along by a brutal 1936 satire by Wolcott Gibbs in the *New Yorker*. The piece was in retaliation for a *Fortune* article about the *New Yorker* by a former staff member, Ralph Ingersoll. Harold Ross, editor of the *New Yorker* responded with Gibbs' devastating "Profile" that seared *Timespeak* and Luce himself.

Time prose was the primary target, but Gibbs' parody also captured Luce as well. If Hadden introduced the innovative *Time* style and coined new words, e.g. kudo, that caught the fancy of readers who sought to become more literate, Luce was responsible for the content of *Time, Life,* and *Fortune*. As editor in chief, Luce read every word of every important story or editorial. If *Time* tempered its exotic style, the influence of Luce's personality and point of view never wavered.

A corps of female researchers–for most of its history no woman would ever be considered for an editorial position in Luce's flagship magazines–would check every fact for accuracy. Correspondents were expected to report facts. Luce himself would read copy carefully for truth. Luce's view of truth often was not factual. Luce's was a higher truth.

If fact clashed with Luce truth, facts would have to yield. The classic example, of course, is related to China. Luce's birthplace was riven by clashes of political ideology before and amidst the Japanese invasion in the 1930s. Luce was one of the leading exponents of what came to be identified as "the China Lobby" in America during the 1950s. His idealized portrait of China and its people presented in the pages of *Life* and *Time* did not square with reality. Whatever reputable correspondents, such as Theodore White and John Hersey, might submit to their New York editors, when their reports failed to reflect the reality that Luce wanted, he either threw out their copy or substituted his version of events. In his magazines, Luce often was neither fair nor objective. Luce never apologized for this prostitution of journalistic ethics; he expected readers to accept his version of the world. The missionary's son never lost his idealized vision of life.

After Luce's death February 28, 1967, his empire continued to grow and prosper and it produced new magazines–*People* and *Money*; published books through its subsidiaries, Time-Life Books and Little, Brown; owned radio and television stations; and cable networks; paper and pulp mills, buildings and real estate. Profit, not publishing became the dominant theme. Luce's stewards lacked his idealism. Time Inc. merged with Warner Communication in 1989-1990–journalism married to show business. And as if a mouse swallowed an elephant, Warner became the dominant partner of the new corporation, Time Warner Communications. What had been Time Inc. was debt-ridden with deflated stock that left shareholders poorer, propped by junk-bonds.

Finally, by the time five-year-old America Online acquired Time Warner in late 2000, *Time,* the linchpin of the enterprise and jewel of the media crown, had become just another magazine. His publishing empire failed to outlast the "American Century" Luce had proudly proclaimed. In the structure of Time Warner, the magazines, led by *Time,* played a significant role, at least from a public relations view. When America Online essentially took over Time Warner, the last vestige of Luce's empire became one of an array of "content providers." The magazines that once were the foundation of the enterprise now represented only twenty-one percent of revenues. Income from cable television, music, and motion pictures accounted for nineteen, sixteen, and thirteen percent, respectively, according to the *New York Times*; by far the major media activity was on the

Internet, with AOL-Time Warner the nation's largest Internet Service Provider (ISP) with 38.6 million subscribers (by 2001 and growing).

Henry R. Luce, who maintained that growing larger in a corporate sense or earning more profits "wasn't the main point," was an evangelist who preached his doctrine to millions of Americans. Luce likened himself to a "Jesuit persuader." His publications were blatant propaganda instruments. Luce did not hesitate to decide what was enduring truth–his truth, despite any facts to the contrary. He was admired–and hated–but millions read and were influenced by his version of truth. Luce once observed that he harbored no hopes to found an institution that outlived him. His successors to Time Inc. obliged him in that regard. In his era, however, Henry Luce was a dominant force in American culture and opinion.

SOURCES:

James L. Baughman, *Henry R. Luce and the Rise of the American News Media* (Boston: Twayne, 1987).

Noel Busch, *Briton Hadden of Time* (New York: Farrar Straus, 1949).

Richard M. Clurman, *To the End of Time* (New York: Simon and Schuster, 1992).

Wolcott Gibbs, "Time...Fortune...Life...Luce," *The New Yorker* Vol. 12 No. 41 (November 26, 1936), pp. 20-25.

Robert E. Herzstein, *Henry R. Luce: A Political Portrait of the Man Who Created the American Century* (New York: Charles Scribner's Sons, 1994).

John Kobler, *Luce: His Time, Life, and Fortune* (Garden City: Doubleday and Co., 1968).

W. A. Swanberg, *Luce and His Empire* (New York: Scribners, 1972).

Loudon Wainwright, *The Great American Magazine: An Inside History of Life* (New York: Knopf, 1986).

SELECTED BOOKS BY LUCE:

The American Century (New York: Farrar & Rhinehart, 1941).

The Ideas of Henry Luce (New York: Atheneum, 1969).

15

Margaret Bourke-White

Photojournalist: Editorials in Pictures

By the beginning of the century, photographic illustrations were staples of American newspapers. Photographs, prompted by the "yellow journalism" of William Randolph Hearst and Joseph Pulitzer in New York, two publishers who exploited the visual image whenever possible, made newspapers more eye pleasing. Yellow journalism–named for the yellow-colored comic strip–was primarily visual. Technological improvements aided in the increasing use of photography; halftone engravings were faster, cleaner, and more accurate than drawings or woodcuts. Printing improvements that enabled rotogravure reproductions were contributing factors to a popular, graphic press. Photographs of news and human interest, added variety to newspapers and prompted street sales. A few magazines used photographs–in 1903, *Leslie's Illustrated Monthly* employed several pages to accompany H.L. Mencken's "Marketing Wild Animals" article with studies of animals in a natural setting. The *National Geographic* was a picture magazine, but with a limited

Margaret Bourke-White: Chronology

1904   born, June 14, the Bronx, N.Y.

1928   cover for *Trade Winds,* lands a five-year cover contract

1929   hired as *Fortune* photographer

1931   *Eyes on Russia*

1936   joins *Life* magazine

1937   *You Have Seen Their Faces*

1939   to Germany and Russia; *North of the Danube*

1941   *Say, is This the U.S.A.;* in Russia for Nazi invasion, photographs air attacks on Moscow

1942   covers air war in England and the invasion of North Africa

1944   covers Italian campaign; *They Called it Purple Heart Valley*

1945   covers war in Europe with Gen. Patton's Third Army

1946   *Dear Fatherland, Rest Quietly*

1949   *Halfway to Freedom*

1952   assigned by *Life* to cover war in Korea

1963   *Portrait of Myself*

1971   dies, August 27, Stamford, Conn.

audience. Edward Bok's *Ladies' Home Journal* was a leader in printing quality photographs for the mass-media magazine field. But these efforts were costly and sporadic. Photographs informed the reader, sometimes educated the reader, often scandalized the reader. By and large, photojournalism, in the early years of the century, followed traditional patterns.

The event that raised photojournalism to an art form arose from one of the greatest catastrophes–economic and social–to strike America, the Great Depression. Literary realism, another element of the new century, led to a demand for pictorial realism. The film documentary showed Americans how America looked, lived, and coped through national adversity. The reporting mind, with a camera and curiosity, opened the way for large numbers of Americans to see what was happening across their vast country.

The camera became an extraordinary medium that reflected with picture and text the testament of social conscience. Exemplary photo-illustrated books recall that era of the share-cropper, the dispossessed, the homeless, hungry, jobless Americans. Excellent books–Walker Evans' *Let Us Now Praise Famous Men,* with text by James Agee; Evans' *American Photographs*–and works by photographers such as Ben Shawn, Dorthea Lange, and Carl Mydans. Margaret Bourke-White's *You Have Seen Their Faces,* with text by Erskine Caldwell, published in 1937, are contributions often forgotten.

Astute publishers, like Henry Luce and Gardner Cowles, saw the immense mass-market potential in photomagazines. Luce's *Life* magazine was launched in 1936 after production problems were resolved: rotary presses were perfected to handle rolls of coated papers; quality coated paper stock was produced in sufficient quantity; and the problems were solved to produce high-speed, quick-drying inks. Cowles, publisher of the Des Moines (Iowa) *Register,* worked with Luce to produce a picture magazine; Luce even invested money in the effort to produce *Look,* published in early 1937, as a a feature-oriented publication with pictures. The primarily photo oriented *Life,* published in 1936, was first, however, and surpassed all of its founder's expectations in its success. Its original cover photograph featured a New Deal dam image captured by Margaret Bourke-White and the entire press run was an instant sell-out. A number of excellent photographers served *Life* and *Look* with distinction, but Bourke-White more than any other, captured the appearance of America, in peace and war, from the Depression to World War II.

Margaret Bourke-White (1904-1971) was born June 14, 1904, in the Bronx. Her father, Joseph White, an Englishman and a Jew, worked as an engineer for R. Hoe, manufacturers of printing presses. Her mother, Minnie Bourke, was Irish-Catholic. In her college years Bourke-White added the Bourke (the hyphen came later), and, mildly anti-Semitic, denied for the rest of her life her Jewish origins. The family moved to Bound Brook, N.J., to be closer to the Hoe factory.

After high school, Bourke-White's higher education began at Columbia University in 1921 where she developed an interest in photography in a class with Clarence H. White (no relation) and ran a photography session at summer camp. She transferred to the University of Michigan and submitted photographs to the school yearbook and conducted a thriving business on the side selling photos to students.

Marriage to a fellow undergraduate, Everett Chapman, took her to Purdue University in 1924. A domineering mother-in-law doomed that marriage–also, she disliked being called Margaret W. Chapman. When her husband took an industrial job, Margaret attempted to complete her education at Case Western Reserve and pursued photographic studies of industrial Cleveland. When her marriage dissolved, she enrolled in Cornell University in 1926 to pursue a degree in biology. Increasingly, however, she continued her photography and ran a business supplying prints of the campus and students to help pay her tuition.

After graduation in 1927, she landed a job with a Cleveland architecture firm–her photographs had a quality that enhanced the romance of industry and buildings. One of her photographs landed her a cover for *Trade Winds,* a trade publication. The magazine paid her $50–her usual fee was five dollars–and ran a Bourke-White cover every month for the next five years. *Architectural Record* published a portfolio of her work and more of her work was appearing in national advertisements. Bourke-White's work displayed the Age of Industry in a booming economy. Her photographs drew the attention of Henry R. Luce, publisher of *Time,* who saw in her work "the smartness and excitement" that he wanted for his new magazine *Fortune.* In 1929, Luce hired Bourke-White as *Fortune's* first and only staff photographer (and the sole woman on its editorial staff).

Now based in New York, Bourke-White went to work on a half-time basis at $1,000 a month to build up stories for the magazine. She photographed foundries, glass-blowing plants, watch-makers–a wide variety of America's booming economy. Between times she filled advertising assignments that paid more. When Big Business took a fall, Luce went ahead with his magazine and Bourke-White's work dominated the first issue.

Fortune, the luxury magazine of big business, managed to survive and in the process became the finest photography magazine in America. Other photographers appeared: Erich Salomon and Walker Evans. With its large pages, lavish layout and display, *Fortune* became a

portfolio for art. Unlike the usual editorial process, stories were not written until the photographs were available. Bourke-White is credited, however, as the creator
of the *Fortune* picture. From coal mines to the Chrysler
Building, Bourke-White patterned the pictures that
helped Americans recognize themselves. More important, *Fortune* made Bourke-White a name people
remembered; her work–often more than one portfolio–
was in every issue but one in *Fortune's* first year and she
was given a prominent credit line. Bourke-White made a
reputation in a man's world.

In 1930 *Fortune* sent her to Germany to photograph
its industry and again in 1933 (she captured the tanks
and guns made of wood, but real armaments eluded her
and she reported that this army was "no threat"), then to
Russia to photograph progress of the Five-Year Plan.
She succeeded where others had failed, and went back
for more pictures in 1932 and 1933. Simon & Schuster
invited her to publish her first book, *Eyes on Russia.*
From that experience, Bourke-White began to empha-
size people in her photographs, where heretofore massive machery and soaring buildings dominated.

Bourke-White became famous and well-paid; in 1930
her income was $25,000; a year later, $50,000; in 1934
her private studio alone brought in $34,000 annually.
Buick automobiles and Goodyear Tire were blue ribbon
accounts. The advertisements, especially, enabled her to
work on perfecting color, enabled by new cameras, film,
and printing processes. In the mid-thirties she
embarked on a new project, a social documentary. Her
partner was Erskine Caldwell, author and playwright,
whose dramatization of "Tobacco Road" was breaking all
records on Broadway. Their joint effort led to publication
of *You Have Seen Their Faces.* The book became an
instant best seller and broke ground because the photographs ranked equally with the text.

Social documentary photography led to a revolution in journalism. The camera no longer illustrated, the camera told; photographs helped form public opinion. Newsreels and Luce's innovative "The March of Time" helped pave the way. The picture magazine conceived by Luce established the camera as a vital instrument of communication. Luce named it the "photographic essay." Henry Luce's new picture magazine *Life* signed on Bourke-White in 1936 as one of its original four photographers. Luce gave Bourke-White her first assignment. The Public Works Administration (PWA) Fort Peck Dam, in New Deal, Montana, became *Life's* first cover, November 23, 1936. Bourke-White led the way for recognition of her–and others'–work. The anonymous journalism at Time Inc. yielded to her demands for photo credit lines.

A 1938 trip to Germany and Czechoslovakia, accompanied by Caldwell, produced another joint book *North of the Danube*. In February 1938, Bourke-White and Caldwell married in Nevada. In August 1939, she sailed to London for *Life* and war broke out the next month. She photographed the war in Rumania, Syria, and Turkey. But she wanted a better salary, more recognition, and to be home–she resigned from *Life* and went to work for Ralph Ingersoll's quirky newspaper *PM,* a creative innovation in journalism that endured for eight years. Bourke-White lasted even less time in that environment. Within four months, Bourke-White returned to *Life,* no longer a staff member, but as a contract employee her salary exceeded pay as a staff member.

Her first assignment, a cross-country trek with Erskine Caldwell, was never published in *Life* but became a book, *Say, is This the U.S.A.* (1941). Anticipating a broadened European war, her editors sent her to Moscow in March; she and Caldwell arrived via the Pacific route. Consequently, Bourke White was on the scene in June 1941 when the Nazis invaded Russia. She photographed graphic scenes of twenty-two air raids on Moscow before she left in September. Later. she was one of the few Western photographers to portray front line conflict. When she returned home in September, *Life* proclaimed her "photographer of the year." Her book, *Shooting the Russian War,* was published the following year.

By spring 1942, Bourke-White was back to the war, this time to photograph the U.S. Air Forces in England. Her photos helped publicize the glamorous B-17 "Flying Fortress" in their daylight raids on Germany. Professionally, Bourke-White was at her peak. Personally, her marriage was dissolving; Caldwell divorced her. In December, on way to cover the invasion, her ship was torpedoed off North Africa. She survived that experience and went on to cover the air war. In Africa, she won permission to accompany a bombing mission and again, under fire, produced notable photographs before she returned home in 1943.

Bourke-White was unable to win accredited status for the European theater. Perhaps unknown to her, she had acquired the reputation as a prima donna, who demanded–and got–special treatment; military personnel had to be designated to carry her equipment, she regularly circumvented channels to get her way and had no compunction to deal directly with the commanding general. She had no hesitation in using her sex to gain favors and access, and if all else failed, she would resort to tears. None of this behavior endeared her to fellow correspondents–or the military people whose basic job was to win a war.

By August, however, she was back on the battlefields. Her assignment was to portray the unpublicized service and supply lines, which the Army wished to publicize. She was sent back to Italy. But by January 1944, she photographed the carnage waged by General Mark Clark's Thirty-sixth Division in Italy's Lin Valley and the activities of the Eleventh Field Hospital, where American readers first witnessed photographs showing the dead and wounded casualties of the Great Crusade. In spring 1944, Bourke-White published *They Called it "Purple Heart Valley,"* an immensely popular book. Bourke-White continued to cover the "forgotten front" with the Army's Eighty-eighth Division and its bloody fight up the Italian peninsula until March 1945.

After she finally won permission to cover the European invasion, Bourke-White accompanied General Geoge S. Patton's Third Army in its race across Europe. She was one of the first correspondents to witness the horror of the Nazi death camps, and she was one of the first correspondents with General Patton's forces to enter Buchenwald, the Nazi death camp, and photograph in graphic detail the horrors that occurred there. She portrayed the total destruction of Germany; *Life* ran her photo essay, "The Face of the Moon" to illustrate the effectiveness of the U.S. aerial saturation bombing.

After the war she put her experiences into another book, *Dear Fatherland, Rest Quietly* (a title taken from the song, "Die Wacht am Rhine," once well-known in America) in which she expressed her anger and hatred, her despair and idealism toward Germany. *Life* regrouped its focus. In March 1946, she went to India, the world's newest democracy, to capture the idealism lost in Germany. Her photographs helped make Mahatma Gandhi an icon in America and became a propaganda tool for the ideals that were expected of India. She was the last correspondent to speak to Gandhi only hours before his assassination. From the India experience came her 1949 book *Halfway to Freedom*.

Not unexpectedly, Bourke-White was attacked in the 1950s as a fellow traveler by columnist Westbrook

Pegler–her sympathies with the sharecroppers, her association with *PM,* her closeness to Russia–combined to make her a target of the McCarthyites. One way to "clear her name," Bourke-White reasoned, was to cover the Korean conflict, a United Nations "police action" manned primarily by U.S. forces. In March 1952, *Life* assigned her to Korea. (North Korea invaded South Korea in 1950. America became involved through President Harry S Truman's decision to support the United Nation's response. More than 130,000 American casualties resulted before a truce was declared in July 1952.) *Life's* photographers had covered the war extensively; Bourke-White was now to cover the intermittent guerrilla warfare that threatened the peace. Her finished picture essay ran as a lead story in *Life* and served, she believed, as a sufficient loyalty oath to silence the Peglers.

On her return and during her subsequent lecture tour, Bourke-White experienced distressing physical symptoms--stiffness and muscle failure in her legs. *Life* kept her busy with assignments, but in 1955, Bourke-White learned she had Parkinson's disease and by 1957 she could no longer handle assignments. She managed to write, however, and produced an autobiography, *Portrait of Myself* in 1963. At the end of her life she was working on a second book of her experiences, but failed to finish it; she died in Stamford, Connecticutt, August 27, 1971. *Life* itself died sixteen months later. The era of the photomagazine was over.

Bourke-White wrote in her unfinished reminiscence: "in the end it is only the work that counts." Omitted is a great deal of Bourke-White's personal life, a stormy and controversial element that in many ways detracts from her idealized self-portrait. The record is clear that Bourke White resorted to any device to get her pictures, with questionable moral and ethical actions. If that behavior was reprehensible, her single-minded determination to complete an assignment must be acknowledged. Her photographs endure, however, and reflect four momentous decades of a tumultous century.

SOURCES:

Eleanor H. Ayer, *Margaret Bourke-White: Photographing the World* (New York: Dillon, 1992).

Michael Carlbach, *American Photojournalism Comes of Age* (Washington: Smithsonian Institution Press, 1997).

Carolyn Daffron, *Margaret Bourke-White* (New York: Chelsea House, 1988).

Vicki Goldberg, *Margaret Bourke-White: A Biography* (New York: Harper & Row, 1986).

Jonathan Silverman, *For the World to See: The Life of Margaret Bourke-White* (New York: Viking, 1983).

SELECTED BOOKS BY BOURKE-WHITE:

Dear Fatherland, Rest Quietly: A Report on the Collapse of Hitler's Thousand Years, (New York: Simon and Schuster, 1946).

Eyes on Russia (New York; Simon & Schuster, 1931).

Halfway to Freedom (New York: Simon and Schuster, 1949).

Portrait of Myself (New York: Simon and Schuster, 1963).

The Taste of War, Edited by Jonathan Silverman (London: Century Publishing, 1985).

They Called it Purple Heart Valley: A Combat Chronicle of the War in Italy (New York: Simon and Schuster, 1944).

Say, is This the U.S.A. (with Erskine Caldwell), (New York: Duell, Sloan and Pearce. 1941).

You Have Seen Their Faces [1937] (Athens: University of Georgia, 1995).

16

Walter Winchell

Reporting Gossip and Rumor

Journalism's definition has changed over the past century. The result is witnessed every day, especially on television which is blamed for practically all the ills that beset modern society. Television news programs–especially local television–are populated by vacuous people who can read reasonably well and smile winningly. Few commentators are journalists in the traditional sense; few have ever covered a beat, fewer still know the definition of news. Typical program fare constitutes of public relations fluff and network promotions. Newspapers began the change long before television.

After the extravagances of end-of-the-century yellow journalism, ethical and factual practices prevailed in many of America's newspapers and magazines, with some notable exceptions. Today, however, the public craving for the lurid and sensational is being satisfied with sustained fare from the "supermarket" tabloid press that purports to report everything from alien sexual encounters to the secret lives of celebrities. Reporting of this nature is a staple of television, modern

Walter Winchell: Chronology

1897   born April 7, New York City

1920   *Billboard,* columnist

1920-24   *Vaudeville News,* columnist

1924-27   New York *Evening Graphic,* columnist

1929-63   New York *Mirror*

1929-63   King Features syndicated columnist

1930-59   radio commentator

1952-64   television commentator

1963-66   New York *Journal-American,* columnist

1966-67   New York *World Journal Tribune,* columnist

1972   dies February 20, Los Angeles, California

media's answer to the lurid penny-press of a century ago. The public views a daily diet of "news" that devotes coverage to marriage, divorce, clinical inquiries into private lives, rumor, speculation, and gossip. Guilty television may be, but it was a newspaper columnist–Walter Winchell–who paved the way for this level of keyhole journalism seventy years ago. Few journalists have managed to exceed Winchell's exploitation of the public's desire for salacious gossip.

Walter Winchell (1897-1972), was born Weinschel (the family changed the name to Winchel, a not uncommon practice in that era) in New York's Lower East side then moved to the Jewish ghetto of Harlem. He was an indifferent student, growing up in poverty in a family beset with strife. Between 1905 and 1908, Walter lived in Danville, Virginia, a poor cotton town. Back in New York, Walter worked at odd jobs and sold newspapers. In 1909 Walter and two classmates won a dancing appearance at a local theater, the Imperial, as "The Little Men with the Big Voices." Renamed "The Imperial Trio," the group won a spot with The Gus Edwards 1910 Song Revue. Gus Edwards, the author of a number of hit songs, including "School Days," retained Winchell.

Winchell left school for the $15-a-week job as a vaudeville performer that ended after three seasons. Winchell, back in New York, took a series of office jobs. By the summer of 1911, however, he was back with Edwards in his School Days troupe. After two years Winchell teamed with Rita Greene to form a dance team; they later married.

In 1918 Winchell enlisted in the Navy and saw limited sea duty stateside aboard the USS *Isis;* his service career lasted only five months. By January, he and Greene were back on a minor circuit. In Chicago, Winchell begged a newspaper acquaintance for an assignment. Jo Swerling, a reporter on the Chicago

Herald Examiner, gave Winchell his entry and Winchell produced a paragraph March 1, 1919, reporting on a Chicago storm that Winchell later embellished as "a blizzard." Through another friend Winchell gained a press card–a newspaperman's I.D.–and as the Imperial Trio moved him out of poverty, so did his press credentials.

On tour through tank-town vaudeville dates, Winchell began submitting items under the heading "Stage Whispers" to *Billboard,* a theatrical trade paper. A few were published. Winchell typed up theatrical items that he posted backstage, called "Newssence," composed of stolen jokes, gossip, and rumor. Winchell mailed copies of his work and managed to get published (at no fee) in the *Vaudeville News,* a newssheet published by NVA (National Vaudeville Artists). By 1920, abandoning show business, Winchell arrived in New York with a job of sorts for the *Vaudeville News,* and a new column, "Broadway Hearsay." Good or bad, his theatrical readers recognized that to be mentioned at all was publicity and Winchell was obliging. Budding newspaperman Winchell neglected his wife and Greene went back on tour. Winchell found a new friend, June Aster, a fellow vaudevillian whom he married in May 1923, neglecting to divorce Greene.

Then Winchell landed a job on a real newspaper, not a trade publication. The New York *Evening Graphic* was a new concept in newspapers, a creation of Bernarr MacFadden, a health advocate who made a reputation with his magazine *Physical Culture* and a fortune with his pulp magazine *True Story.* His newspaper creation was a tabloid that would tell the truth and present human interest stories, not news. Winchell began his column, "Your Broadway and Mine," on September 24, 1924. Illiterate, gossipy, full of "gags" and aimed at the lowest common denominator, Winchell's column was a success. Winchell became a Broadway staple, initially guided through its people and places by Mark Hellinger and

Damon Runyon, fellow columnists. Winchell became known, feared and respected as a diligent digger of information. His background as a street-fighter provided his education and vocabulary. Winchell did not invent slang; he improved upon it.

Winchell's contemporaries knew the rules of English grammar; Winchell could write. He expressed himself in his column with the words of a new era–the actor, the gangster, the speakeasy, the self-promoter–the denizens of Broadway employed a slang that Winchell exploited. What he heard, Winchell improved upon. He coined new words that entered the nation's lexicon. H.L. Mencken's *The American Language* is studded with Winchellisms: the Main Stem, giggle-water and similar concoctions were also found in a contemporary source of coinage, Henry R. Luce's *Time*–"cinemactress," for example.

The *Graphic* was a vulgar paper, bereft of news, that stressed sex, contests, and human interest stories. One of its dubious contribution to journalism was the "composograph"–faked photographs, that were decried by reputable newspaper critics like Guy Fawkes [Robert Benchley] in the *New Yorker*. The tabloids, led by the *Graphic,* paved the way for later journalistic vulgarities.

Winchell's Monday column, headed "Mainly About Mainstreeters," was gossip, unlike his other columns with anecdotes, poems, and press agent plugs. It became "This Town of Ours" in 1927 with a venue much wider than Broadway. Widening his circle created new opportunities, but also created new animosities. Winchell's feud with the brothers Schubert (because he panned their productions) led to problems with his editors and the *Graphic*. Moreover, Winchell wanted more money and a greater share of his growing syndication income and by 1929, Winchell sought new opportunities.

William Randolph Hearst's *Evening Journal* lured Winchell with a signing bonus, $500 weekly, and fifty percent of syndication fees. Winchell managed to have himself fired from the *Graphic* (his contract had two years to run) to work for Hearst's New York *Mirror,* another tabloid, until 1931. Hearst agreed, when the *Graphic* contract expired. His first column ran June 10, 1929. His schedule was arduous by modern standards: six columns a week (sometimes two full columns) but Winchell, with a secretary only, produced the copy needed. By 1930 Winchell found something more to do.

Radio was a growing medium and Winchell had appeared from time to time as a guest on a number of shows, including Rudy Vallee's. The money was good, the exposure enormous, and Winchell wanted a show of his own. By May 12, 1930 at 7:45, CBS aired Winchell on WABC in New York. His quarter-hour show, "Before Dinner–Walter Winchell" (shortly after renamed "Saks Broadway with Walter Winchell" to identify the sponsor) was little more than gossip, delivered in his distinctive staccato style. He found time to make a Vitaphone movie, "Bard of Broadway," filmed at their Queens studio. Hollywood, with its glamour–and money–beckoned. By August, when his radio show ended, Winchell had managed a new five year contract with the *Mirror*–for $121,000 a year–and a new weekly radio contract with the Wise Shoe Company for $1,000 weekly.

Vaudeville was dying, but in 1930 the New York Palace theater in an effort to attract customers in a Depression economy, lured Walter Winchell to appear as an M.C. for a $3,500 weekly appearance. In that era, newspaper columnists, popular personalities, did this kind of thing–Heywood Broun and Mark Hellinger performed similar stints at the Palace. For Winchell, however, the one-time vaudevillian who had never been good enough to play the Palace, the job was a vindication of sorts. Getting even was a Winchell trait. Despite more profitable offers, Winchell declined to extend his appearances–the strain was too demanding--and the one-time three-a-day hoofer had made his point.

Winchell acquired a new radio show and a new sponsor, La Gerardine, a women's hair preparation. Then Lucky Strike paid him $35,000 to announce for their NBC program, "The Lucky Strike Dance Hour" three times a week for a coast-to-coast and international audience–the kind of audience Winchell sought–immense, influential, and unseen. In order to get out of the local-only broadcast contract for Le Gerardine and sign a $6,000-a-week contract with Lucky Strike, Winchell talked a young *Graphic* gossip columnist into being his replacement–Ed Sullivan. Sullivan went on to his own Broadway column, more radio shows and, eventually, his own television show and became a national personality. (Expectedly, Winchell and Sullivan became enemies.) Winchell benefited from the Lucky Strike connection; the advertising people used his photograph and phrases in print and on billboards.

By 1930 Winchell was America's best-known newspaperman and to many he typified newspapermen–and the image was not at all good. A large number of the public loved him. More importantly, an increasing number of his fellow journalists questioned his ethics, his reporting, his biases, and his character. Winchell was a major force on American opinion, unquestionably.

When his contract with Lucky Strike ended, Winchell signed with the Andrew Jergens Company, for a fifteen minute Sunday night radio broadcast over the NBC Blue Network. It began December 4, 1932. Winchell's sign-on, "Good Evening Mr. and Mrs. America and all the ships at sea. Let's go to press. Flash," began in 1934. The broadcast contained all the elements of his column–gossip, rumor, innuendo, with crime and train wrecks, punctuated with an occasional "flash" or "just in" to add verisimilitude. His eclipses between items in his column became, for the listening audience, the clicks of a telegraph key. By 1934, Winchell received $2,500 weekly for a thirty-nine week contract for his "Jergen's Journal," and it was one of America's top-rated shows. Winchell described himself as "your newsboy."

Winchell continued off and on with his work for Hollywood, personal appearances, along with his column and radio show—all were lucrative fields and Winchell was insulated from the Great Depression. But along with Broadway gossip and cafe society rumors, Winchell commented on politics and plugged President Franklin Roosevelt's New Deal. Roosevelt, as adroit a manipulator as any president, gave Winchell an audience. Winchell, who never forgot nor ever denied his Jewish origins, was one of the first newspaper people to oppose Adolf Hitler and American Nazis. Winchell was an ally of FDR in this cause and also worked closely with FBI Director J. Edgar Hoover. In his zeal, Winchell applied for a commission in Naval Intelligence in 1934 (his request was rejected).

Winchell covered the major crime stories of the time and this strengthened his ties with Hoover—along with the fact that Winchell was helpful to Hoover, who liked to party in the bright spots, like the Stork Club, where WW reigned. For Hearst, Winchell played a major role in the Lindbergh kidnapping case. The trial became a three-ring media circus for newspaper circulation excess and Winchell was more culpable than most for this travesty of journalism. Press critic Benchley, writing in the *New Yorker,* was "disgusted" and "ashamed."

Winchell's 1936 Twentieth Century-Fox film, "Wake Up and Live," for which he received $75,000, was unmemorable, except it enabled an audience to actually see Winchell—a graying man with a receding hairline, with a slight, five-foot, seven-inch frame—who affected a tough guy pose. Nevertheless, he followed with "Love and Hisses," again co-starring orchestra leader Ben Bernie. Winchell's 1937 contract with Jergens raised his radio salary to $4,000 weekly. By 1938, Winchell reported earnings of $362,145 and *Time* magazine featured him on a cover July 18, 1938.

Winchell's preoccupation with politics and his unabashed support of FDR's policies, however, were becoming an irritant to his publisher, Mr. Hearst, who thought that Winchell should stick to Broadway gossip. Winchell increasingly saw himself as a pundit. The *New Yorker,* in 1940, ran one of its longest "Profiles" to deflate Winchell, much as it had dealt with Henry Luce in 1934. Winchell was incensed and began a sustained campaign to smear *New Yorker* editor Harold Ross. Winchell was a gutter fighter and his "drop dead" list (to be purged in and from the column) was infamous.

With the war in 1941, Winchell, now forty-four, again sought a commission in the naval reserve for active duty. Until this came through in 1942, WW fought for FDR's liberal programs and withstood an increasing assault from the conservative press, who not only disliked Winchell, but his outspoken stand for the common man. A secret "fact-finding" mission to Brazil satisfied Winchell's military ambitions. A three-day mission seemed hardly of any significance to the Navy and State Department, especially by someone unable to speak the language, but it satisfied Winchell. He continued his attacks on members of Congress who opposed Roosevelt and aided Hoover in rooting out crime and Nazi sympathizers. General Geoge C. Marshall tried, unsuccessfully to get NBC to muzzle Winchell's broadcasts on the grounds that he was giving away war information that aided the enemy. But Winchell played a major role in home-front morale.

After the war and Roosevelt's death, Winchell—no longer in favor with presidents Truman, Eisenhower and

Kennedy–switched his allegiance to fighting communism in America, real and imagined. Winchell became a
staunch supporter of Senator Joseph R. McCarthy.

    In 1949 Winchell left his old sponsor Jergens for a
new $650,000 contract and moved to ABC with his top-
rated show. By 1951, his radio show had slipped out of
the top ten and Winchell signed with another radio sponsor–and a television show. Radio was losing its audience.
His 1952 venture was less than successful–Winchell was
aging, if not old; his high-intensity, rapid fire delivery
was dated as was his trademark fedora. In 1955 ABC
severed Winchell's contract. He managed to sign a contract with a minor network, Mutual, for his radio show.
In October 1956, NBC produced "The Walter Winchell
Show," a variety hour modeled after Ed Sullivan's popular CBS "Toast of the Town." Winchell lasted only one
season. His next effort, "The Walter Winchell Files" also
failed. Ironically, Winchell later made an impressive success with his masterful voice-over introduction to the
television series, "The Untouchables" (1959-64). He was
heard, not seen.

    Winchell's listening and viewing audience eroded; his
radio career ended in 1959 when his sponsor canceled
and Mutual announced its unwillingness to sustain the
program. He lost a larger audience when the New York
Mirror went out of business in October 1963, a victim of
labor strife. Winchell's column moved to the other
Hearst outlet, the *Journal-American,* but Winchell no
longer commanded the audience, and the prestige, he
once enjoyed with the *Mirror.* His columns were reduced
in content and frequency and he took a pay cut–to
$57,000 a year, a handsome fee for many, but far below
Winchell's standards. His syndication customers now
totalled 125, a respectable number for almost anyone,
but far below Winchell's once-lofty 1,000 subscribers.

    The slide continued when more labor strife forced

Hearst to merge the *Journal-American* with the New York *Herald Tribune,* and the *World-Telegram* and *Sun* to form a newspaper called the *World Journal Tribune.* Bad as it was, the hybrid newspaper had no place for Winchell and Hearst canceled Winchell's contract in May 1967, a humiliating rebuff.

Winchell, denied a New York outlet, obtained a column in *Variety* and *Film Daily,* and even in an obscure racing sheet. Winchell finished his autobiography in 1967, but was unable to find a publisher. With its posthumous publication in 1975, critics dismissed Winchell's interpretation of events as self-serving and cynical. A 1970 effort to revive Winchell's column in a proposed New York newspaper to be called the *Mirror* failed and Winchell's "retirement from retirement" never materialized. Winchell died February 20, 1972. Winchell, the individual, undoubtedly had a number of faults, professional and personal, and may have been unlikable. The mid-1950s motion picture "Sweet Smell of Success," portrayed a powerful and malevolent national Broadway columnist, generally interpreted as a thinly-veiled portrait of Winchell–an interpretation that Winchell himself accepted. "Success" was a devastating portrait of the power of a gossip columnist.

The growth and power of gossip in journalism is Winchell's legacy; he introduced that now-dominant element into newspapers and later, radio and television. Clearly, his was the vehicle. His column, when it began in the *Graphic,* was little more than a pallid imitation of FPA's popular "Conning Tower," complete with witticisms, mentions, and even a diary. Winchell gradually introduced gossip, and when circulation soared, the *Graphic* gave him space to include personal tidbits once deemed unsuitable in American journalism.

In the mid-1920s Winchell fostered a form of journalism that came to dominate news–print and electronic–for the remainder of the century. Gossip, bred by Winchell, influenced the attitudes of journalists in every medium. The goals and responsibility of journalism was altered for better or worse by Winchell. The ideal that journalism should strive to elevate the public's taste and intelligence, not pander to the lowest common denominator, has disappeared and might strike readers today as quaint and old-fashioned. Journalistic standards altered and its role became entertainment, primarily. Whether or not that notion is accepted, Walter Winchell unquestionably helped to define journalism's role in contemporary American culture.

SOURCES:

Neal Gabler, *Winchell: Gossip, Power and the Culture of Celebrity* (New York: Vintage, 1994).

Herman Klurfied, *Winchell: His Life and Times* (New York: Praeger, 1976).

St. Clair McKelway, *Gossip: The Life and Times of Walter Winchell* (New York: Viking Press, 1940).

John Mosedale, *The Men Who Made Broadway: Damon Runyon, Walter Winchell and Their World* (New York: Marek, 1981).

Bob Thomas, *Winchell* (New York: Doubleday & Co., 1971).

BY WINCHELL:

Winchell Exclusive: "Things that Happened to Me–And Me to Them" (Englewood Cliffs: Prentice-Hall, 1975).

17

Robert Benchley

Press Criticism with Humor

Press criticism has not been the same since "The Wayward Press" disappeared from the *New Yorker*. Most people associate A. J. Liebling with that work, remembered through several books–*The Wayward Press* (1947) and *The Press* (1975). But the excellent press criticism of Robert Benchley, dating several decades earlier, is little known. Benchley, preceded Liebling's work by twenty years and originated "The Wayward Press" in 1927 and continued for more than a dozen years. Academic critics dismiss this work as "light, chatty and superficial." Benchley's writing was graceful and light, but neither frivolous nor superficial–humorous, surely. He christened the department with its whimsical title. Benchley is remembered primarily as a major American humorist of the 1920s and 1930s and his accomplishments as a humor writer, drama-critic, radio commentator and motion picture actor overshadow his solid credentials as a critic: he was a newspaperman and sometime public relations practitioner and advertising writer in his early years.

Robert Benchley: Chronology

1889   born, September 15, Worcester, Mass.

1904   attends local public schools, high school drama

1907   attends Phillip Execeter Academy

1908   enters Harvard College, contributes to *Lampoon*

1910   elected to Board of Editors of *Lampoon*

1912   employment with Boston Museum of Fine Arts; then
         Curtis Publishing Co.

1913   graduates from Harvard, edits Curtis *Obiter Dicta*

1914   fired by Curtis; hired by Russel & Bros., a paper
         manufacturer, as "welfare secretary"

1916   hired by New York *Tribune,* later with *Tribune Magazine*

1917   theatrical press agent for William A. Brady

1918   censor for Aircraft Board, Washington, D.C.; joins the
         Tribune Graphic; works for Liberty Loan

1920   *Vanity Fair* managing editor; begins column, "Books and
         Other Things," New York *World;* writes column for *Life*

1921   *Of All Things!*; syndicated column for David Lawrence

1922   *Love Conquers All*

1923   appears in Irving Berlin's "Music Box Review" with
         sketch "Treasurer's Report"

Sixteen books of Benchley's have been published; none include his "Wayward Press" pieces. Benchley wrote the series under a pseudonym, Guy Fawkes. Undoubtedly, his puckish sense of humor prompted the name selection. But one motivation was the need to conceal his identity. He had contractual commitments elsewhere. Harold Ross, editor of the *New Yorker,* commanded a small army of anonymous contributors.

Benchley was a writer with extensive experience: a broad background with institutional public relations; work as a publicity man, advertising writer, and former newspaperman acquainted him with an intimate knowledge of the press. In that pre-television era, with only the early beginnings of radio and a still-young motion picture industry, newspapers dominated.

Robert C. Benchley (1889-1945), even before he left Harvard in 1912 (lacking a degree), demonstrated promising talent as a humorist and writer. The legend persists that he passed an International Law exam dealing with the Newfoundland fisheries dispute with an essay on the issue from the point of view of the fish. He wrote from that view, but failed the exam and had to return to Harvard to pick up his degree a year behind his class. His reputation as a humorist was secure. In college, he served as president (editor) of the *Lampoon* and his comic skits generated wide attention.

His first job was brief service with the Boston Museum of Fine Art (he declined an offer from the Boston *Journal* as a humor columnist) and then became an advertising-publicity man for the Curtis Publishing Company, where he produced a monthly magazine and wrote trade advertisements. Fired from this job, partly because his boss did not enjoy Benchley's parody issues of the magazine and impromptu comedic sales presentations, he moved to Russell & Brothers, a Boston paper manufacturer, to edit the house newspaper and perform

1925   *Pluck and Luck*

1926   writes subtitles for Paramount Studios

1927   *The Early Worm;* first "Wayward Press" for the
       New Yorker

1928   *20,000 Leagues Under the Sea, or David Copperfield;*
       appears in first of forty-nine movie short subjects

1929   leaves *Life,* joins *New Yorker* as drama critic

1932   *No Poems;* first feature film

1933   begins column for King Features Syndicate

1935   receives Academy Award for best short subject

1936   *My Ten Years in a Quandry;* ends King Features affiliation

1938   *After 1903–What?;* first radio program

1939   ends "Wayward Press" for *New Yorker*

1940   ends drama column for *New Yorker*

1942   *Inside Benchley*

1943   *Benchley Beside Himself*

1945   last film short; dies in New York City, November 21

1947   *Benchley–or Else!*

1949   *Chips Off the Old Benchley*

1954   *The Benchley Roundup*

company social-welfare work. The job allowed him time to pursue free-lance writing that came to the attention of Franklin P. Adams–F.P.A., writer of "The Conning Tower" in the New York *Tribune,* at that time one of the most-influential newspaper columnists in America.

Adams rescued him with an offer of a newspaper job in 1916. Later, Benchley admitted that he was "the worst reporter, even for his age, in New York City." Less than three months later, Adams helped him move to the *Tribune Magazine* with Sunday feature work where writing opportunities were more amenable to his style and temperament. Meanwhile, Benchley penetrated the free-lance markets with *Vanity Fair,* the *Saturday Evening Post* and other magazines.

Again fired after a brief time, Benchley spent the next three months as a public relations-publicity man for a theatrical producer. Benchley cared neither for the job nor his client, William A. Brady. Nevertheless, Benchley learned a great deal about the theatrical world and the efforts required to get a client talked about in the newspapers and, conversely the means to stop uncomplimentary items from appearing. He next spent a short, unhappy time writing advertising copy (for Dr. Lyon's Tooth Powder) for the Andruss Peterson agency.

Benchley drifted into public relations work through assistance from a Harvard classmate in wartime Washington as chief of publicity for the Aircraft Board. His duties were more of a censor than information vendor and he churned out the necessary press work until he left quietly after a few months. With a connection made in Washington by former Harvard classmate Ernest Gruening, who became managing editor of the New York *Tribune* (later Governor and U. S. Senator from Alaska), Benchley joined the *Tribune* as editor in May. By July, he and Gruening were both out after a dispute with publisher Ogden Reid and the Justice

Department over a story and photographs deemed pro-German (and pro-black as well).

Benchley returned to public relations work for the Liberty Loan. With the war's end, that work came to a close. Benchley then landed a job as managing editor of *Vanity Fair,* under Frank Crowninshield. His work companions were Dorothy Parker and Robert E. Sherwood. Benchley wrote the light and humorous material for which he discovered a liking, and produced free-lance articles for a number of magazines.

In January 1920, he and Sherwood resigned in protest when Parker was fired for a critical review of actress Billie Burke, when Burke's husband, Florenz Ziegfeld, complained to management. Benchley again retreated to writing advertising copy, this time for the Logan agency's aniline dye account, and free-lance book reviews for the New York *World.* By spring, however, Benchley was hired by Charles Dana Gibson as drama critic for *Life,* in those years a leading humor magazine (later purchased by Henry Luce for its title alone). He spent nine happy years in a job he had sought since the dreary days at Curtis. It was the era of the Round Table at the Algonquin. Benchley was inspired to perform his classic "Treasurer's Report" for a Round Table production and then invited to appear in Irving Berlin's "Music Box Review;" he became a celebrity. By 1926 he was in Hollywood writing dialogue and subtitles for Jesse Lasky. Two years later Benchley appeared in the first of a series of movie shorts that continued until 1945. (He won an Academy Award in 1935.) Benchley continued to submit free-lance work to a number of popular magazines. Increasingly, in the late 1920s, more of his articles, signed and unsigned, began to appear in Harold Ross's new magazine.

The *New Yorker* had published a number of press criticisms under various titles, beginning as early as its second issue: "Behind the News," "The Current Press," "In the Press," "Reviewing the News," and "The Press in Review," written by a number of people including Benchley. He eventually came up with the title that became a permanent department, "The Wayward Press," written as Guy Fawkes. Legally, Benchley could not write for other magazines and continue as drama critic for *Life*. Nonetheless, he contributed his "Wayward Press" reviews on a free-lance basis.

Two years later he assumed the drama post at the *New Yorker* and wrote the "Theatre" department until 1940, frequently appearing in both capacities in the weekly magazine. These combined efforts produced hundreds of columns over the years and his theater reviews are classics. But his wry assessments of news coverage brought a particular point of view to press criticism: engaging and perceptive observations humorously couched to cushion the barbed comment.

Liebling later dismissed Benchley's work, observing that it was done "in the same spirit as he would have reviewed the vaudeville shows we then still had." Liebling lacked Benchley's humor and sense of the absurd. Benchley's satire was tempered with gentle wit. Unlike H.L. Mencken's scalding attacks (a contemporary whose comments Benchley read with approval), Benchley avoided partisan politics and personal attacks; he directed his attention to how the New York City press dealt with news. He focused his enquiry into what defined news; he examined the appearance of newspapers and editorial content; he looked at advertisements, the placement of ads. He was a gadfly, amiable but thorough. Benchley directed his comments to the average reader. The focus of attention was the press in New York City, which at that time had a dozen or so daily newspapers. Benchley read them all.

Press criticism was in that era a random and sometime thing. From time to time Walter Lippmann or H. L. Mencken, for example, would impart a critical comment on press behavior. But until Benchley undertook a periodic examination no one appraised newspaper performance on a sustained and methodical basis.

He began with a chiding of the New York press coverage of Commander Richard E. Byrd's explorations of the North Pole, and the fusillade of stories based on little more than speculation: "Might it not be well if the correspondents refrained from sending anything until they were sure of it, even at the cost of being suspected by the New York office of sleeping on the job?" Similarly, his piece on President Calvin Coolidge's "I do not choose to run" statement again took the press to task for coverage "rivalling the signing of the Emancipation Proclamation by Abraham Lincoln" and "glutting the market" with overblown stories.

Benchley's public comment on the Sacco-Vanzetti execution expressed his contempt for the New York *World's* position: "...after leading the field in the fight for the two men, it suddenly prostrated itself... and developed a serious streak of yellow...[and] lost the services of Heywood Broun." Benchley marched in the protest staged over the trial. His criticism flayed the craven position of the traditionally-liberal *World.* Benchley's contempt was clear.

His columns maintained a watchdog role on sloppy and sentimental stories, and the fawning of the press over empty items–John D. Rockefeller greeting the first cool days of autumn golfing. Similarly, he noted blatant advertising plugs on the news pages when respected newspapers paid editorial homage to Ford and General Motors: "to give the greatest possible value in their respective classes." Free advertising, of course, lurks on modern news pages; examine the typical contemporary travel or real-estate section. Benchley watched carefully the advertising-news content ratio. He commented acidly: "*The Sun* has finally capitulated and given in completely to the department stores" when an entire insert was placed into "what was left of the *Sun*...next we may look for a four-page insert...in which there may be nothing but news." Genuine news was hard to come by and Benchley resented anything less. The shameless mixture of advertising ballyhoo for local auto shows and boat shows into the news pages prompted criticism–a questionable practice continued on modern newspapers.

Poor writing aroused his ire. No idols were sacrosanct. One searching examination of the purple language of football reporting indicted Grantland Rice, the dean of America's sportswriters, for colorful excess: "an autumn sky heavily tinted with flames and flashes of orange and black [Princeton's colors] turned suddenly into the shining glow of Yale's triumphant blue." For that matter, Benchley did not hesitate to take the entire New York City press corps to task. He disparaged its effusive excess of trivia devoted to the "second coming of Lindbergh." This was a whimsical way to point out that the excessive outpouring was characteristic of the press at its carnival worst. Like the target of many of Benchley's scoldings, it is a practice indulged in to this day by even the better newspapers for topics of far less importance or consequence.

Benchley took aim at the public relations practice of generating "insipid" puffery for presidential candidates Alfred E. Smith and Herbert Hoover. Today, of course, better-trained professionals in well-paid posts do precisely the same thing, and similarly insipid stories emanate from the White House dealing with dogs or other pets. The formula still works.

Similarly, he consistently harpooned the public relations-inspired antics of theater figures followed by the press–David Belasco, Florenz Ziegfeld, and others–and concluded: "we thought there was a law against this sort of thing." He continued to chide the "better" newspapers for "mangled prose" and falling for other public relations-inspired "sucker stories." As a one-time newsman and a former press agent, Benchley knew all the tricks of both trades. Today, of course, modern readers are constantly kept apprised of the doings of people like Madonna and O.J.; the "sucker" stories persist.

Benchley tried to be helpful; coverage of the World Series "seemed readable" but he noted that the "literary flavor" in baseball reporting had "started a movement which has now assumed proportions of a menace." Today's readers detecting a sportswriter's stream-of-consciousness might recall Benchley's warning.

Benchley, as press watch-dog, got his point across when it came to questionable journalistic practices. He warned readers that the New York *Graphic* followed a practice to "never use a real photo if you can fake one" and that its self-described "composograph" (a doctored photograph) of a shipwreck was "as bad a piece of journalism as a metropolitan newspaper has ever pulled." Photographic fakery continues to be practiced to this day. Computers have replaced the air-brush, but readers still wonder if what they see is genuine.

Poor editing distressed Benchley. How news was written and the form in which it was presented were matters of importance. He examined the graphic aspects of newspapers: layout, good and bad; inept typesetting; and poor placement of advertisements that disfigured page makeup. The appearance of a newspaper's masthead was cause for comment. Editorial content received Benchley's diligent attention; he was a stickler for accurate reporting. From time to time he would run samplings of quotes "that we think...do not ring true...and we do not believe them to be accurate quotations." He went on to observe that "they have no particular importance" except to demonstrate that "reporters and rewrite men put words into the mouths of their characters which no one could ever say." The practice continues.

What constitutes news and how it should be played was a constant Benchley theme. The elaborate and excessive coverage of the death of Tex Rickard in 1929 (the one-time-famous fight promoter), offended his sense of balance and rightness. The story really belonged in the sports section (where too much was made of the event as well, in Benchley's opinion) and Rickard's death was discussed for days. Benchley had similar reservations when newspapers devoted excessive attention to the death of politicians, gangsters and bootleggers ("gurry" was one of his terms for this news). He lamented the fact that genuine news was often overshadowed by "genial junk," supplied for the most part by public relations people who found ready accomplices for their efforts in accommodating newsrooms.

Benchley disclosed that reports of foreign events were "doctored and censored" by the New York press, and that the pundits altered their views after events. Benchley singled out Lippmann, but made the point in a brief paragraph to remind prognosticators that "predictions are going to be read...after the event has taken place." Benchley examined the foreign press, compared to the New York product. During a trip to Europe, he was not impressed: "News is the last thing a French editor worries about, for crime dominates."

After his look-round at the French, German and English newspapers, Benchley took the American press to task for the vast amounts of public relations fillers masquerading as news. He singled out the aviation industry, the trans-Atlantic liner companies and theatrical producers—all areas of public relations activity that irritated him, especially when editors used these items as legitimate news.

Benchley's primary focus was how the press handled news. At times his sense of propriety was outraged. He took the press to task for its handling of the Lindbergh kidnapping. In a searing indictment: "Not only did they make up news, but they made up disgusting news, news which, even had it been true, was the sort of thing that no self-respecting paper in its right mind would have printed...we cannot even read them without nausea."

A recurring Benchley theme concerned news manipulation by the Federal government. His charges were direct and specific. He fingered the Treasury Department "as a pretty obvious propagandist" by timing its "inspired" stories dealing with the dire federal deficit to coincide with the congressional hearings on the World War Veterans Compensation bill. He pointed out that the Administration did not want the measure passed. Accordingly, it sent out press releases headed "Shadow of Deficit Concerns Treasury; Any Extra Outlay A Peril," which the *Times* blazoned on the front page. Benchley labeled the story for what it was and inquired: "Why not, when stories as palpably inspired as the Surplus Deficit-Surplus rotation are printed, run a little credit-line above them reading 'Treasury Department, Adv.'?"

Benchley's work for the *New Yorker* as press critic ended in 1939; his days as a press gadfly were over. For more than a decade Benchley presented a view of press criticism in self-deprecating prose, unerringly aimed at specific failings of the daily press. His style was light, lucid, and personal. He was a humorist and never forgot it. But, like Mark Twain, Benchley's humor held a bite often overlooked. Clearly, his judgmental outlook is evident in every piece he wrote. Benchley was not unkind, but his disapproval was evident. In many respects his rectitude displays a shade of puritanism.

Robert Benchley compiled an indictment of misdeeds committed by the press. He consistently deplored careless writing that compromised news content; repeatedly exposed flimsy stories devoid of substance and drew attention to questionable personality puff-pieces that trivialized news; criticized public relations features that eroded the integrity of genuine news; documented the growing influence of advertising on the content and presentation of news; exposed conflict-of-interest issues, manufactured quotes, questionable news sources, unethical conduct; and alerted readers to government propaganda and its attempts at news manipulation.

Benchley's legacy of criticism of the daily press, itself written on deadline, provides a useful and formidable agenda to assess the quality of modern media. The measures by which he assessed the press remain valid.

Hollywood's abundant money provided Benchley an escape from "real work." He made forty-nine shorts for Fox, M-G-M, Universal, and Paramount (his first feature was "China Seas;" in 1939 he was in Alfred Hitchcock's "Foreign Correspondent." Acting lured Benchley from further literary output, a serious loss for writing in America. He officially ended his writing career in 1943: "I've run out of ideas." Benchley was a humorist without parallel. His press criticism remains a singular contribution to journalism.

SOURCES:

Altman, Billy *Laughter's Gentle Soul: The Life of Robert Benchley* (New York: W. W. Norton, 1997).

Benchley, Nathaniel *Robert Benchley: A Biography* (New York: McGraw-Hill, 1955).

Yates, Norris W. *Robert Benchley* (New York: Twayne, 1968).

SELECTED BOOKS BY BENCHLEY:

After 1903-What? (New York: Harper & Bros., 1938).

Benchley at the Theatre: Drama Criticism: 1920-1940 Charles Getchell, ed. (Ipswich: Ipswich Press, 1988).

Benchley Beside Himself (New York: Harper & Bros., 1943).

Benchley–Or Else! (New York; Harper & Bros., 1947).

The Benchley Roundup, Compiled by Nathaniel Benchley (New York: Harper & Bros., 1954).

Chips Off the Old Benchley (New York: Harper & Bros., 1949).

Inside Benchley (New York: Harper & Bros., 1942).

Love Conquers All (Pleasantville: Akadine Press, 1999).

Of All Things! (Pleasantville: Akadine Press, 1999).

The Treasurer's Report and Other Aspects of Community Singing (New York: Harper & Bros., 1930).

18

John Gunther

Journalism Becomes History

In his time John Gunther was one of America's most widely-read and popular journalists. He was the inventer, said Eric Sevareid, of "book-length reporting." Gunther was a reporter who could write and make sense of complex and distant events for Americans when the world was changing from the dreary days of isolationism and Depression into a confused chaos of upheaval and conflict abroad. The 1930s are so remote that few people today appreciate the hungry desire for news describing war-threatened Europe and the even-more arcane regions of the Far East. After writing several autobiographical novels, Gunther's first great literary success came with *Inside Europe,* a chatty, insightful look at the various capitals with informed detail, pertinent quotes and cogent summaries. The book sold well, went into six editions, and was translated into seventeen languages. Before people were saturated with daily news-pictures from television, Gunther made a superb contribution to journalism. His book enabled Gunther to quit full-time newspaper employment and

John Gunther: Chronology

1901   born, August 30, Chicago

1918   University of Chicago, staff of the *Daily Marion*

1922   reporter, Chicago *Daily News*

1924   to Europe for the United Press; appointed assistant to
        Daily News London bureau chief

1926   *Red Pavilon* (novel)

1927   *Eden for One* (novel)

1929   *The Golden Fleece* (novel)

1931   Vienna bureau chief, Chicago *Daily News*

1932   *Bright Nemesis* (novel)

1935   London bureau chief, Chicago *Daily News*

1936   *Inside Europe* (six editions over next four years);
        resigned from Chicago *Daily News*, August 1

1937   signed with NANA (North American Newspaper Alliance)

1938   began series of articles for *Reader's Digest*

1939   *Inside Asia; High Cost of Hitler*

1941   *Inside Latin America*

1942   Office of War Information (OWI), screenwriting

1943   war correspondent, NANA and NBC Blue Network, Sicily

1944   *D-Day; The Troubled Midnight* (novel)

write at his own pace for syndication and magazines for a great deal of money. Magazine articles in the mass circulation markets and several radio appearances brought more fame.

Beyond financial success, his work was unique. Gunther's several *Inside* books were products of their times, and–like journalism itself–the first draft of history. Few of Gunther's works have endured, consequently, Gunther and his books are largely forgotten and often as dated as yesterday's newspapers. None of his novels have survived as notable literature; his biographies of world leaders, balanced and useful, in their time, have been largely superseded. Perhaps his only enduring work is *Death Be Not Proud,* a moving elegy for his son, John, who died a tragically early death. As a reporter, however, Gunther was one of the best. For the historian, investigation reveals that much of what he reported is valid still. Few books on Africa, for example, are better, even today.

John Gunther (1901-1970) began his journalistic career by contributing work to the University of Chicago college newspaper and wrote a column, "Literary Leaders," dealing with books and authors. As a college student, Gunther dismissed Ben Hecht's *Eric Dorn* as lacking "solidity." His column was a popular feature and Gunther sold two articles to H.L. Mencken's magazine, the *Smart Set.* Mencken was the leading critic at the time; the two were never close, but continued correspondence for a number of years. Gunther's *Smart Set* work earned modest fees, but appearance in the *Smart Set* was an accomplishment that helped make him known locally and in New York.

Gunther joined the Chicago *Daily News*–the city's largest-circulation newspaper–in 1922, on the basis of his college writing, after a summer vacation exploring in Europe. His salary was fifteen dollars weekly. The news-

1947 *Inside U.S.A.*

1948 *Death Be Not Proud;* contributor to *Look,* New York
      Herald Tribune

1949 *Behind the Curtain*

1950 *Roosevelt in Retrospect: A Profile in History; The Riddle
      of MacArthur*

1952 *Eisenhower: The Man and the Symbol*

1955 *Inside Africa*

1956 *Days to Remember: America 1945-1955;* articles
      for *Collier's* dealing with USSR

1958 *Inside Russia Today*

1959 ABC weekly television program

1960 *Taken at the Flood: The Story of Albert D. Lasker*

1961 *Inside Europe Today*

1962 *A Fragment of an Autobiography*

1964 *The Lost City*

1965 *Chicago Revisted; Procession*

1967 *Inside South America*

1969 *Twelve Cities*

1970 *The Indian Sign;* dies May 29, New York City

room of the *Daily News*–earlier the home of Carl
Sandburg and Ben Hecht–proved to be a useful step
toward Gunther's goal of becoming a writer.

He demonstrated uncommonly good qualities as a
reporter. During the Tea Pot Dome scandals in 1924 during the Harding Administration, Gunther suggested a
story on the geographic area itself, while the rest of the
nation was being told about the political shenanigans of
oil-land leases. It proved to be one of the best feature stories of the year, the second time that one of Gunther's
stories had been selected.

In late 1924 Gunther decided he wanted to cover
events abroad and went off to Europe–with no job. He
sailed First-class; Gunther always preferred the best.
On board, Gunther managed an interview with the
Prince of Wales. United Press and the London bureau of
the *Daily News* were interested in his story. This led to
a post with the *Daily News'* London bureau.

Gunther met and interviewed interesting people, literary and journalistic–Arthur Conan Doyle, Rebecca
West, Raymond Gram Swing, Dorothy Thompson, and
Cass Canfield, representative for Harper's publishers.
Gunther became the "swingman," alternating among the
various European bureaus of the *Daily News*. Between
times Gunther was working on novels.

His first novel, a thinly-veiled autobiography, *Red
Pavilion,* was published in 1926. The book drew mixed
reviews, but received some notoriety when it was
banned in Boston. The next year Gunther's second novel
appeared, *Eden for One* (published in London as *Peter
Lancelot*). In 1929 Gunther's third novel in as many
years appeared, *The Golden Fleece*. The recognition, and
acclaim, that he sought as a novelist eluded him, however. Gunther, meanwhile, was sending dispatches from
abroad, covering the French-Arab conflicts in North
Africa and events in Greece and Albania. His travels

included Russia and the Balkans. His wide coverage was being used by other newspapers and increasingly Gunther's stories earned him fame. Gunther flirted briefly with a career in Hollywood, prompted by his modest success with his novels. The abundant, and easy, money held little attraction, however. Writers risked a short life in Hollywood, despite the high salary. Journalism remained Gunther's major goal. He returned to Europe after the *Daily News* offered him the post of bureau chief in Vienna in 1930.

On the scene, Gunther was witnessing the rise of Nazism and published a series of articles for *Harper's* and the *Nation* that described the unrest in Europe. Cass Canfield, president of Harper & Brothers publishers conceived the idea of a book describing the increasing turmoil in Europe. He finally convinced Gunther to undertake the project with a tempting $5,000 advance, a handsome sum for that time. Beginning in 1932, Gunther worked on the project, an immense undertaking that encompassed all the countries, capitals and notable personalities of Europe. Then in 1935 Gunther was promoted to bureau chief of the *Daily News* in its London office.

Gunther used his contacts with journalistic colleagues in Europe to acquire information and he proved most apt–some of whom later complained that he "picked their brains." He did, but he knew how to use every scrap of information and had the initiative to exploit it. He finished the 190,000 word manuscript and came up with the title, *Inside Europe.* Early portions of the book were published in *Harper's,* the *Reader's Digest,* and *Cosmopolitan;* Gunther's diary appeared in a two-part installment in the *Atlantic.* Gunther, more properly his agents, had the ability to publicize his work, but the work was timely, informative and satisfied a public desire for news about a confusing situation. *Inside*

Europe was an instant success, leading to Harper's request for an updated edition and an offer of a lucrative lecture tour at $500-per appearance. Subsequently, Gunther resigned from the Chicago *Daily News,* not without some feeling in Chicago that he had let the newspaper down.

Inside Europe was a Book-of-the Month-Club (BOMC) selection. Beyond that, sales topped 500,000, the book was translated into seventeen languages. Canfield wanted another book, this time dealing with Asia. Gunther started on a fact-finding journey and signed with NANA (North American Newspaper Alliance) and the *Saturday Evening Post* to print his dispatches from the mid-East and India along the way. Gunther found himself a celebrity being interviewed by local press people as his book was selling in the United States at a rate of 1,000 copies a month. The chatty, informative book of current events was itself outdated in chaotic Asia within the same period of time.

His fame from the *Inside Europe* book plus magazine articles to a mass audience enabled Gunther to have access to leaders in India, the Philippines, China, and Japan. Back in the United States, Gunther was booked for another cross-country lecture tour and this time his fee was $750 for each of the seventeen appearances. Excerpts of the new book appeared in a number of publications; the *Reader's Digest* paid $1,500 for several selections and was the beginning of a long association with Gunther. Other excerpts appeared in the *Atlantic,* the *Nation, Harper's* and *Current History.* When *Inside Asia* appeared in April 1939, it was met with enthusiastic reception; a lively, gossipy book, and not too profound. Gunther concluded that America was unlikely to avoid further trouble in Asia.

With a contract from NANA, the *Reader's Digest,* and the NBC Red Network, Gunther sailed for Europe and broadcast his comments from Geneva, Moscow and, on the day war broke out, London. He produced a quicky book, *The High Cost of Hitler,* based on his radio broadcasts. This book was rejected by Harper's, but published by Hamish Hamilton in Britain; expectedly, the book sold poorly and did little to contribute to Gunther's literary or journalistic reputation.

With war raging in Europe and Japanese aggression in the Far East, Gunther returned home to begin his next formula book dealing with Latin America. Starting in October 1940, Gunther embarked on a five-month fact-finding tour, beginning in Mexico to Central and South America. He visited all twenty nations with contracts from the *Reader's Digest* and the NBC Blue Network to help pay expenses and armed with letters of introduction from high-level U.S. officials. *Inside Latin America* was published in October 1941 and Gunther's findings exposed the heavy political influence of the Roman Catholic church, the Nazi espionage rings that were operating, and the corruption and instability in the region. This brought attacks from church leaders and the German government. The book earned Gunther a personal interview with President Franklin Roosevelt, who was greatly interested.

His overview of Latin America, despite being written under deadline, presented a comprehensive picture of that continent, but was attacked as "superficial." Later in October, Gunther flew to London to begin coverage of the war in Europe with a series of broadcasts. He spent the next two months as a correspondent, broadcasting on-the-scene reports for NBC.

Gunther's income was approximately $65,000 annually and he was a regular in New York cafe society; he was a celebrated author with a number of popular books to his credit. In the early days of the war after Pearl Harbor was attacked, Gunther went to Hollywood and

Twentieth Century-Fox studios to work on war documentaries for the Office of War Information. He contributed narrative texts for an Air Force film "Thunder Birds" and "The Battle of China." He was also a popular figure in Hollywood social life, but found time for a weekly radio broadcast for NBC in 1943. Early that year, with a contract from NBC and NANA, Gunther left for England to again take up work as an on-the-scene correspondent based in Malta.

Gunther covered Operation Husky, General Dwight D. Eisenhower's invasion of Sicily in July 1943. Gunther interviewed Eisenhower and the two got on well. Gunther covered the invasion, led by General George Patton and Field Marshall Bernard Montgomery, and came under fire. He filed more than fifty dispatches and made more than a dozen broadcasts. Back home, Gunther again tried his hand at another novel–*The Troubled Midnight,* a tale of Viennese intrigue–that met with only moderate success. His wartime book *D-Day,* recounting his Sicilian experiences, drawn from his dispatches and radio broadcasts, met better success. Wartime journalism ended for Gunther; by mid-1944 he was at work researching material for his next *Inside* book to be focused on the United States.

With a healthy $25,000 advance, Gunther began his book that examined all forty-eight states, a portrait of the United States. A thirteen month tour took him to every state where he met with officials–local and in Washington–the result was *Inside U.S.A.,* published in 1947, to great acclaim and rewarding sales; the book was an instant best-seller.

News that his son John, a pupil attending Deerfield Academy, had a brain tumor was devastating. From this tragedy emerged Gunther's one enduring work, *Death Be Not Proud* (1948), his only book that remains in print.

A trip to Eastern Europe resulted in another timely

book, *Behind the Curtain* (1949)–the title from Winston Churchill's "Iron Curtain" speech in Fulton, Missouri –that established the idea of the post-war threat of Stalinism and the Communist menace. Public opinion was mobilized with excerpts in the *Reader's Digest* and the book's selection as a BOMC choice guaranteed high sales. It helped identify the Cold War as a concept, but with an even-handed approach to its solution.

In a change of pace, Gunther expanded an earlier article into a full-length biography in 1950, *Roosevelt in Retrospect: A Profile in History,* a laudatory account that has subsequently suffered when more recent elements of FDR's life became known. Later in the same year, he published *The Riddle of MacArthur,* initially prompted by MacArthur's rule in post-war Japan, but hastened by the conflict in Korea. Richard Rovere's profile of Gunther written for the *New Yorker*, published some years earlier, resurfaced in the critical reviews that charged Gunther with being a "superficial" writer. But no one could gainsay that Gunther was a writer of world-wide fame with an uncommon grasp of international events and access to influential leaders.

Based on two lengthy articles for *Look* magazine– already touting the former Supreme Commander as a possible presidential candidate–Gunther expanded his research and drew on his brief wartime acquaintance to explore Ike's personal side. *Eisenhower: The Man and the Symbol* was published in 1952.

Gunther returned to his winning formula, beginning work on an investigation of Africa. Again financed by articles in the *Reader's Digest,* Gunther examined the disintegrating colonies and the rise of African nationalism. *Inside Africa* was published in 1955, and once again a book of Gunther's was guaranteed heavy sales and exposure when the BOMC named it as a feature selection; the book was a sensational best-seller and it shed light on the political and economic upheavals of an entire continent that had been neglected for many years.

In 1956, in collaboration with Bernard Quint, *Life* magazine art director, Gunther wrote the text for a picture book, *Days to Remember: America 1945-1955.* It sold well, but was dismissed as a "picture book." His next important project was a book dealing with the Soviet Union. *Collier's* magazine contracted to publish the early chapters, but the magazine folded in October. Television was becoming the nation's major media source; book sales were slumping. Nevertheless, *Look* published the reports. Gunther undertook a free-lance assignment to raise money–the annual report for a pharmaceutical company. *Inside Pfizer* did not add to his reputation.

Inside Russia Today (1958) was another Book-of-the-Month-Club selection and attained best-seller status. Gunther presented a balanced account of the Soviet Union and avoided the hysteria of the Cold War mentality that colored most topics Russian in that era. Gunther's fame earned him a *Time* magazine cover story in April 1958 that reported no other newsman had made more money (an estimated million dollars annually) or had written more successful books. Sales of Gunther's books exceeded four million copies.

In a change of pace, Gunther wrote a biography of pioneer advertising man Alfred Lasker. *Taken at the Flood: The Story of Alfred D. Lasker* (1960) sold moderately well. Gunther had moved into television with a weekly show, "High Road to Adventure" for ABC in September 1959, that disappeared after a year. A series of articles for the *Reader's Digest* became the basis for another book, *Inside Europe Today* (1961), an entirely new book–not merely a revision of the earlier look at Europe. The book was another best-seller.

Gunther had begun to donate his notes and correspondence to the University of Chicago and based on this material with two articles for *Harper's,* he produced a modest 116-page *A Fragment of an Autobiography: The Fun of Writing the Inside Books* (1962).

He contemplated an autobiography, that was never finished. An autobiographical novel, *The Lost City* (1964), dealt with his years in pre-war Vienna. Sales were slight and BOMC passed; it was a Literary Guild selection, not bad for others, but a step down for Gunther. Gunther turned to articles for *Esquire* and *Playboy* and a brief tribute to the University of Chicago in *Chicago Revisited* (1965). The same year *Harper's* published *Procession,* material culled from his earlier books dealing with world leaders.

His next *Inside* book, planned to focus on Australia, was shelved when the *Reader's Digest* asked for an update on Latin America. The result in 1967 was *Inside South America.* Again the formula worked and with the BOMC's selection, the book became another Gunther best-seller. Again spurred by a series of articles in the *Reader's Digest,* Gunther compiled a collection of world city profiles; *Twelve Cities* (1969) also reached the best-seller list. That success spurred Gunther to undertake the extensive research to conquer the last unexplored literary frontier, Australia. When he returned from Australia in 1970, an exhausted Gunther entered a New York hospital. The diagnosis was incurable cancer. Gunther died May 29, 1970.

His posthumous novel, *The Indian Sign* (1970), another thinly veiled autobiographical examination, was poorly received. John Gunther's *Inside Australia,* with the authors listed as Gunther and William Forbis (who completed the last portion), was, expectedly, the least-successful of the *Inside* books.

John Gunther unquestionably contributed significantly to American thought through his journalism in the twentieth century. His journalism was lively, informative, and timely. Like most journalism, however, it was ephemeral. In its time, Gunther's work was recognized as unique. His commentary has not endured, however, and is largely neglected today, even as historic artifact. Despite his driving ambition to become a recognized novelist, Gunther was unsuccessful and his efforts at fiction are also largely forgotten.

His one-time mentor, H.L. Mencken, assessed him as a "third-rater" and thought only *Inside Asia* really worthwhile. Gunther made much money and lived well; he liked the good life and café society. Despite the fact that he spent a good deal of time living the good life, Gunther worked hard and produced a prodigious amount of copy for mass-market consumption that paid well. This work, produced on deadline, was often superficial lacking depth and penetrating insight, but with an excellent news sense. At bottom, Gunther was a superlative newspaperman.

As a reporter, Gunther was an excellent example of a newspaper legman who had the knack of getting facts and raw information into a compelling narrative to explain complex issues. He benefitted from a publisher who knew how to market books and authors and obtain exposure. Millions of American readers benefited from news and information that John Gunther provided. Gunther was a product of his time, and his books exemplify those times. That era was disappearing, even during Gunther's lifetime. Television emerged–book and magazine sales waned, Gunther's metier. His only lasting literary legacy, *Death Be Not Proud,* remains one of the finest tributes to human courage and is likely to endure. Gunther himsel, ever the newsman, demonstrated a passion for factual accuracy and an enthusiasm for information unmatched by few other journalists in his time or our own.

SOURCES:

Ken Cuthbertson, *Inside: The Biography of John Gunther* (Chicago: Bonus Books, 1992).

John Gunther, *A Fragment of Autobiography* (New York: Harper & Row, 1964).

Jay Pridemore, *John Gunther: Inside Journalism* (Chicago: University of Chicago Press, 1990).

Richard Rovere, "John Gunther" *The New Yorker* (August 23, 1947), 30-40.

SELECTED BOOKS BY GUNTHER:

D-Day (New York: Harper & Bros., 1941).

Death Be Not Proud (New York: Harper & Bros., 1949).

Eisenhower: The Man and the Symbol (New York: Harper & Bros., 1951).

Inside Africa (New York: Harper & Bros., 1955).

Inside Asia (New York: Harper and Bros., 1939).

Inside Europe (New York: Harper & Bros., 1936).

Inside the U.S.A. (New York: Harper and Bros., 1947).

19

H.L. Mencken

Influence on a Whole Generation

Early into the twentieth century, America under the influence of Manifest Destiny entered the international stage. For most, at home the nation remained under the spell of its mythic past; rural life predominated even as its cities burgeoned with growth of new industry, fueled by immigrants. The Progressive Era was beginning; muckrakers exposed the seamy side of government and industry. Nevertheless, America's life and literature remained under the restrictive influence of its Puritan origins. The realism of Frank Norris and Jack London made its uneasy presence felt; the examinations of government and industry by Lincoln Steffens and Upton Sinclair acquainted large numbers of Americans with the less-attractive elements of the American Dream. Mass immigration and mass industrialization was changing the face of America.

The excesses of yellow journalism committed by Joseph Pulitzer and William Randolph Hearst were confined to New York. For the most part, newspapers were content to report the happenings of the day, and

H.L. Mencken: Chronology

1880	born, September 12, Baltimore, Maryland

1896	graduates from Polytechnic High School, enters family cigar business

1899	joins Baltimore *Evening Herald*, reporter

1903	city editor of *Morning Herald; Ventures Into Verse*

1904	city editor of *Evening Herald*

1905	managing editor of *Herald; George Bernard Shaw: His Plays*

1906	*Herald* folds, joins Baltimore *Evening News,* then the Baltimore *Sunday Sun*

1908	*The Philosophy of Fredrich Nietzsche;* joins *Smart Set* as book review editor

1910	appointed associate editor, Baltimore *Evening Sun;* coauthor of *The Man Versus the Man*

1911	begins "Free Lance" column in the *Evening Sun*

1914	appointed co-editor, with George Jean Nathan, of the *Smart Set*

1915	"Free Lance" column ends in October

1916	*A Book of Burlesques; A Little Book in C Major;* in December goes to Germany as a "war correspondent" for the *Sunpapers*

1917	writes for the New York *Evening Mail* (June through July 1918); *A Book of Prefaces*

who was to prove the most-influential of the century was just beginning his career in Baltimore. Henry Louis Mencken, shortened to H.L. Mencken on his byline, was destined to make his mark as a newspaperman– perhaps the most influential of the twentieth century– as a columnist, editor, author, literary critic, and philologist. Among the literate, Mencken's reputation as "disturber of the peace" endures.

An iconoclast, with an invective and inventive style, H.L. Mencken began his newspaper career in Baltimore with a column that brought him local fame for his attacks on the accepted standards. He became a national figure with a magazine venue that enabled him to demolish with gleeful gusto the shams and pretensions of his day. Mencken was, first and foremost, a journalist of the highest caliber, but he also played a role that significantly altered the American literary landscape. Mencken, Walter Lippmann wrote in 1926, was "the most powerful personal influence on this whole generation of educated people."

Henry Louis Mencken (1880-1956) was born in Baltimore, September 12, 1880. His parents were third-generation Baltimoreans of German stock; his father, a successful merchant, owned his own tobacco firm. Henry, the eldest of three boys and a girl, led a comfortable, upper-middle-class life. Mencken attended a private German school and later the Polytechnic Institute, a public high school. That constituted his formal education; he declined to attend college. After graduation, Mencken joined his father's cigar business as a salesman, but Mencken yearned to be a newspaperman. After his father's death in January 1899, Mencken for weeks besieged the offices of the Baltimore *Morning Herald,* until editor Max Ways gave him a job to cover a story in a distant suburb in the middle of a blizzard. He did the job. From then on, Mencken was a newspaper-

1918   *Damn! A Book of Calumny; In Defense of Women*

1919   *Prejudices: First Series* (continues through 1927 with the Sixth series); *The American Language*

1920   begins "Monday Articles" in *Evening Sun; The American Credo* and *Heliogabalus* (with George Jean Nathan)

1923   ends association with *Smart Set*

1924   founding editor of the *American Mercury;* begins column for the Chicago *Sunday Tribune* (until January 1928)

1925   Scopes "monkey" trial

1926   *Notes on Democracy*

1927   *Selected Prejudices*

1928   *Menckeniana: A Schimpflexikon*

1930   *Treatise on the Gods*

1933   December, resigns as editor of the *American Mercury*

1938   editorial page editor (January-May) the *Evening Sun*

1940   *Happy Days*

1941   *Newspaper Days*

1942   *A New Dictionary of Quotations*

1943   *Heathen Days*

1956   dies, January 27, Baltimore, Md.; *Minority Report: H.L. Mencken's Notebooks* (posthumously)

man. Briefly, he held both jobs, working day and night.

Mencken worked hard, a credo he followed all his life. In the evenings he worked at free-lance–he published pieces under pseudonyms in *Leslie's Monthly* and wrote for other journals. From 1901 through 1903, he wrote a daily column of dramatic criticism, along with his editorials and verse. His book of verse, with the influence of Kipling and George Ade evident, was published in 1903, the same year he became city editor of the *Morning Herald.* In 1905 Mencken published *George Bernard Shaw: His Plays,* the first collection of Shaw ever attempted. Shaw's thinking influenced young Mencken. The same year he was promoted to managing editor. The rise of Mencken led to a description as "the boy wonder." He earned more celebrity when he managed to get his newspaper printed and published–from Philadelphia and Washington–during the vast devastation of the Baltimore fire in 1904.

When the *Herald* folded in 1906, Mencken joined the Baltimore *Sunpapers* as editor of the *Sunday Sun,* one of the newspapers published by A. S. Abell. He mainly occupied himself with editorial writing and continued to review drama until his (fair but harsh) criticism brought protests from local producers. He pursued his personal literary career with continued free-lance articles and published another book, *The Philosophy of Friedrich Nietzsche,* (with his translation from the German) in 1908. One biographer reports "it was more Mencken's Nietzsche than Nietzsche's Nietzsche," but the book added to Mencken's literary reputation. Theodore Dreiser, editor of the *Delineator*–another Mencken free-lance outlet–helped Mencken land a position writing a book review column in 1908 for a monthly magazine, the *Smart Set.* Mencken acquired a national forum–and met George Jean Nathan, a young drama critic--and helped the *Smart Set* acquire a literary reputation. His books and articles were part-time jobs. His headquarters was Baltimore and would remain so for the rest of his life. Mencken's targeted the shallowness of most American writing and his goal was to sweep away the rubbish that passed for literature.

At the *Sunpapers,* Mencken helped establish an afternoon paper with personality and verve, the *Evening Sun,* where Mencken began a column in 1911, the "Free Lance." His column soon became one which none dared not read; his targets were every form of sham and pretense, politicians and the Ku Klux Klan. Mencken attacked whatever came into his head with impertinence, humor, and a high degree of literacy.

In the book page of the *Smart Set,* his iconoclastic views of the passing scene, presented with an invective style that combined wit and humor, reflected all aspects of behavior and literary opinion. He had license to attack all icons. Like his early guide Shaw, Mencken enjoyed a zestful delight in destroying society's icons, and the "boobs" who practiced Democracy. Mencken led the growing rebellion against the genteel tradition of American writing. He lauded the group of American realists, particularly Dreiser, whose *Sister Carrie* helped pave the way for Frank Norris' *Octopus,* Edith Wharton's *House of Mirth,* and Upton Sinclair's *The Jungle.* Mencken encouraged a vibrant American literature and critiques on American culture. One of his favorite targets was William Dean Howells for his "niceness." Even so, he did not hesitate to castigate writers, like Sinclair and Drieser, when they undertook crusades.

Mencken's own tendency to crusade landed him in trouble with his "Free Lance." As the coming war encroached onto America, Mencken's pro-German, anti-British, anti-Woodrow Wilson commentary led to protests. Consequently, *Sunpapers* management cancelled the column in 1915. Free and open discussion of the war–the propaganda, the issues that made war seem to be a crusade–was impossible in those times. The restriction imposed by management was a move that Mencken bitterly recalled to the end of his days as a curtailment to free speech. Mencken did not dispute the fact that management always has the right to decide what it will publish, however, and he found other outlets.

In 1914 new ownership offered Nathan the post as editor of the *Smart Set,* which he accepted with the proviso that Mencken be co-editor. Under that duo the *Smart Set* became one of the leading organs of the cultural conflict. Comment was confined to literary rebellion; the war, even after America entered in 1917, was never mentioned in the *Smart Set.* Mencken visited Germany as a "war correspondent" by the *Sunpapers* in 1916 before America entered the conflict and he sent back fair dispatches that presented the German view. Upon his return, he learned that most of his copy had been suppressed. With the outbreak of war in 1917, he severed writing for the *Sunpapers* and turned to the New York *Evening Mail* with a series of columns. Ironically, the *Evening Mail* itself was eventually shut down by the Administration under the Sedition Act as a pro-German newspaper. Mencken published two of his notable columns there, however: "Sahara of the Bozart," an attack on the literary desert of the American South; and "A Neglected Anniversary," a spoof of the first White House bathtub, that endures to this day as literal truth in certain reference journals. During the war years, Mencken himself was not only silenced, but spied upon by the Justice Department; he became even more embittered. Literary subjects occupied his attention.

In 1917 he published a collection of his *Smart Set* commentaries for Knopf, *A Book of Prefaces* and in 1918, *In Defense of Women,* a book that some critics today accept as the title advertises, even though its thesis was anything but a defense–women are only better than men; neither are much good. His wartime years were occupied with *The American Language,* a major work.

Knopf published other books that added to Mencken's fame: *Prejudices: First Series,* a collection from the *Smart Set*–six subsequent collections were published from 1920-1927. In 1920 Mencken returned to the *Sunpapers* and began a series of Monday columns. If the wartime rancor was forgiven, it was not forgotten; the "Free Lance" was not revived. His "Monday Articles" served as an outlet for ideas and as immediate drafts for topics that made their way into the *Smart Set* and, eventually, books. If Mencken or Nathan had too many articles in a particular issue, both employed Major Owen Hatterras as a convenient pen name. In 1923, however, Mencken left the *Smart Set* over a disagreement with management–Mencken unkindly dealt with President Warren G. Harding's death. Mencken was undisturbed; he felt the *Smart Set* lacked the stature he sought for a first-rate magazine. Consequently, the next year, again with Nathan, he established a new magazine backed by publisher Alfred Knopf, the *American Mercury.* This time, however, it was to be a magazine of Mencken's design and planning.

Mencken's journalism career was punctuated with the 1925 "Monkey trial" in Dayton, Tennessee, where the teaching of Christian Fundamentalism clashed with Darwinian theory. A high school teacher, John T. Scopes, was accused of teaching evolution in conflict with state law (which he freely admitted) and the ACLU brought the issue to trial in state court. Mencken convinced his newspaper the *Evening Sun* to back Scopes and pay his bond. Famed national lawyer Clarence Darrow defended Scopes against the prosecutor, three-time Democratic presidential candidate William Jennings Bryan. Mencken was the most prominent of the 300-odd newsmen at the trial which created a sensation. Mencken's copy was itself sensational and his national fame grew. Myth has created the impression that the trial was one about free speech and religion; it was not, although Mencken's copy blistered the "Holy Rollers," "morons" and "imbeciles" who interpreted the Bible as literal truth. Mencken's assault on Bryan as a "fraud" and "charlatan" was the real issue. Bryan won, but destroyed himself politically, Mencken's real aim. The next year his work was syndicated nationally by the *Chicago Tribune* and Mencken's reputation soared even higher.

Many newspaper publishers disliked Mencken, undoubtedly because he belittled their efforts in the Fourth Estate, as much as he abused the narrow and limited views of college professors and ineffectual journalism schools. Mencken assumed sole editorship of the *Mercury* within a year after its founding and encountered trouble for his controversial articles and topics. One chapter from a book, "Hatrack," led to Mencken's arrest in Boston as the Watch and Ward Society attempted to suppress his magazine on a morals issue. In this clear instance of First Amendment infringement, Mencken was astounded to find that a good portion of America's press failed to support him. Mencken was clear in his stand for free press and free speech, and his contempt for much of America's press hardened.

Mencken's stature as an editor soared while he labored to build the *Mercury* into an influential voice in American letters. From its inception the *Mercury* received literary acclaim and its circulation matched or exceeded its competition. Pages in the magazine reflected Mencken's scathing commentary on American manners and morals. Mencken was no reformer, but he was a rebel without peer. Mencken was a satirist who could—and did—attack, attack, attack. Mencken contrasted the past, usually favorably, with the present restrictions on Constitutional freedom. Prohibition was a prime target. The *Mercury* was lively and discordant-- and read by an audience receptive to the derision that Mencken employed. Writers of stature, many of whom Mencken had developed and encouraged, helped make the *Mercury's* pages the most-read and talked about in America. Mencken was America's taste-maker; looked on as a demigod by many. In that era, the *New York Times* described Mencken as "the most powerful private citizen in America." Walter Lippmann wrote that this "Holy Terror from Baltimore" was "the most powerful personal influence on this whole generation of educated people."

With the onset of the Great Depression, Mencken lost touch and his audience eroded; negative commentary was no longer welcome in an economically crippled America that looked for hope and expectation. In December 1933, with mounting debt and loss of circulation, Mencken abandoned the *Mercury*. In that era, while still editor of the *Mercury,* Mencken published *Notes on Democracy* (1926), that exposed its proponents and their faults; a slim volume, *James Branch Cabell* (1927); *Treatise on the Gods* (1930); and *Making a President* (1932). His first book after departing the *Mercury* was *Treatise on Right and Wrong* (1934), a companion volume to his essay on religions, which sold well but was a disappointment. Mencken continued the *Prejudices* series and added supplements to the *American Language*. Journalistically, he continued his weekly articles for the *Evening Sun,* where he concentrated on the political scene–the socialistic trends of the New Deal concerned and disturbed Mencken. He coauthored *The Sunpapers of Baltimore* (1937) with Frank R. Kent, Gerald W. Johnson, and Hamilton Owens.

Mencken was appointed interim editor of the editorial page of the *Evening Sun* in 1938 and this whirlwind episode brought drastic change and revisions to a newspaper that he thought had become "flatulent." Mencken proved to be a poor administrator who was unable to delegate, but an innovative and creative editor. Few of his changes lasted under a new editor, however.

Mencken again was denied his column by *Sunpapers* management in February 1940. As in 1916, he again opposed the coming war as a device to inveigle the United States into a conflict that he felt was largely England's problem, and continued to castigate in brutal terms President Franklin Roosevelt and the New Deal. Mencken continued his association, but withdrew from active newspaper work until 1948. In the 1940s a new Mencken emerged.

Mencken mined a new vein, nostalgia. If he was unhappy with present events, he looked back at the past as things once were. Beginning with a series of articles for Harold Ross' *New Yorker,* Mencken produced a biographic trilogy: *Happy Days* (1940), his Baltimore boyhood reminiscences; *Newspaper Days* (1941), his turn-of-the-century years; and *Heathen Days* (1943), a series of sketches. These charming books met with enthusiastic reception from a generation unfamiliar with the combative Mencken. *A New Dictionary of Quotations* (1940), *A Christmas Story* (1946), and his *Chrestomathy* (1949) capped Mencken's writing career.

As a newspaperman, he had one last hurrah covering the 1948 presidential nominating conventions--there were three that year–in Philadelphia. Fittingly, the last piece he wrote, in November 1948, was a strong defense of individual liberties, protesting segregation in Baltimore's public parks. To the end of his career, Mencken battled vestiges of the Ku Klux Klan and Jim Crow. Two weeks later a stroke deprived him of speech and the capacity to write. He died January 29, 1956.

Mencken's posthumous works include: *Minority Report* (1956) and books compiled from his papers *H.L.*

Mencken's Diary (1990); *My Life as Author and Editor* (1993); and *Thirty-five years of Newspaper Work: A Memoir* (1994). Several anthologies and more than thirty biographies give evidence that Mencken's presence remains a vital element. He is a "monument to American journalism"–the phrase is Russell Baker's.

Mencken played a pivotal role in the first half of the twentieth century during his productive life–as a newspaperman, for forty-three years; twenty years as an editor; forty years as an author, twenty-five as a literary critic; and thirty years as a philologist–any one of which would have sufficed as a career for most ambitious individuals. Mencken did them all, and his record makes clear that each was performed magnificently.

Mencken made a national reputation–even world renown–from his base in Baltimore; his office was in New York, he once observed, but his home was in Baltimore. His later writings reveal that the basic verities of "those gaudy times" endured and his early lessons of honor and propriety may have provided the skepticism with which he viewed a world changing around him.

With all his faults–and Mencken had many–nothing can detract from his accomplishments. He discovered and nurtured talent; some of America's best writers benefited from Mencken's recognition and encouragement. He recognized literary merit, and never hesitated to expose the pompous and fraudulent. For a man now labelled a bigot, he encouraged–and published–works by women, and blacks and other minorities, when it was not popular to do so. He battled with lively humor the pretensions and puritanical influence of the meretricious. His journalism reflects the contributions of the workaday and also the constructive criticisms that established goals to help make a newspaper of distinction. As a journalist he viewed the world with wit and acerbic humor. Mencken, a staunch defender of individual liberty and freedom, gleefully attacked "quacks" and "mountebanks" and "charlatans." However "idiotic," their point of view, he never denied opponents the right to respond. Through his career, Mencken battled those forces that attempted to muzzle free speech, free thought, and free press.

SOURCES:

Carl Bode, *Mencken* (Baltimore: Johns Hopkins University Press, 1986).

Charles A. Fecher, *Mencken: A Study of His Thought* (New York: Knopf, 1978).

Vincent Fitzpatrick, *H.L. Mencken* (New York: Ungar/Continuum, 1989).

S. L. Harrison, *Mencken Revisited: Author, Editor & Newspaperman* (Lanham: University Press of America, 1999).

Fred Hobson, *Mencken: A Life* (New York: Random House, 1994).

William Manchester, *Disturber of the Peace: The Life of H.L. Mencken* (Amherst: University of Massachusetts Press, 1986).

William H. Nolte, *H.L. Mencken: Literary Critic* (Middletown: Wesleyan University Press, 1966).

SELECTED BOOKS BY MENCKEN:

A Bathtub Hoax & Other Blasts and Bravos from the Chicago Tribune, Robert McHugh, ed. (New York: Knopf, 1958).

A Book of Prefaces (New York: Knopf, 1917).

A Carnival of Buncombe, Malcolm Moos, ed. (New York: Johns Hopkins University Press, 1956).

A Mencken Chrestomathy (New York: Knopf, 1949).

Happy Days: 1880-1892 (New York: Knopf, 1940).

Heathen Days: 1890-1936 (New York: Knopf, 1943).

Minority Report (New York: Knopf, 1956).

My Life as Author and Editor, Jonathan Yardley, ed. (New York: Knopf, 1993).

Newspaper Days: 1899-1906 (New York: Knopf, 1941).

The American Language (New York: Knopf, 1919).

Thirty-five Years of Newspaper Work, Fred Hobson, Vincent Fitzpatrick and Bradford Jacobs, eds. (Baltimore: Johns Hopkins University Press, 1994).

Treatise on the Gods (New York: Knopf, 1930).

20

Walter Lippmann

The Last Titan

For more than sixty years of the twentieth century, Walter Lippmann played a major part in American political thought; his was an unparalleled role in American journalism. Unquestionably, Lippmann was a dominant figure of his profession, with unprecedented influence on American opinion and thought. His "Today and Tomorrow" column was read by and influenced national and international leaders, as well as millions of newspaper and magazine readers. Walter Lippmann transcended journalism; he was public philosopher, a moral leader, and a first-rate newspaperman. Unlike many journalists, Lippmann dominated his trade and earned that title, with no apology.

Beyond theories or academic exercise, Lippmann experienced gritty politics. His background included practical experience in public service at the state and local level as well as national and international circles; he served president Woodrow Wilson during World War I and at the Paris Peace Conference. The author of more than seventeen books, Lippmann's work endures

Walter Lippmann: Chronology

1889   born, New York City

1908   Harvard Socialist Club, contributes to school publications

1910   reporter, *Boston Common;* assistant to Lincoln Steffens's
        Everybody's Magazine

1913   *A Preface to Politics*

1914   *Drift and Mastery;* editorial board of *New Republic*

1917   assistant to Secretary of War, Secretary to Inquiry

1920   joins New York *World* as editorial writer

1922   *Public Opinion*

1923   editor, New York *World*

1925   *The Phantom Public*

1931   begins "Today and Tomorrow" for *Herald Tribune*

1955   *Essays in the Public Philosophy*

1958   awarded Pulitzer prize

1962   second Pulitzer prize; George Foster Peabody Award;
        moves column to *Washington Post*

1963   begins column for *Newsweek*

1964   awarded Presidential Medal of Freedom

1971   ends "Today and Tomorrow"

1974   dies, New York City

through such classics as *Public Opinion* (1922) and *Essays in the Public Philosophy* (1955). Lippmann was the voice and conscience of America during demanding times of this nation's experience.

Walter Lippmann (1889-1974) was born in New York City into advantaged circumstances; his German-Jewish parents were upper middle class. His father was a clothing manufacturer and real estate broker who made wise investments. Young Lippmann was a distinguished student at Dr. Sach's School for Boys, a private school for the well-to-do; he regularly took trips to Europe with his family. In 1906, at seventeen, he entered Harvard College and graduated in three years Phi Beta Kappa. His classmates included John Reed, Alan Seegar, Robert Benchley, T.S. Eliot, Heywood Broun, Conrad Aiken, Stuart Chase, and Samuel Eliot Morison. In college, none was more distinguished than Lippmann; he became president of the Harvard Socialist Club, which he helped found, and during his student days served the poor in the Boston slums as a volunteer social worker.

Lippmann's writing for the *Harvard Illustrated Review* brought him to the attention of philosopher William James. James, recently retired, was one of Harvard's faculty who influenced Lippmann's intellectual development. As a student, Lippmann was well on his way to becoming well connected. George Santayana and Graham Wallas also contributed to the formulation of Lippmann's social thought. Lippmann served as an assistant to Santayana in 1910, and the possibility of an academic career seemed appropriate.

After graduation, however, Lippmann joined the reformist newspaper the *Boston Common* as a reporter. That stint–beat reporting was tedious and boring–lasted only six weeks before the muckraking journalist Lincoln Steffens, then editor of the national magazine

Everybody's, invited Lippmann to be his assistant. By 1910, the muckraking era was over and when Steffens retired from his post, Lippmann also left.

He joined the socialist administration of Mayor George Lunn, of Schenectady, New York, an experience frustrating and eye-opening. Lippmann loathed the pettiness and mind-numbing meetings that led nowhere. Victorious at the polls, Lunn's movement lacked a firm political base. After three months, Lippmann left his job as Lunn's secretary and turned to writing. Muckraking had waned and the Progressive Era was coming to a close. Reform, its leaders, and its attendant movements occupied Lippmann's thoughts. He produced two books: *A Preface to Politics* (1913) and *Drift and Mastery* (1914). These two books brought Lippmann attention as one of the nation's foremost political thinkers.

In 1913 Herbert Croly invited Lippmann to become an editor of the *New Republic,* a new progressive journal Croly founded with Walter Weyl. The *New Republic* soon became an influential voice in American journalism and was courted by President Woodrow Wilson in his re-election effort and to win support for American intervention in the European war. Even-handed editorially, the *New Republic* was accused of being anti-British. The editors and Lippmann, who had earlier attacked William Jennings Bryan (Wilson's Secretary of State) and Wilson himself for their political views (Lippmann admired Theodore Roosevelt), were won over, however. The *New Republic* supported Wilson. Lippmann's 1917 book, *The Stakes of Diplomacy,* argued for international controls and a "balance of power."

Lippmann took a leave of absence from the *New Republic* during the war years to serve in Wilson's administration in several capacities. First, he served in Washington as an assistant to Secretary of War Newton D. Baker. Then, after several months, Colonel Edward

M. House, Wilson's key advisor, invited Lippmann to serve as secretary to the Inquiry, a New York City-based secret panel of scholars selected to provide Wilson with advice on post-war peace proposals. Commissioned a captain in June 1918, Lippmann served in Europe in Army Intelligence specializing in propaganda work for Wilson's Fourteen Point peace plan. This work in public opinion persuasion took Lippmann to the highest levels of London and Paris diplomatic circles. Later he joined the United States delegation to the Versailles Peace conference. In 1919, "what began as a crusade ended in confusion" Lippmann wrote, and he returned to New York and the *New Republic*.

In addition to his editorial duties at the magazine, Lippmann became American correspondent for the *Manchester Guardian*. Disillusioned with the harsh peace imposed on Germany that contained the seeds for future conflict, the editors of the *New Republic* unanimously condemned the treaty and America's role in the League of Nations. Lippmann's questions and concerns, originally an essay in the *New Republic,* was published as *The Political Scene* (1919).

Press criticism, specifically a case study of the *New York Times* and its handling of the Bolshevik revolution, was the focus of Lippmann's *Liberty and the News* (1920). In this neglected aspect of Lippmann's thought, he argues that government institutions operate often upon the engine of opinion. Therefore, the press is obligated to present facts accurately and reliably. *Liberty and the News,* based originally on an extended essay, "The Test of the News," in the *Atlantic Monthly* demonstrates that the Russian revolution, as reported in the *Times* was inaccurate and biased. The *Times,* Lippmann clearly proved, printed stories of atrocities that did not happen, described events that did not occur, and reported the "collapse" of the Bolshevik regime more than ninety times. Sloppy, partisan, and inaccurate reporting were no help to the public in forming intelligent opinion. Few critics were examining the role of the press. Lippmann's analysis of the moral and professional deficiencies of journalism was ground-breaking and remains a largely neglected contribution.

Lippmann looked beyond the failures of the press to examine the means by which the public formed its opinion. He relinquished his ties with the *Manchester Guardian* and in 1921 took a six-month leave of absence from the *New Republic* to devote time to a book dealing with public opinion. But Lippmann found time to write a column for *Vanity Fair*, a monthly magazine dealing with the arts, where the writing was freer with less ponderous subjects. He continued with *Vanity Fair* until 1934 and published a collection *Men of Destiny* (1937) selected from the *Yale Review, Harper's, Atlantic,* and others. *Men of Destiny* presents thumbnail appraisals of Lippmann's candid opinion of a number of significant literary and political figuress.

Before his new manuscript had gone to the publisher, Lippmann was visited by Herbert Bayard Swope, the energetic editor of Joseph Pulitzer's New York *World,* one of the nation's most influential newspapers. Swope made Lippmann a tempting offer: to become Frank Cobb's deputy editor of the editorial page, with a great deal more salary and write editorials of his own choosing that could influence millions. The *World* offered a greater scope than the limited, intellectual readership of the *New Republic;* he joined the New York *World* in January 1922, and his monumental book, *Public Opinion* was published in August 1922.

Drawing on his war-time experience of observing government manipulation facts and molding and suppressing information, Lippmann was acutely aware that the press is not objective and that the average citizen is not rational and lacks the capacity to make intelligent decisions. *Public Opinion* explained the failure of traditional political mechanisms in American democracy.

The distortions come, not from governments alone, but the distortions in our head. People are educated and conditioned to understand what they are trained to comprehend. Emotions, habits, and prejudices make reality. "We do not first see, then define," wrote Lippmann, "we define first then see." He explained that stereotypes are essential to understanding and help define what is factual. The "fact" is judgment, and the rationale is that "fact" does not have more than one dimension. Lippmann employed Plato's analogy of the man chained in a cave observing only the dancing shadows from the firelight as reality. In the modern culture it is similarly impossible for the self-contained individual to know all that is necessary concerning the manifold issues of government. Modern democracy must be modified. Modern man, Lippmann temporized, was simply too busy to accumulate all of the facts and information to reach sound decisions. (H.L. Mencken, in his review, flatly stated that Lippmann declined to acknowledge that most of the body politic were boobs and morons, incapable of analytical judgment.) Lippmann's analyses were correct, whatever reasons he advanced, but they were jarring to democratic theory.

Lippmann was an elitist and his writings reflect elitism. His solution was a "specialized class" of leaders. Modern political correctness rejects Lippmann's elitism, just as modern political correctness rejects his notion of stereotypes to circumvent thinking. Stereotypes–"the pictures in our minds"–are necessary. However sterotypes may be rejected, to echo Galileo, they exist, nonetheless. Stereotypes (a term borrowed from an obsolete newspaper printing process) prevail for the same reasons that Lippmann advanced seventy years ago.

He took up his duties writing editorials for the *World,* for a much larger, if less learned, audience. Swope had built a newspaper of substance and influence after the wild years of "yellow journalism" between Joseph Pulitzer and William Randolph Hearst. Among Lippmann's colleagues in the editorial rooms were Maxwell Anderson, Laurence Stallings, and Arthur Krock; Cobb was the boss, but Lippmann had a virtual free hand as his deputy. The editorial page had the added impact of Rollin Kirby's cartoons, the best in America. During his nine years at the *World,* Lippmann wrote some 1,200 editorials, a third of which dealt with international issues, a high proportion during the era of American isolationism.

In 1924 Lippmann became editorial page editor, when cancer killed Cobb. Lippmann also became a director of the Council, the *World's* policy making body. Swope's connection as a paid public relations advisor to financier Bernard Baruch distressed Lippmann. But Arthur Krock's relationship—he quoted Baruch often in his column—and his after-hours job as "private counsel on public relations" for the banking firm of Dillon, Reed led Lippmann to banish Krock from the editorial offices. Lippmann's ethics caused hard feelings between the two men (Krock left the *World* in 1927 to join the *New York Times*). Lippmann's code of ethics led him to defend some censorship—the press' sensationalism in murder trials was attacked by Lippmann. He was no crusader and Lippmann was no absolutist with regard to the First Amendment. He broke with former classmate Heywood Broun over the Sacco-Vanzetti case. Broun's outspoken column was banished from the *World's* op-ed page. A newspaper, Lippmann maintained, should speak with "one voice," a point of view that Lippmann altered when his was the dissenting voice. Oswald Garrison Villard, editor of the *Nation,* charged that

Lippmann's elegant and even-handed editorials in the *World* were "Machiavellian."

The Phantom Public (1925), a sequel in a sense to *Public Opinion,* demonstrated Lippmann's intellectual ambivalence. Here, he set straight some points: voters were not intellectually equipped; enlarging the suffrage and getting out the vote do not solve democracy's problems. Mencken agreed with brutal candor: the masses were ignorant and unteachable. The 1925 Scopes trial in Dayton, Tennessee, confirmed Lippmann's unease on the principle of majority rule. Ironically, Lippmann sat out this episode tending his wife's illness in Baltimore, where he was able to read Mencken's slashing attacks in the local *Sunpapers*. Lippmann's interpretation can be read in his *Vanity Fair* columns and his series of lectures at the University of Virginia, published as *American Inquisitors* (1928). The Scopes episode and Bryan's ploy for majority rule convinced Lippmann more than ever that majority rule can endanger liberty.

His 1929 book, *A Preface to Morals,* reflected the end of the Progressive Era and the electorate's growing cynicism. Lippmann prescribed the "detached" and "disinterested" man who could find his way through a stoic humanism. The book was a popular success, a Book-of-the Month selection that went into many printings and help make Lippmann a well-known personality. Lippmann was wooed by the University of North Carolina to be its president; Harvard offered him a chair in government; the Council of Foreign Relations sought him to head its studies. He declined all offers.

Then, the *World* ended. Joseph Pulitzer's heirs broke his will and in a craven act of cowardice and greed, sold the newspaper to Scripps-Howard. Lippmann rejected offers to write for the new *World-Telegram,* $50,000 from Hearst to write for the New York *American,* and an offer from the *New York Times* to head a Washington office.

He accepted an offer from the conservative Republican *Herald Tribune* to write his decidedly liberal views. In September 1931, Lippmann began his column "Today and Tomorrow" that was to continue for the next thirty-six years. From the beginning the column was a success; from its initial 100 subscribers, it eventually included more than 200 newspapers, with a combined circulation of twelve million readers. Lippmann enjoyed public popularity–the *New Yorker* ran a cartoon; the Rodgers and Hart musical "Pal Joey" noted his expected "brilliance." Lippmann was a major personality.

Lippmann reluctantly supported the candidacy of Franklin Roosevelt, but became an avid supporter of the New Deal. By the 1936 election, however, he supported Republican candidate Alf Landon and became disillusioned with FDR and his policies. *The Good Society* (1937) was Lippmann's intellectual repudiation of the New Deal, but to an extent it revealed his own confusion. Totalitarianism was a threat and FDR's liberal policies (which Lippmann endorsed) were "administrative" not truly "lawful." In the pre-war years, he supported armed neutrality and warned against the Nazis under Hitler. He was silent toward the moral plight of the Jews and their abuse by the Nazis (he remained mute even when official news of the death camps came out after the war). FDR and the British used Lippmann to prepare the public for the destroyers-for-bases deal. First, Lippmann dealt with the British Ambassador, and then floated the proposal in his column with favorable comment.

After the Pearl Harbor attack plunged America into war, Lippmann endorsed the evacuation by citizens of Japanese ancestry from the West Coast, "for security reasons," although in later years he argued that it was "to protect" the Japanese. This is a sorry episode in his career. His 1943 book, *United States Foreign Policy: Shield of the Republic,* rejected the Wilsonian goal of international organizations for strong nationalistic military alliances. His follow-up book, *United States War Aims* (1944) placed Lippmann as America's foremost commentator on foreign affairs and diplomatic issues writing in the popular press.

No better guide to United States foreign policy can be provided through the 1950s and 1960s than Walter Lippmann's columns. Not that he was always correct or suggested the course taken. He often disagreed with Secretaries of State–Dean Acheson, under President Harry S Truman, and John Foster Dulles, under President Dwight Eisenhower. Lippmann opposed collective security under the United Nations. He opposed the central role of Germany in NATO and argued against a European Union dominated by Germany. Nevertheless, his wise counsel and rational arguments played an influential role with decision-makers in America and abroad.

His 1955 book, *Essays in the Public Philosophy,* was a disappointment to many, who expected much more than its message of "a retreat from liberalism." Lippmann's resort to natural law traditions dismayed many, and his message of a strong executive within the bounds of constitutionalism, reason, and consent was viewed as the summation of a tired liberal. The book, however, deserves continued attention for its message that reaches beyond its times.

Lippmann endorsed John F. Kennedy and was influential in the selection of Dean Rusk as Secretary of State. He vetted Kennedy's inspiring inaugural address (but years later deplored it as "jingoistic rhetoric"). Lippmann's 1958 interview with Soviet Premier Nikita Khrushchev earned him a Pulitzer prize. He won another in 1962, along with a George Foster Peabody Award, for a series of CBS television interviews. In 1964 he was awarded the Presidential Medal of Freedom during his period of favoritism with President Lyndon Johnson.

In 1962 he severed his long connection with the *Herald Tribune* for a better financial arrangement with the *Washington Post*–more than seventy thousand dollars a year–syndication of "Today and Tomorrow" and publication in *Newsweek* magazine, beginning January 1963. Lippmann initially enjoyed a close relationship with President Johnson, but that soured when Lippmann opposed the Administration's deepening involvement in Vietnam. The break was bitter on both sides and the White House began a campaign of denigration. In May 1967 the final "Today and Tomorrow" column appeared and Lippmann admonished an audience at the National Press Club to "Put not your trust in Princes" and reminded that journalists should always have "air space" between themselves and the President, advice he himself did not follow. In his final years Lippmann continued to publish occasional pieces in *Newsweek*–the last appeared in January 1971. Advancing age and heart trouble enfeebled Lippmann and he died December 14, 1974.

Lippmann was an institution for three generations of Americans, who conveyed the complexities of a changing world in terms understandable. He was not always correct and was on occasion inconsistent, but his detached observations were crafted in a superb literary style. Influence was his stock in trade and he influenced millions, from the mighty to the average reader. His advice to journalists to keep an "air space" between themselves and the President did not apply to him: he was close to Wilson, Franklin Roosevelt, Kennedy, and finally Johnson. He often took an active and hidden role in government policy and programs–conduct that clearly violates rules of journalism ethics. Lippmann was an intellectual who stood apart emotionally from the tempests of his times. Lippmann, perhaps more than any practicing journalist, exemplified the ideal press in its search for truth. In that regard he was deadly serious, in contrast to Mencken, perhaps his only peer, who always saw the uproarious humor in government and politics.

Lippmann's moral compass always held hope. He described eloquently in *Public Opinion:* the ideal role of the press. The press, if it did its job well, must be "like the beam of a searchlight that moves restlessly about, bringing one episode and then another out of the darkness into vision." Lippmann, who never failed to pursue that relentless search, was the last of the Titans of the twentieth century.

SOURCES:

Larry L. Adams, *Walter Lippmann* (Boston: Twayne, 1977).

Marquis Childs and James Reston, eds., *Walter Lippmann and His Times* (New York: Harcourt, Brace, 1959).

John Luskin, *Lippmann, Liberty and the Press* (Montgomery: University of Alabama Press, 1972).

Edward L. Schapsmeier, *Walter Lippmann: Philosopher-Journalist* (Washington: Public Affairs Press, 1969).

Ronald Steel, *Walter Lippmann and the American Century* (Boston: Atlantic/Little, Brown, 1980).

David Elliott Weingast, *Walter Lippmann: A Study in Personal Journalism* (New Brunswick: Rutgers University Press, 1949).

Charles Wellborn, *Twentieth Century Pilgrimage: Walter Lippmann and the Public Philosophy* (Baton Rouge: Louisiana State University Press, 1969).

SELECTED BOOKS BY LIPPMANN:

A Preface to Morals (New York: Macmillan, 1929).

A Preface to Politics (New York: M. Kennedy, 1913).

Drift and Mastery (New York: M. Kennedy, 1914).

Essays in the Public Philosophy (Boston: Little, Brown, 1955).

Liberty and the News (New York: Harcourt, Brace, 1920).

Men of Destiny (New York: Macmillan, 1927).

Public Opinion (New York: Harcourt, Brace, 1922).

The Cold War: A Study in U.S. Foreign Policy (New York: Harper, 1947).

The Good Society (Boston: Little, Brown, 1937).

The Phantom Public (New York: Harcourt, Brace, 1925).

21

Edward R. Murrow

Broadcast Journalist Nonpareil

Radio, patented in the United States in 1891 by Thomas Edison, was in its infancy in the early years of the twentieth century. The first voice broadcast waited until 1907. Radio's role was seen as similar to the telegraph and telephone, a possibly useful adjunct that could assist with breaking news events, little more. When news of the sinking of the North Star passenger liner *Titanic* occurred in April 1912, real news reporting of the tragedy awaited the landing of survivors in New York. Parades or sporting events–prize fights or the World Series–constituted radio fare. The sensational 1925 Scopes trial, in Dayton, Tennessee, was the first trial to be broadcast nationally–real journalism was found in the print media.

The Radio Corporation of America (RCA) was organized by Owen D. Young in 1919. The first station, WWJ, Detroit, went on the air in 1920; by November, Westinghouse reported the presidential elections. Network radio emerged in the mid-1920s. The first, the National Broadcasting Company (NBC), a subsidiary of

Edward R. Murrow: Chronology

1908   born, April 25, Greensboro, North Carolina

1926   student at Washington State, Pullman; after graduation

1930   elected president, National Student Federation of America

1930   joined CBS's "University of the Air"

1935   Director of Talks for CBS education broadcasts in Europe

1939   When Britain enters war, broadcasts London "blitz" and
        assembles CBS radio news team

1945   CBS vice president and director of Public Affairs

1947   resigns CBS administrative posts, begins nightly news
        program "Edward R. Murrow and the News"

1948   television coverage of presidential conventions

1950   begins end-of-year news roundup (through 1961)

1951   "See it Now" begins on television; canceled in 1957

1956   resigns from CBS Board of Directors

1959   *Radio Television Daily* names Murrow "Commentator of
        the Year"; takes sabbatical from CBS

1960   returns to "CBS Reports" briefly, accepts President
        Kennedy's invitation to serve as director of the USIA

1964   resigns from USIA; recieves Presidential Medal of
        Freedom from Lyndon Johnson

1965   dies April 27, in Pawling, New York

RCA was formed in 1926; William S. Paley's Columbia Broadcasting System (CBS) followed in 1927. By the 1930s radio was an indispensable part of American life, with a fourth of the nation unemployed, free radio entertainment became a staple. President Franklin D. Roosevelt, with a masterful voice, used radio for his "fireside chats" to assure Americans that their government cared. Reporting news from radio, however, was left mostly to "commentators."

An early radio reporter, Floyd Gibbons, broadcast for NBC his "Headline Hunter" program. Gibbons, a veteran Chicago *Tribune* war correspondent who reported on the Sino-Japanese war and other events, retired in the early 1930s. The NBC network had Lowell Thomas, described as a man "with a million-dollar voice and not a nickel's worth of news." Boake Carter, flamboyant and meretricious, was CBS's commentator. Carter was entertaining, but devoid of any journalistic sense; moreover, he was little more than a shill for his commercial sponsors. The CBS "Special Events" (i.e. news division) also employed announcer Robert Trout, who did the commercials for "Jack Armstrong, All-American Boy" between parades, prize fights and other news announcements. Such was the state of radio news in America in the late 1930s when war intervened.

In 1935, Paley hired Edward R. Murrow as radio education director to handle CBS special events in Europe–not news, but "educational" and cultural events. Murrow changed the journalistic world, however, with his broadcast reporting, beginning with the outbreak of the European war.

Edward R. Murrow (1908-1965) was born in Greensboro, North Carolina (named Egbert Roscoe), to a family of the working-poor that moved to Everett, Washington in 1913. His father worked the logging camps and this is the kind of work young Murrow did through his school years. He attended Edison High, was active in the debate club, and graduated in 1925. He was accepted at Washington State, in Pullman, in 1926, and paid his tuition with money earned in the lumber camps.

Murrow became a speech major and a star debater, was elected class president, a top ROTC student who was active in the student theater, and by his senior year, president of the Pacific Student Presidents Association. (About this time, he dropped the Egbert.) He graduated in 1930 and was elected president of National Student Federation of America, an influential organization. He went to New York City in that capacity. In July he landed a position as group leader for a delegation to tour Europe. Upon his return after eight weeks, Morrow landed a job with CBS's University of the Air, a weekly talk show that led to Murrow's first real job with the Institute of International Education for student events. That led him to Europe again in 1932. He came in contact with leading intellectuals and thinkers in his work for the IIE. In 1935 he left for a position with CBS as "Director of Talks" for their education broadcasts in Europe. Murrow was no broadcaster, his job was to be an administrator who sought speakers.

Wartime events in Europe gave Murrow opportunity to access CBS with on-the-spot reports. When Germany "annexed" Austria, Murrow's news roundup format from London, Vienna, and Paris was a breakthrough in reporting. The CBS officials in New York authorized Murrow to hire a team of correspondents. Murrow engaged William L. Shirer, in Berlin; Eric Sevareid, in Paris; and the first female correspondent, Marvin Breckinridge, in Amsterdam. When England entered the war, Murrow's nightly broadcasts during the London blitz by the Germans gave Americans a word picture of the Battle of Britain. Murrow was an eyewitness to the events he was describing, on the rooftops describing the bombs, the fires, the ack-ack. He returned home a famous correspondent. Murrow scripted his commentary for the ear–words to be heard. Moreover, his radio reports were immediate and he beat newspapers by hours, if not days. His audience numbered in the millions. When the United States entered the war after the Japanese attack on Pearl Harbor in 1941, CBS returned Murrow to Europe with authority over the entire European theater of war. He also flew with U.S. A.A.F. bombers; he covered the war until Germany surrendered in May 1945. Broadcast journalism, under Murrow's impetus, became a preeminent source of information and communication in America. Radio news under Murrow's direction was real, immediate, and compelling.

After the war Murrow became Director of Public Affairs for CBS. Vice president Murrow discovered that sponsors and politics would influence his ideas for programming. A series of documentaries–hard-hitting social commentary–were deemed too controversial and CBS marketing people were unhappy. Murrow discovered that the bottom line mattered most to his good friend Paley. Murrow was overruled on who would–or would not–be hired as a broadcaster at CBS. The beginnings of the McCarthy blacklist were being felt at CBS.

In July 1947, CBS announced Murrow's resignation as vice president and director of public affairs to return to "other duties." The ideals that Murrow sought for broadcast journalism were found wanting at CBS. Publicly, CBS retained and lauded the radio journalist that the American public viewed as having the highest integrity in the profession, but privately Murrow was frustrated.

Officially, "not happy as an administrator," Murrow returned to radio with his own nightly news program, "Edward R. Murrow with the News." Along with Fred Friendly, Murrow also produced a Columbia LP album "I

Can Hear it Now: 1933-45" that was a great commercial success. Later, the two collaborated in a weekly CBS show, "Hear it Now." Murrow was the senior partner and made the decisions for topics and editorial content. Sponsors were often unhappy with Murrow's liberal view and the contents of both programs were often viewed with dismay by CBS itself. Campbell's Soup, the sponsor of his news program, canceled because of "ratings"–although Murrow's was the nation's top-rated CBS news program.

In 1948 Murrow reluctantly covered the presidential nominating conventions for CBS television–all three political parties held their sessions in Philadelphia–and CBS linked the Eastern cities with an audience of less than one million. Radio was still king, with an audience ten times that size, but television–soon to be paramount–made its entrance that year. By 1949 more than ten million sets were in American homes. Television was where the advertising dollar would create future wealth for the networks. It marked the beginning of a new era. Murrow never really liked television–the awkward apparatus, the lights, the stage craft–and clearly preferred radio. "I wish," Murrow once said, "goddamned television had never been invented." Murrow prompted by CBS, moved with the trend, however.

In December 1950 Murrow created a program–an end-of-year discussion–that presented viewers with an analysis of foreign and domestic issues. Participants were "Murrow's boys"–and strictly limited to that group of people he had hired for CBS–already identified as an elite group. The program aired every year sometime in the week between Christmas and New Year's for eleven years. This was Murrow's kind of television–a group of "talking heads" making intelligent and thoughtful comments. "Dull" thought CBS executives.

In 1951 Murrow's radio documentary moved to television, with a new title–"See It Now"–a recreation of current and historical events, that became widely popular. Murrow's coverage of the Korean War was graphic depiction that people saw in their living rooms. With the Communist witch hunt in full cry, led by Senator Joseph R. McCarthy, a Republican from Wisconsin, Murrow devoted an entire 1954 broadcast to an exposure of his bullying and reckless charges that had destroyed many careers. McCarthy, given equal time to reply by CBS, accused Murrow of supplying "propaganda for communist causes." By year's end, however, McCarthy himself had been censured by the United States Senate and was finished as a political force. Murrow was given a large share of the credit for bringing to an end one of the most disgraceful episodes in American politics. Alistair Cooke, writing in the [Manchester] *Guardian Weekly,* described the program as "a stunning endorsement of Murrow's courage." Endorsement at CBS was lukewarm.

"See it Now," one of television's best documentaries of all time, relentlessly engaged in controversial issues that lost sponsors and revenue for CBS. In 1955 after sponsor Alcoa dropped its backing, the network canceled the series. Murrow played host to celebrities and the rich and famous on the popular "Person to Person," a program that brought the network high revenues and generated no controversy.

Murrow worked the 1956 Chicago presidential nominating conventions; he was not the lead anchor, but was reduced to charting regional returns on election night. The CBS network, long atop the ratings, was buried by the NBC team of Chet Huntley and David Brinkley. In October Murrow resigned from the CBS board of directors, a position that he had held for seven years. The atmosphere was changing at CBS. Blacklisting for suspected communist sympathies was prevalent still. Even with McCarthy a fading memory, CBS remained a willing participant. Many of Murrow's friends had suffered and Murrow himself was listed in FBI files as "suspect." Inside CBS the battle for control of programming was a sore point with management.

"See it Now" was canceled in 1957; it cost too much, explained the network as the show won another Emmy award for excellence. In a speech that year Murrow angered the executives at CBS, when he told the annual meeting of the Radio and Television News Directors that television was being used "to distract, delude and amuse and insulate" the viewer. Television, he concluded "can teach, illuminate; yes, it can even inspire. But it can do so only to the extent that humans are determined to use it to those ends. Otherwise, it is merely lights and wires in a box." Paley was "disappointed" and other CBS television executives openly furious.

Murrow, increasingly frustrated with the inner workings, angered others, particularly CBS president Frank Stanton, whose background was research. Murrow in another comment that year attacked the quantitative reliance on statistics that reduced people to "charts and graphs" and raised questions about the quality of television content. Murrow sent Paley an intemperate letter that announced he "wanted out."

With the cancellation of "See it Now," CBS gave Murrow a show that had been on the back burner for some time. "Small World," a talk show that featured world leaders, intellectuals, and other notable people, was buried in the Sunday afternoon time slot, a ghetto so far as ratings were concerned. "Small World" won wide critical acclaim but minuscule ratings. In 1959 the *Radio Television Daily* polls placed Murrow as the Commentator of the Year for both radio and television. In February Murrow requested a leave of absence from CBS, as allowed in his contract. Before he left for his sabbatical, Murrow was told the arrangements for the shows upon his return. Fred W. Friendly would be the executive producer of "CBS Reports" and Murrow would be consulted. In essence, Friendly was in charge, but under the direct control of the CBS hierarchy as to topics, content, costs, and comment. Murrow, in effect, was now no more than a hired hand. Newsmen were no longer in control of news at CBS. Management, now in total command, decided what constituted news. By December 1959 Murrow's programs disappeared and so did Murrow—his face, his name. Paley wanted his network to belong to him.

In April 1960, Murrow returned and "CBS Reports" went ahead on a truncated schedule with Murrow playing a limited, allotted role. The most remembered of these programs was the acclaimed "Harvest of Shame" report on migrant farm workers. To many viewers, CBS was still personified by Edward R. Murrow's reporting, but he was playing a decreasing role. When the quiz show scandals broke—many popular television quiz programs were rigged—Stanton announced that CBS would cancel its shows. Further, he announced a policy that linked Murrow's "Person to Person" with the "deceits" of the quiz shows. Murrow's program was, of course, show business and participants were well aware of the general line of conversation. Stanton, who disliked Murrow (the feeling was mutual) took a cheap and cowardly shot that infuriated Murrow.

In the 1960 Democratic convention Murrow served as a floor reporter, one of the lowliest assignments—and a tiring chore. Murrow, who had not been really healthy since 1957, showed the strain that was probably aggravated by his reduced role. Later, when he shared a portion of the booth with Walter Cronkite, the strain showed. The two shared the work in Chicago when the Republicans met, but the NBC duo of Huntley-Brinkley swept the ratings, more than doubling CBS's ratings.

Before his inauguration, President-elect John F. Kennedy sought nominations for his new administration. Stanton says that he suggested Murrow as director of the United States Information Agency. Blair Clark, a CBS correspondent with connections to the new president, suggested Murrow as USIA head. The appointment of Edward R. Murrow as Kennedy's USIA director was announced December 27. In his meetings with Stanton and Paley, Murrow learned that his future role at CBS would be limited. Murrow chose to accept Kennedy's appointment to go into government service rather than accept exile at CBS. Murrow declined to accept an offer from ABC to head their news division for reasons known only to him.

Washington in the era of the "New Frontier" was an exciting place and Murrow early in his tenure was caught in the aftermath of the abortive CIA-backed Cuban invasion. Not consulted, he stayed out of it. Through his term with the USIA, Murrow had no problems playing the activist role that Kennedy sought for the agency. Murrow's personal reputation for integrity and credibility enhanced USIA's stature. He represented USIA in meetings with the Pentagon's Joint Chiefs of Staff, the CIA, the State Department, and was a member of the National Security Council. His administrative skills helped improve the Voice of America, with director Henry Loomis as a loyal ally. As a bureaucrat, Murrow did well. On one of his many trips abroad in 1962, he collapsed in Tehran, and was diagnosed with cancer upon his return home. In early fall 1963, Murrow had his left lung removed. He was recuperating when President Kennedy was assassinated November 22. Shortly after, Lyndon Johnson–an old adversary–was sworn in as president; Murrow found that no one would take his calls at the White House. He resigned from the USIA. In September 1964, Murrow received from Johnson the

Presidential Medal of Freedom, the nation's highest civilian peacetime honor. On April 27, 1965 Murrow died at Quaker Hill, his home in Pawling, New York.

Murrow was responsible for creating broadcast journalism that was without precedent or tradition. Murrow and his team made it up as they went along–his contribution to radio as a preeminent medium for news left a legacy of professionalism unmatched to this day. When the crisis of World War II required news reporting, Murrow hired correspondents with no regard for their radio background; his requirements were for people of intelligence and knowledge. Voices mattered little.

Murrow's correspondents–known later as Murrow's Boys–became leading broadcast journalism figures in post-war America. Each shared a background in print, were good reporters, and more important to Murrow, could write. Many applicants were found wanting and Murrow chose his people with care. Murrow's group is worth remembering.

William L. Shirer, despite his thin and reedy voice, was the first. Shirer had come from the *Paris Tribune,* the Chicago *Tribune* and the International News Service. He covered Vienna and later Berlin for Murrow. Eric Sevareid, with no radio experience, could write. He had been fired from the Minneapolis *Journal* and was in France with the *Paris Herald.* Larry LaSuer, who worked for the United Press, covered Russia for Murrow and CBS.

Murrow made no sex distinctions. He hired Mary Marvin Breckenridge, a writer in Europe on assignment for *Town and Country* and *Life* magazine, to report from Norway. The New York "bastards" (as Murrow referred to management) fired her for "too sensational" reports. Breckenridge was fired because she was a woman. Murrow was prevented from hiring Helen Kilpatrick, with the Chicago *Daily News* because of her sex by the same "bastards."

Charles Collingwood, called "Bonnie Prince Charlie" by Murrow for his flamboyance, was a reporter for United Press. He made a name with his distinguished coverage of North Africa for CBS. Winston Burdett, once an obscure staffer for the Brooklyn *Eagle,* was Murrow's man in Norway. Cecil Brown had worked for INS, Hearst's International News Service, covered Italy and Africa and was an eye-witness reporter of the Japanese sinking of the British battleships H.M.S. *Repulse* and the *Prince of Wales* off Singapore.

Howard K. Smith was working for United Press when Murrow hired him to cover Berlin. Smith remained a close Murrow disciple even after he left CBS much later to become an anchor with ABC. Bill Downs, a friend of Collingwood, and another United Press reporter, was tapped by Murrow to cover Moscow. Bill Shadel, a reporter for the National Rifle Association magazine, *American Rifleman,* was hired by Murrow as a CBS stringer to cover the European invasion. Richard Hottelet, known to Murrow and Smith, was also a United Press reporter, who covered the air forces and rode B-26 bombers on their raids into Germany. This was the corps of Murrow's boys.

Later, after the war, Murrow brought other distinguished people to CBS: Alexander Kendrick, George Polk, and David Schoenbrun. For a few brief years, Sevareid later observed, "the Murrow team was nonpareil." Murrow inspired other, later, CBS correspondents: Charles Kuralt, Dan Rather, and Daniel Shorr.

Edward R. Murrow, and the team he carefully assembled, brought broadcast journalism—radio and television—to its Golden Age. Sevaried mourned the loss of his "incandescence." In retrospect, CBS looks to Murrow's heritage, but the network treated him, and a number of his colleagues, shabbily. Finally, Murrow was a victim of television's growth—and corporate greed and jealousy—that could not tolerate newsman being in charge of programs. Television has emerged into the vehicle that Murrow warned it could become. The new electronic age belongs to corporate people little interested in journalism as news. Television journalism is now comprised in large part as entertainment-infotainment- geared to produce viewers and income, with little regard for the important values that Murrow cherished—integrity, courage, and the free expression of thoughtful analysis. Edward R. Murrow set a standard of excellence that presents a formidable challenge to twenty-first century broadcast journalism.

SOURCES:

Stanley Cloud and Lynn Olson, *The Murrow Boys: Pioneers in the Front Lines of Broadcast Journalism* (Boston: Houghton Mifflin, 1996).

Norman H. Finkelstein, *With Heroic Torch: The Life of Edward R. Murrow* (New York: Clarion, 1997).

Alexander Kendrick, *Prime Time: The Life of Edward R. Murrow* (Boston: Little, Brown, 1967).

Joseph E. Persico, *Edward R. Murrow: An American Original* (New York: McGraw-Hill, 1988).

A. M. Sperber, *Murrow: His Life and Times* (New York: Freundlich Books, 1986).

SELECTED BOOKS BY MURROW:

In Search of Light: The Broadcasts of Edward R. Murrow, 1938-1961 Edward Bliss, Jr., ed. (New York: Knopf, 1967).

This Is London Elmer Davis, ed. (New York: Simon & Schuster, 1941).

With Fred Friendly, *See It Now* (New York: Simon & Schuster, 1955).

Selected Bibliography

These books may prove useful beyond the references cited in the several chapters for other individuals and should be helpful for further investigation into more information pertaining to people and events of twentieth-century journalism.

Ade, George *The Permanent Ade: The Living Writings of George Ade* Fred C. Kelly, ed. (Indianapolis: Bobbs-Merrill, 1947).

Alsop, Joseph and Alsop, Stewart *The Reporter's Trade* (New York: Reynal & Co., 1958).

Alterman, Eric *Sound & Fury* (New York: HarperCollins, 1992).

Anderson, Jack with James Boyd *Confessions of a Muckraker* (New York: Random House, 1979).

Baer, Arthur ("Bugs") *The Family Album* (New York: Boni, 1925).

Baker, Russell *The Good Times* (New York: Wm. Morrow, 1989).

Baldwin, Gerald J. *E.W. Scripps and the Business of Newspapers* (Urbana: University of Illinois, 1999).

Barnouw, Erik *The Golden Web: A History of Broadcasting in the United States: 1930-1953* 2 vols. (New York: Oxford University Press, 1970).

_____ *Tube of Plenty: The Evolution of American Television* (New York: Oxford University Press, 1979).

Barrett, James W. *The End of the World* (New York: Harper & Bros., 1931).

Beasley, Norman *Frank Knox, American* (New York: Doubleday, Doran, 1936).

Beebe, Lucius *The Lucius Beebe Reader* Charles Clegg and Duncan Enrich, eds. (Garden City: Doubleday, 1967).

Benson, Jackson J. *The True Adventures of John Steinbeck, Writer* (New York: Penguin, 1984).

Berger, Meyer *The Story of the New York Times* (New York: Simon and Schuster, 1951).

Bernstein, Burton *Thurber: A Biography* (New York: Arbor House, 1975).

Bierce, Ambrose *The Collected Works of Ambrose Bierce* (New York: Citadel Press, 1989).

Bishop, Jim *The Mark Hellinger Story* (New York: Appleton-Century-Croft, 1952).

Bliss, Edward Jr. *Now the News: The Story of Broadcast Journalism* (New York: Columbia University Press, 1991).

Block, Herbert *A Cartoonist's Life* (New York: Macmillan, 1993).

Bloom, James D. *Left Letters: The Culture Wars of Mike Gold and Joseph Freeman* (New York: Columbia University Press, 1992).

Bowles, Jerry *A Thousand Sundays: The Story of the Ed Sullivan Show* (New York: Putnam, 1980).

Bradlee, Ben *A Good Life: Newspapers and Other Adventures* (New York: Simon & Schuster/Touchstone, 1995).

Braley, Russ *Bad News: The Foreign Policy of the New York Times* (Chicago: Regnery/Gateway 1984).

Brash, Walter *Forerunners of Revolution: Muckrakers and the American Social Conscience* (Lanham: University Press of America, 1990).

Breslin, Jimmy *Damon Runyon* (New York: Ticknor and Fields, 1991).

Brinkley, David *A Memoir* (New York; Ballantine, 1995).

____ *Washington Goes to War* (New York: Knopf, 1988).

Brisbane, Arthur *Today and the Future Day* (New York: Alberson Publishing, 1925).

Broder, David S. *Behind the Front Page: A Candid Look at How the News is Made* (New York: Simon & Schuster/ Touchstone, 1987).

Broun, Heywood *Sitting on the World* (New York: Putnam, 1924).

Brown, Les *Televi$ion: The Business Behind the Box* (New York: Harcourt Brace Jovanovich, 1971).

Cahan, Abraham *The Education of Abraham Cahan* 2 vols. (Philadelphia: Jewish Publication Society of America, 1969).

Caen, Herb *Only in San Francisco* (Garden City: Doubleday, 1960),

Canham, Erwin D. *Commitment to Freedom: The Story of the Christian Science Monitor* (Boston: Houghton Mifflin, 1958).

Carlson, Oliver *Brisbane–A Candid Biography* (New York: Stackpoole Sons, 1937).

Cater, Douglass *The Fourth Branch of Government* (Boston: Houghton Mifflin, 1957).

Catledge, Turner *My Life and The Times* (New York: Harper & Row, 1971).

Chapman, Elisabeth Cobb *My Wayward Parent: A Book about Irvin S. Cobb* (Indianapolis: Bobbs-Merrill, 1945).

Childs, Marquis *Write from Power* (New York: Harper, 1942).

Churchill, Alan *Park Row* (New York: Rinehart, 1958).

Clapper, Raymond *Watching the World* Olive Ewing Clapper, ed. (New York: Whittlesey House, 1944).

Cobb, Irvin *Exit Laughing* (Indianapolis: Bobbs-Merrill, 1941).

Cochran, Negley D. *E.W. Scripps* (New York: Harcourt, Brace, 1933).

Cohen, Lester *NY Graphic: The World's Zaniest Newspaper* (Philadelphia: Chilton, 1964).

Commanger, Henry Steele *The American Mind: An Interpretation of American Thought and Character Since the 1800's* (New Haven: Yale University Press, 1954).

Conrad, Will et al *The Milwaukee Journal: The First Eighty Years* (Madison: University of Wisconsin Press, 1984).

Considine, Bob *It's All News to Me* (New York: Meredith, 1967).

Cook, Fred *The Muckrakers* (New York: Doubleday, 1972).

Cooke, Alistair *Memories of the Great & the Good* (New York: Arcade, 1999).

Cooper, Kent *Cooper and the Associated Press* (New York: Random House, 1959).

Cort, David *The Sins of Henry R. Luce* (Secaucus, N.J.: Stuart, 1974).

Cowley, Malcolm *A Second Flowering* (New York: Viking/ Compass, 1973).

Cox, James M. *Journey Through My Years* (New York: Simon and Schuster, 1946).

Cronkite, Walter *A Reporter's Life* (New York: Knopf, 1996).

Croy, Homer *Our Will Rogers* (Boston: Little, Brown, 1953).

Dates, Janette and Barlow, William *Split-Images: Afro-Americans and the Mass Media* (Washington: Howard University Press, 1990).

Davis, Richard Harding *Notes of A War Correspondent* (New York: Scribner's & Sons, 1912).

Diamond, Edwin *Behind the Times: Inside the New York Times* (Chicago: University of Chicago Press, 1995).

Dolmetsch, Carl, ed. *The Smart Set: A History and Anthology* (New York: Dial, 1966).

Donovan, Hedley *Right Places, Right Times* (New York: Henry Holt, 1989).

Dreiser, Theodore *Newspaper Days* (Philadelphia: University of Pennsylvania Press, 1991).

Driscoll, Charles B. *The Life of O.O. McIntyre* (New York: Greystone Press, 1938).

Dunne, Finley Peter *Mr. Dooley* Barbara Schaef, ed. (Springfield: Lincoln Herndon Press, 1938).

Ellis, Elmer *Mr. Dooley's America* (New York: Knopf, 1941).

Endres, Kathleen L. and Lueck, Theresa L., eds. *Women's Periodicals in the United States Consumer Magazines* (Westport: Greenwood Press, 1995).

Ernst, Robert *Weakness is a Crime: The Life of Bernarr MacFadden* (Syracuse: Syracuse University Press, 1991).

Fanning, Charles *Peter Finley Dunne and Mr. Dooley: The Chicago Years* (Louisville: University Press of Kentucky, 1978).

Fang, Irving E. *Those Radio Commentators* (Ames: Iowa State University Press, 1977).

Farr, Finis *Fair Enough: The Life of Westbrook Pegler* (New York: Arlington House, 1975).

Farson, Negley *The Way of a Transgressor* (New York: Zenith, 1983).

Febenthal, Carol *Power, Privilege and the Post* (New York: G.P. Putnam, 1993).

Fetherling, Doug *The Five Lives of Ben Hecht* (Toronto: Lester & Orpen, 1977).

Fielding, Raymond *The American Newsreel: 1911-1967* (Norman: University of Oklahoma Press, 1972).

Fischer, Roger A. *Them Damned Pictures: Explorations in American Political Cartoon Art* (North Haven: Archon Press, 1996).

Fisher, Charles *The Columnists* (New York: Howell, Soskin, 1944).

Folsom, Michael *Introduction to Mike Gold* (New York: International Publishers, 1972).

Forman, Bess *By-line: The Personal History of a Newspaperwoman* (New York: Knopf, 1949).

Fountain, Charles *Sportswriter: The Life and Times of Grantland Rice* (New York: Oxford University Press, 1993).

Fowler, Gene *Skyline: A Reporter's Reminiscences of the Twenties* (New York: Viking Press, 1961).

Frankel, Max *The Times of My Life* (New York: Random House, 1998).

Friendly, Fred W. *Due to Circumstances Beyond Our Control* (New York: Vintage, 1968).

Gatewood, Wirth *Fifty Years in Pictures: The New York Daily News* (New York: Doubleday, 1979).

Gies, Joseph *The Colonel of Chicago: A Biography of Robert R. McCormick* (New York: E.P. Dutton, 1980).

Gibbons, Edward *Floyd Gibbons: Your Headline Hunter* (New York: Exposition, 1953).

Golden, Harry *Harry Golden: An Autobiography* (New York: Putnam, 1949).

Goulden, Joseph C. *Fit to Print: A.M. Rosenthal and His Times* (Secacus: Stuart, 1988).

Graham, Katharine *Personal History* (New York: Knopf, 1997).

Grauer, Neil *Wits & Sages* (Baltimore: Johns Hopkins University Press, 1984).

Halberstam, David *The Powers That Be* (New York: Knopf, 1979).

Hamill, Pete *Irrational Ravings* (New York: Putnam, 1971).

Hansen, Harry *Midwest Portraits: A Book of Memories and Friendships* (New York: Harcourt Brace, 1923).

Harris, Michael David *Always on Sunday, Ed Sullivan: An Inside View* (New York: Meredith, 1968).

Harris, Sydney *Strictly Personal* (Chicago: Regnary, 1953).

Hecht, Ben *A Child of the Century* (New York: Simon & Schuster, 1954).

Hellinger, Mark *Moon Over Broadway* (New York: W. Faro, 1931).

Hertsgaard, Mark *On Bended Knee: The Press and the Reagan Presidency* (New York: Farrar, Straus Giroux, 1988).

Hess, Stephen and Northrop, Sandy *Drawn & Quartered: The History of American Political Cartoons* (Montgomery, Ala.: Elliott and Clark, 1996).

Hicks, Granville *John Reed: The Making of a Revolutionary* (New York: Macmillan, 1936).

Hill, Edwin C. *The Human Side of the News* (New York: Black, 1934).

Hohenberg, John *Foreign Correspondents: The Great Reporters and Their Times* 2nd ed. (Syracuse: Syracuse University Press, 1995).

Hoopes, Roy *Ralph Ingersoll* (New York: Atheneum, 1985).

Husk, Bill *Thunder in the Rockies: The Incredible Denver Post* (New York: Morrow, 1976).

Hoyt, Edwin Palmer *Alexander Woollcott: The Man Who Came to Dinner* (Radnor: Chilton Books, 1973).

Humes, Joy D. *Oswald Garrison Villard* (Syracuse: Syracuse University Press, 1960).

Inabinett, Mark *Grantland Rice and His Heroes: The Sportswriter as Mythmaker* (Knoxville: University of Tennessee Press, 1994).

Ingersoll, Ralph *Point of Departure: An Adventure in Autobiography* (New York: Harcourt Brace & World, 1961).

Israel, Lee *Kilgallen* (New York: Dial, 1980).

Johnson, Haynes *Sleepwalking Through History* (New York: Anchor, 1991).

Juergens, George *Joseph Pulitzer and the New York World* (Princeton: Princeton University Press, 1966).

Kahn, Jr., E.J. *The World of Swope* (New York: Press Publishing, 1965).

Kaplan, Justine *Lincoln Steffens* (New York: Simon & Schuster, 1974).

Keeler, Robert E. *Newsday: A Candid History of the Respectable Tabloid* (New York: Arbor House/Morrow, 1990).

Kelly, Fred *George Ade: Warmhearted Satirist* (Indianapolis: Bobbs-Merrill, 1947).

Kempton, Murray *Rebellions, Perversities, and Main Events* (New York: Times Books/Random House, 1994).

Kenny, Herbert A. *Newspaper Row* (Boston: Globe/Pequot Press, 1987).

Kilgallen, Dorothy *Girl Around the World* (Philadelphia: McKay, 1936).

Kluger, Richard *The Paper: The Life and Death of the New York Herald Tribune* (New York: Knopf, 1986).

Kluger, Steve *Yank, The Army Weekly* (New York: St. Martin's Press, 1991).

Knightly, Phillip *The First Casualty* (New York: Harcourt Brace Jovanovich, 1975).

Kozel, Wendy *LIFE's America: Family and Nation in Post-War Photojournalism* (Philadelphia: Temple University Press, 1954).

Krock, Arthur *In the Nation: 1932-1966* (New York: McGraw-Hill, 1969).

Kroeger, Brooks *Nellie Bly* (New York: Times Books/Random House, 1994).

Kunkel, Thomas *Genius in Disguise: Harold Ross and the New Yorker* (New York: Random House, 1995).

Lawrence, David *Diary of a Washington Correspondent* (New York: Kinsey, 1941).

Leonard, John *Private Lives in the Imperial City* (New York: Knopf, 1979).

Lendt, David L. *Ding: The Life of Jay Norwood Darling* (Ames: Iowa State University Press, 1984).

Lerner, Max *Actions and Passions: Notes on the Multiple Revolution of Our Time* (New York: Simon and Schuster, 1949).

Lewis, Alfred Allen *Man of the World–Herbert Bayard Swope* (Indianapolis: Bobbs-Merrill, 1978).

Lewis, David Levering *W.E.B. DuBois: The Fight for Equality and the American Century, 1919-1963* (New York: Henry Holt, 2000).

Lewis, Tom *Empire of the Air: The Men Who Made Radio* (New York: Harper/Perennial, 1993).

Lewinski, Jorge *The Camera at War* (New York: Simon & Schuster, 1978).

Liebling, A.J. *The Press* 2d ed. (New York: Ballantine, 1975).

Lippmann, Walter *Interpretations: 1933-35* (New York: Macmillan, 1936).

Lukas, J. Anthony *Big Trouble* (New York: Simon & Schuster, 1997).

Lutz, William W. *The News of Detroit* (Boston: Little, Brown, 1973).

Lyon, Peter *Success Story: The Life and Times of S.S. McClure* (De Land: Edwards, 1967).

MacCambridge, Michael *The Franchise: A History of Sports Illustrated Magazine* (New York: Hyperion, 1997).

Mahon, Gigi *The Last Days of the New Yorker* (New York: McGraw-Hill, 1988).

Maier, Thomas *Newhouse: All the Glitter, Power & Glory of America's Richest Media Empire and the Secretive Man Behind It* (Boulder: Johnson Books, 1997).

Manchester, William *The Glory and the Dream: A Narrative History of America, 1939-1972* 2 vols. (Boston: Little, Brown, 1972).

Martin, Harold *Ralph McGill: Reporter* (Boston: Little, Brown, 1973).

Martin, Ralph *Cissy: The Extraordinary Life of Eleanor Medill Patterson* (New York: Simon & Schuster, 1979).

Marzolf, Marion Tuttle *Civilizing Voices: American Press Criticism 1800-1950* (New York: Longman, 1991).

Matusow, Barbara *The Evening Stars: The Making of the Network News Anchor* (Boston: Houghton Mifflin, 1983).

MacAdams *Ben Hecht: The Man Behind the Legend* (New York: Charles Scribner's Sons, 1990).

McClure, Samuel S. *My Autobiography* (New York: Stokes, 1914).

McGill, Ralph *Fleas Come with the Dog* (Nashville: Abingdon, 1954).

McIntyre, O.O. *The Big Town: New York Day by Day* (New York: Dodd Mead, 1935).

McKee, John DeWitt *William Allen White: Maverick on Main Street* (Westport: Greenwood Press, 1975).

Mencken, H.L. *A Gang of Pecksniffs and other Comments on Newspaper Publishers, Editors and Reporters* Theo Lippman, ed. (New York: Arlington House, 1975).

Meade, Marion *Dorothy Parker: What Fresh Hell is This?* (London: Heineman, 1988).

Meyer, Karl E. *Pundits, Poets, and Wits: An Omnibus of American Newspaper Columnists* (New York: Oxford University Press, 1990).

Miller, Leo *The Story of Ernie Pyle* New York: Viking, 1950).

Milton, Joyce *The Yellow Kids* (New York: Harper & Row, 1989).

Moore, William T. *Dateline Chicago* (New York: Taplinger Publishing, 1973).

Moorehouse, Ward *Just the other Day: From Yellow Pines to Broadway* (New York: McGraw-Hill, 1953).

Morris, Sylvia Jukes *Rage for Fame: The Ascent of Clare Booth Luce* (New York: Random House, 1997).

Nasaw, David *The Chief: The Life and Times of William Randolph Hearst* (Boston: Houghton Mifflin, 2000).

O'Brien, Frank M. *The Story of the Sun* (New York: George H. Doran, 1918).

O'Connor, Richard *Ambrose Bierce: A Biography* (Boston: Little, Brown, 1967).

O'Neil, William J. *The Last Romantic: The Life of Max Eastman* (New York: Oxford University Press, 1978).

Osgood, Charles *The Osgood Files* (New York: Fawcett, 1991).

Parenti, Michael *Inventing Reality: The Politics of the Mass Media* (New York: St. Martin's Press, 1986).

Parsons, Louella O. *Tell It To Louella* (New York: Putnam, 1961).

Patner, Andrew. *I.F. Stone: A Portrait* (New York: Pantheon, 1988).

Pilat, Oliver *Drew Pearson: An Unauthorized Biography* (New York: Harper Magazine Press, 1973).

Pyle, Ernie *Here Is Your War* (New York: Henry Holt, 1943).

Reasoner, Harry *Before the Colors Fade* (New York: Knopf, 1981).

Rascoe, Burton *We Were Interrupted* (Garden City: Doubleday, 1947).

Reston, James *Deadline: A Memoir* (New York: Random House, 1991).

Rich, Everett *The Man From Emporia: William Allen White* (New York: Farrar and Rinehart, 1941).

Rivers, William *The Opinionmakers* (Boston: Beacon Press, 1965).

Roberts, Chalmers M. *The Washington Post: The First 100 Years* (Boston: Houghton Mifflin, 1977).

Robertson, Michael *Stephen Crane, Journalist, and the Making of Modern American Literature* (New York: Columbia University Press, 1997.)

Rogers, Will *The Autobiography of Will Rogers,* Donald Day, ed. (Boston: Houghton Mifflin, 1949).

Rooney, Andrew A. *My War* (New York: Times/Random House, 1995).

Roosevelt, Eleanor *This I Remember* (New York: Harper, 1949).

Rosenstone, Robert A. *Romantic Revolutionary: A Biography of John Reed* (New York: Vintage, 1975).

Royster, Vermont *My Own, My Country's Time: A Journalist's Journey* (Chapel Hill: Algonquin, 1983).

Runyon, Damon *A Treasury of Damon Runyon* (New York: Modern Library, 1958).

Safire, William *Safire's Washington* (New York: Times Books, 1980).

Schoenbrun, David *On and Off the Air: An Informal History of CBS News* (New York: E.P. Dutton, 1989).

Schroth, Raymond A. *The American Journey of Eric Sevaried* (South Royalton: Steerforth Press, 1995).

Shaw, Archer H. *The Plain Dealer: 1842-1942* (New York: Knopf, 1942).

Seitz, Don C. *Artemus Ward: A Biography and Bibliography* (New York: Harper, 1919).

Seldes, George *Witness to a Century* (New York: Ballantine, 1987).

Shivel, Gail L. *New Yorker Profiles: 1925-1992, A Biblioraphy* (Lanham: University Press of America, 2000).

Sloat, Warren *1929: America Before the Crash* (New York: Macmillan, 1979).

Smith, Sally Bedell *In All His Glory* (New York: Simon and Schuster, 1988).

Smith, Red [Walter] *To Absent Friends* (New York: Signet, 1986).

Smith, Richard Norton *The Colonel: The Life and Legend of Robert R. McCormick: 1880-1955* (Boston: Houghton Mifflin Co., 1997).

Sokolov, Raymond *Wayward Reporter* (New York: Harper & Row, 1988).

Squires, James D. *Read All About It! The Corporate Takeover of America's Newspapers* (New York: Times/Random House, 1993).

Stevens, John D. *Sensationalism and the New York Press* (New York: Columbia University Press, 1991).

Stone, I.F. *The Haunted Fifties: 1953-1963* (Boston: Little, Brown, 1989).

Sullivan, Mark *Our Times: 1900-1925,* 6 vols. (New York: Scribner's, 1936).

_____ *The Education of an American* (New York: Doubleday, 1938).

Sulzberger, C.L. *A Long Row of Candles: Memoirs and Diaries, 1934-1954* (New York: Macmillan, 1969).

Swanberg, W.A. *Citizen Hearst* (New York: Scribner's, 1964).

Swing, Raymond Gram *How War Came* (New York: W.W. Norton, 1939).

Taylor, Bert Leston *The So-Called Human Race* (New York: Knopf, 1922).

Tebbell, John *The Life and Good Times of William Randolph Hearst* (New York: E.P. Dutton, 1952).

Teichman, Howard *Smart Aleck: The Wit, World and Life of Alexander Woollcott* (New York: Morrow, 1976).

Thomas, Lowell *Good Evening Everybody* (New York: William Morrow, 1976).

Tifft, Susan E. and Jones, Allen S. *The Patriarch: The Rise and Fall of the Bingham Dynasty* (New York: Summit: 1991).

_____ *The Trust: The Private and Powerful Family Behind the New York Times* (Boston: Little, Brown 1999).

Tobin James *Ernie Pyle's War* (New York: The Free Press, 1997).

Wainwright, Loudon *The Great American Magazine: An Inside History of LIFE* (New York: Knopf, 1986).

Wall, Joseph *Henry Watterson: Reconstructed Rebel* (New York: Oxford University Press, 1956).

Walker, Stanley *City Editor* (New York: Frederick A. Sokes, 1934/Johns Hopkins University Press, 1998).

Weiner, Ed *The Damon Runyon Story* (New York: Longman Green, 1948).

Wendt, Lloyd *Chicago Tribune: The Rise of a Great American Newspaper* (New York: Rand MacNally, 1979).

_____ *The Wall Street Journal* (New York: Rand MacNally, 1982).

Westin, Av *Newswatch: How TV Decides the News* (New York: Simon & Schuster, 1962).

Westin, Mary Ann *Native Americans in the News: Images of Indians in the Twentieth Century* (Westport: Greenwood Press, 1996).

White, Theodore H. *In Search of History: A Personal Adventure* (New York: Harper and Row, 1978).

White, William Allen *The Autobiography of William Allen White* (New York: Macmillan, 1946).

Wicker, Tom *On Press* (New York: Viking, 1978).

Wills, Gary *Lead Time: A Journalist's Education* (Garden City: Doubleday, 1983).

Wills, Kendall J., ed. *The Pulitzer Prizes* (New York: Simon & Schuster, 1988).

Wilds, John *Afternoon Story: The History of the New Orleans States-Item* (Baton Rouge: Louisiana State University Press, 1976).

Williams, Harold A. *The Baltimore Sun: 1837-1987* (Baltimore: Johns Hopkins University Press, 1987).

Wilson, Clint C. *Black Journalists in Paradox: Historical Perspectives and Current Dilemmas* (New York: Greenwood, 1991).

Wolsey, Roland E. *The Black Press, U.S.A.* 2nd ed. (Ames: Iowa State University Press, 1990).

Woodress, James *Willa Cather: A Literary Life* (Lincoln: University of Nebraska Press, 1987).

Woodward, Bob and Bernstein, Carl *All the President's Men* (New York: Simon and Schuster, 1974).

Woollcott, Alexander *Shouts and Murmurs: Echoes of a Thousand and One First Nights* (New York: Century, 1922).

Yoder, Edwin M. *Joe Alsop's Cold War: A Study in Journalism Influence and Intrigue* (Chapel Hill: University of North Carolina, 1995).

Young, Art, *Art Young: His Life and Times* (New York: Sheridan House, 1939).

Zumwalt, Ken *The Stars and Stripes: World War II & the Early Years* (Austin: Eakin Press, 1989).

Name Index

S. L. Harrison, author of *Mencken Revisited: Author, Editor & Newspaperman,* and other books, was a staff member of the Baltimore *Sun,* the Baltimore *News-Post,* the Washington *Times-Herald* and the *National Journal.* He served as a legislative assistant in the U.S. House of Representatives and the Senate, and as a senior staff member with the Institute for Defense Analyses and the Research Analysis Corporation. During the Korean War, he served with the USAF Air Training Command as a cryptographer-analyst. He has taught at the University of Maryland (College Park), the American University (Washington) and the University of Miami. He was a Public Affairs Fellow, Stanford University, Hoover Institution and is editor of *Menckeniana,* published quarterly by the Enoch Pratt Free Library, Baltimore, Maryland.

DATE DUE

AUG 2 1 2002